95

W9-BWS-258

Madonna of the Trail. Statue presented to Illinois, 1928, to honor the frontier mother.

THE ROADS THEY MADE:

Women in Illinois History

by

Adade Mitchell Wheeler

with

Marlene Stein Wortman

1977 Chicago
CHARLES H. KERR PUBLISHING COMPANY

HQ
1438
.I3
W48
c.2

Deborah Bright, Design

TO WOMEN OF THE PAST:
  Rizpah de Laittre Mitchell
  Elizabeth Ann Mitchell Bacon

and

TO WOMEN OF THE FUTURE:
  Megan Rachel Wheeler
  Leonie Wortman

" 'We shall not travel by the
roads we make.' We may not,
but someone else will, and
someone made roads for me."
                    Agnes Nestor

ACKNOWLEDGMENTS

In writing this narrative and analysis of women's experience in Illinois—the roads they have taken and are—taking and making—the assistance of many people has been welcome and invaluable. There are many with whom I talked as I traveled around Illinois and who gave me more leads than I was able to use. We thank them all, but there are some whose assistance we must acknowledge.

First, acknowledgement and thanks must go to Bruce Thomas and his Center for Illinois Studies, Inc., without whom this manuscript would never have been written. The idea of "Essays in Practice" to complete the picture is his; we think the reader will find that they add immeasurably in describing the efforts of some of today's roadmakers. When the Center brings out its studies, excerpts from this book will be part of them.

I am also particularly indebted to those good friends who not only encouraged me to dig farther, but who helped me to do so: Joyce Breiseth of Wheaton who combed literally dozens of books, culling any mention of an Illinois woman; historian Terry Allen of College of DuPage; and Edith Fejer and Mattie Choice who made editing suggestions.

In my travels around the state in the fall of 1975 I met many who helped then and later: Billie and Frank Brown and librarian Vera Millhouse of Galena; Margaret Allen of Western Illinois University; Katy Fiene, president of the State Historical Society; Adele Hahn and Jessie Lee Huffstutler of Chester; historians Charles Hosmer and Paul O. Williams of Principia College, Elsah; Annetta Cronin long time resident of Jersey County; Tom and Virginia Beadle, Jack and Jerran Beadle and Halley N. Thistlewood of Cairo; Margaret Logsdon of Shawneetown; Mary Burtschi of Vandalia; The Carbondale Women's Center; Gertrude Brainard of Belleville Area College, Librarian Margaret Meyer of Decatur; Marilyn Blaze of Knoxville and Marilyn Millard Harper of the Galesburg Library. In Springfield, I want to thank Roger Bridges of the Illinois Historical Library and Gloria Craven, member of the State Board of the League of Women Voters.

In the Chicago area are many scholars and organization women who have suggested resources or who have given me information: Jacquelyn Peterson, Perry Duis and Richard Jensen of the Circle Campus of the University of Illinois and Virginia Stewart of its library; Lorraine Passovoy on Indian history; Corey Venning of Loyola; Marcie Love, member of the Board of Directors of Planned Parenthood; Zola Groves, former state president of the Business and Professional Woman's Club; Nan Wood, Mary Jean Collins and Mary Ann Lupa of the National Organization of Women; Donna Schiller, state president of the League of Women Voters; Marget Hamilton, former mayor of Wheaton; Rebecca Anne Sive-Tomashetsky of the Institute on Pluralism and Group Identity; Heather Booth of the

Midwest Academy; Margaret Cowden of Macomb, executive director of the Illinois Commission on the Status of Women. We would also like to acknowledge all those who filled out the forms we sent them which gave us so much material on their organizations. We wished we were writing a book just about today's women's groups!

Advice and sources of information came from Betty Ziegler of Illinois College, Jacksonville; Reverend Landry Genovsky of Quincy College; John Simon of Southern Illinois University and Ruth Strand, formerly of the Elmhurst Library. Among those active in politics who located valuable information for us were Giddy Dyer, member of the General Assembly, and Joanne Maxwell of Rep. John M. Erlenborn's office, who obtained census statistics on Illinois women. Cody Hofmann of Wheaton gave us permission to use the artist's sketch of her mother, Dr. Ellen Flower Hancock. Probably the most essential assistance has been that of Ann Foley, editor, who has spent countless hours making sense of my rhetoric.

Marlene Stein Wortman, who co-authored the last two chapters, would like to thank Illinois Institute of Technology for a Junior Research Fellowship to study the issue of governing nineteenth century cities.

Adade Mitchell Wheeler
September 1976

TABLE OF CONTENTS

Acknowledgments 7

Introduction 11

1 INDIAN WOMEN.................................. 13

2 WOMEN ON THE ILLINOIS FRONTIER........... 21

3 WOMEN THROUGH THE CIVIL WAR............. 35

4 WOMEN AND CHANGE TO 1920.................. 51

5 FROM FLAPPER TO LIBBER......................111

6 ESSAYS IN PRACTICE
   The Carbondale Women's Center
       by Rita Lovell Moss..........................146
   The Institute of Women Today
       by Sister Margaret Ellen Traxler, SSND........153
   The Illinois Women's Agenda
       by Rebecca Anne Sive-Tomashefsky............159
   Women's Health Care
       by Abby Pariser..............................164
   The Coalition of Labor Union Women
       Interview with Barbara Merrill................172
   The ERA in Illinois
       by Charlotte Hunter Waters....................180

Chapter Notes 189

Bibliography 204

Index 208

(Artist, Deborah Bright)

Illinois

Introduction

In the Capitol Building in Springfield, there are thirteen statues of famous men, with six more on the grounds.Until last fall, the only statue of a woman was the anonymous figure who welcomed visitors to the Women's Building of the 1893 Columbian World Exposition in Chicago, moved to Springfield to serve the same function. Due to the growing awareness of women's participation in Illinois life, a statue of Lottie Holman O'Neill, Illinois' first woman legislator, has at last been added to the group in the rotunda.

Another statue, an 18 foot marble monument of the "Madonna of the Trail," a child in her arms and another tugging at her skirts, was designed to commemorate the sacrifices of pioneer mothers. The Daughters of the American Revolution donated the statue to mark the end of the National Old Trails Road in Vandalia. "The Madonna" stands on her pedestal while the two inscriptions on the base commemorate Abraham Lincoln and the Cumberland Road. The statue was unveiled in 1928 by a woman before a crowd of 10,000 people. The dedication did not reenact a scene from the life of the "Madonna," it did not present the work she did along the trail nor an Indian capture. For the dedication of the woman's statue, the first meeting of Lincoln and Douglas in Vandalia was dramatized.[1]

The woman was on her appropriate pedestal—ignored.

The O'Neill statue is evidence of a slowly growing awareness that women—as people—do have a place in history. But the attitude toward the "Madonna" is still far more typical. Women are treated as abstractions or as symbols; their real accomplishments are rarely recorded. History books mention women so seldom that they seem to fade into the woodwork of the home. A woman is mentioned in her relationship to men and through the eyes of men. Her birth is recorded, if her father was prominent, or her marriage, if to an important man. At death, a minister will elaborate on what she meant to her family, especially if she was a "good mother" or "gracious hostess." Women have been relegated to a subservient, secondary role, which in men's estimation is not the stuff of which history is made.

Even the majority of people have been excluded from mention in history books; for the most part, heroes—military, political or financial—fill these studies; and they are heroes as seen by men. In the past few decades, many historians have broken with this pattern, investigating not only the roles but the importance of the unnamed people of whom the world is made. History as a whole and women's history in particular have benefited.

But what purpose does it now serve to write about the experiences of women in Illinois? Is it to try to show their importance? to give life to our foremothers in order to give pride to ourselves? to dramatize the drudgery and difficulty of women's lives? to show their influence on men—through manipulation or other uses of what power they could wield? Or are we filling in the gaps caused by a history of only half the human race?

Certainly it is time to take women down from their pedestals, to dust them off and to allow them to replay their parts in Illinois history. We need to be able to see the importance of their contributions. Our state has a plethora of "notable women"—women like Jane Addams and Frances Willard—who were of great benefit to the people of Illinois. But there is much more to women's experience than their activities alone. In *The Roads They Made* we have tried to describe the contributions of many different groups of women and to relate them to the larger process of historical development.

The history of women and women's efforts is complex; women relate to men's historical experience, but their experience differs; they relate to other women but are unique. We can often only discuss the roads made by different groups—club women, working women, professionals and homemakers—in a limited way; limited not only due to a lack of space but to a lack of adequate sources to present a balanced picture. Much more research is needed.

We have tried to show how the roads of these groups have sometimes converged; how women have worked together with more consciousness of helping each other; how at other times women have seemed isolated from each other, struggling to survive. We need to understand more about how such patterns develop. We need to know more about how laws have been passed which concern women and why the enforcement of such laws has been so difficult. We need to determine the relationship of law to reality in regard to women.

These are some of the avenues we have tried to explore in *The Roads They Made*. We have covered only a few of the main highways. Much more needs to be done to explore the side roads and the byways before we can build a structure which will be of service to the road builders of the future. We hope this book will be a beginning.

Adade Mitchell Wheeler, August 1976.

CHAPTER 1
Indian Women

Many thousands of books have been written setting forth the
gallant deeds of men, . . . but few books have been devoted
to the patience and the energy of the other actor in the drama.

—Otis Mason

"The only flesh-and-blood wife you can take's a squaw. Squaws
are the only wives for traders. God Damm it! White women are about
as useful as silk fans."[1] This was the advice given by an old-timer to a
young Frenchman considering becoming a fur trader. Apparently
the advice was taken by most of the early traders, trappers and
explorers, some of whom already had a wife back home. Just what
did the Indian women have to make them so attractive?

Aside from monopolizing the marriage market, they were, of
course, in tune with the environment. They knew how to survive in
the wilderness; better yet, they had the skills to make life pleasant,
even comfortable. Considering the hazards of the Illinois frontier,
such a helpmeet would seem not only desirable but indispensable.
And while some white men found Indian women "ugly," others
reported them as "good-looking," and some, especially half-breeds,
were described as "beautiful." By marrying an Indian woman, a man
could be clothed, the results of his hunting made palatable, his
shelter assured; he would have the best care available if he became ill
and in addition would enjoy protection when Indians were on the
warpath against whites. There is much evidence that Indian women
were loyal and loving. What more could he ask? Indian women were
one of the greatest assets the white man had in the wilderness.

Prior to the end of the Revolutionary War, there were many
different tribes in Illinois country. The Illini group included the
Kaskaskia, Kahokia, Michigames, Peoria, Tamoroa and the
Moingwena. All of these were linked by language to the Algonquin.
The men had several wives and seem to have been less warlike than
some other groups. Although the number of wives may or may not
have been the motivation for peace, Indian women did have a
reputation as peacemakers.[2]

At various times the Potowatomi, Miami, Winnebago, Chippewa,
Sauk, Fox and Kickapoo roamed through Illinois as they moved west
to escape the encroachment of whites and other tribes. The Shawnee
were in the southeast, and for a while the Ottawa under Pontiac
lived along the Kankakee River in the north.

Although each of these groups had its own customs and
ceremonies, it is possible to summarize the division of labor. While
the men did the hunting and fought to protect the tribe, women
were the producers, a role similar to that of white women in pre-
industrial Europe and colonial America. But in white society women

only helped in the fields while Indian women took primary responsibility for agricultural production. All accounts picture her as seldom idle, very industrious—a regular Puritan of the wilderness. One observer says this was especially true of married women.[3]

There was little hierarchy among the women in Indian life. The chief's first wife might have more helpers than the other wives or the wife of an outstanding warrior might get help from the captives he brought back. But for the most part all women worked equally hard on the same tasks and did not have to see others in idleness while they worked. Indian women worked no harder than lower class white women have always worked.[4] Moreover, they worked together, so that they did not suffer the isolation many pioneer women experienced.

Women's work varied with the seasons. They were responsible for planting and hoeing the gardens of wheat or corn, squash, melons and beans. They gathered the wood needed for fires and tended them, brought water, built the shelter. When the tribe moved the women dismantled the cabins or tepees, carrying them on their backs. The Flemish priest-explorer. Hennepin, reported that they were "so lusty and strong that they carry on their backs 2 or 300 weight besides their Children, and not withstanding the Burthen can run as swiftly as any of our Soldiers with their Arms."[5]

During harvest time, they gathered the wheat, if that were the main crop, and threshed it. They had ways of roasting or boiling and drying the wheat to preserve it. If corn were the staple, they husked and ground it. They also dried pumpkins, gathered berries and nuts, found many roots which they knew how to cook, and picked and prepared herbs for medicinal use. The bounty of the hunt was theirs to prepare; they were the butchers and cooks for the feast and the preservers of meat for the future. They readied the skins for use, made clothing from the skins, often decorating it with ribbons, porcupine quills, tufts of dyed deer hair or even elaborate and lovely beadwork; they were artists.

Marriage customs included an exchange of gifts between the families as an indication of serious intent. Not unlike the traditions of many non-Indian cultures, the women of some tribes did not have much control over whom they would marry; other family members usually made the decision for them. Among the Shawnees, for example, these negotiations were carried on between the mothers of the couple.

It was difficult for the white observers to judge the feelings of the men and women for each other; some have written that the men never showed any affection for their wives. Appearances could be deceiving, however; the Indian prides himself on controlling his feelings and would show indifference to his wife when others were present. Those who knew them best felt that they did have very strong affections.

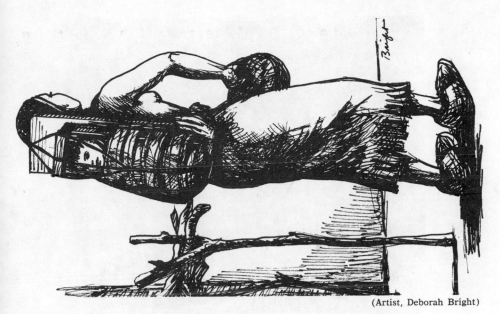

(Artist, Deborah Bright)

Indian woman with papoose, from the Chicago
region, as portrayed in exhibit at Field Musuem.

When it came time for childbirth, the woman retired to a small hut,
either the one used for isolation during her menstrual periods or
another at the edge of the village. As in most primitive and frontier
cultures women were in charge of this process and the men were
relegated to the background. Among the Miami, if there were
difficulty with the birth, 40 or 50 men would descend on the spot,
yelling as though they were attacking an enemy, shooting guns,
even hitting the cabin "which brings about immediate deliverance."[6]
But since the women knew a good deal about various mixtures of
herbs which would ease the pain of childbirth and help recovery,
perhaps the men's diversionary tactics were only a male response to
something they did not understand and may have merely
contributed to their own satisfaction. The women seem to have
failed to comment.

Sometimes mother and child stayed in the small cabin several days
while the main lodge was cleaned and carefully prepared for their
return. At other times the mother seemed to be back at work almost
immediately. These Indian women had many convenient ways of
solving problems of child care never adopted by the white culture.
The papoose cradle, or the board to which the infant was bound,
controlled the child with safety while freeing the mother to do other
things, much the same as the swaddling clothes of white cultures.
These contrivances were adapted to suit the area where they were

(Photographer Barry Wheeler)
Mother with child in carrier today; child has freedom
to move and can view the world from many angles.

used—fur lined in the north, made of reeds in the south with perhaps
an awning to shade the baby's face from the sun.[7] There seems to be
no evidence that the confinement harmed the children. Moss was
used as a disposable diaper long before white women had such a
luxury. Children were treated with kindness and affection. Mothers
taught the girls skills they needed while the fathers took over the
training of the boys.

For a woman adultery was a serious offense, though there seems
to have been no punishment for rape. Among several tribes a woman
would suffer some kind of mutilation, such as the cutting off of her
nose or an ear. This marked her, certainly more permanently than a
scarlet letter, and could spoil her chance for another marriage.
However, Juliette Kinzie, in her book of experiences on the frontier,
Wau-Bun, tells of one case where a husband, furious because his wife
refused to live with him, bit off the end of her nose so no one else
would have her. But she was so well thought of that she "was not
made to suffer."[8] Other tribes punished adultery by whipping.
Among the Miamis it was thought appropriate to have the culprit
brought to the middle of the village and offered to all who wanted to
have her. This could be as many as 200 and she sometimes died from
their assaults. Under French influence, the Miamis gave up that
form of punishment.[9]

In recording their impressions, the first white men to become familiar with Indians on the frontier seem to have viewed the activities of Indian women from the standpoint of white European culture. Since many of the Indian women's chores would have fallen to the men in white family life, these men perceived her as a slave to the Indian man, someone who obeyed his commands and was consigned to a life of hard work, doing the lowliest tasks. Typical statements might be "from an economic viewpoint, she was a beast of burden,"[10] or "Indians in general were not kind and affectionate to their women, whom they treat rather as slaves than as companions, compelling them not only to perform the drudgery of the household, but even to work in the field. . . . I have often seen families travelling and while the poor squaw, bending under the weight of a heavy load, and the girls carrying packs or the smaller children on their shoulders, were laboring along, the Lazy Indian in front might be seen with nothing but his rifle and blanket and boys with only bow and arrows or a blowgun."[11] Hunting was sport and recreation for most white males; thus, the figure of the male Indian with only a rifle or bow and arrow put him into a relaxing occupation.

It does not seem to have occurred to these white men that hunting and protecting, as male functions, were essential to the survival of the tribe. In moving camp sites, in any travel on the trail or even at their living quarters, the males had to be alert and ready to defend, both against animals and against any surprise attack. Perhaps by the time the white men were making their notes such constant guardedness was not essential, but habits and attitudes do not change as rapidly as conditions.

In northwest Illinois, Indian women worked the mines and the crude smelters which the Indians owned. The wife of one Indian chief, Peosta, struck a lode of lead which helped her group occupy that region. Again the women were doing what the whites considered their work, while the "braves looked on."[12] But the white men continued to use the women as miners when they took over; they really were in no position to criticize the Indians for overworking women.

From the evidence of captives who lived with Indians, the women did not protest the demands made upon them. They worked cheerfully. There are stories of their helping each other, sharing their meager food supplies—even with the whites. Jennison, an Englishman who was captured by the Indians, felt that the women's labor was "not severe." Their jobs, he wrote, were no harder than those of white women, and their cares "not half so numerous nor as great." They could work "as they please, . . . in a leisurely fashion . . . many of the skills of the colonial women were not known, so not practiced." This he felt was the reason why some women captives were so willing to stay with the Indians.

Certainly something in the Indian way of life attracted whites. From the earliest times there have been stories of the chagrin and surprise of the whites when a rescued white woman showed a lack of enthusiasm for returning to white society. Children too seemed to have become accustomed to Indian ways and wanted to stay with them. The Indians often raided in order to take captives to be adopted into the tribe to replace members who had been killed or captured. As ransoms paid by the whites grew higher, those who were returned had to be watched to prevent their escape and return to the Indians. Some had married and had children; they remembered their Indian families as kind and affectionate. In fact, the Americans wondered at the "extraordianary drawing power of the Indian culture."[13]This was not true in reverse; Indians did not acculturate readily into white society.

The experiences of captives in Illinois were mixed but several gave testimony to good treatment by Indian women. During the Fort Dearborn Massacre, the wife of Captain Helm was saved by Black Partridge; when the wife of an Indian chief saw her condition, she took water from the stream, added maple sugar to it and gave it to her to drink, "This act of kindness . . . touched me most sensibly," said Mrs. Helm, later ransomed at Detroit.[14]

Mrs. Simmons and a six month old infant became captives of a brave after the Fort Dearborn episode. She was hiked 200 miles to Green Bay and then forced to run the gauntlet. She managed to survive the ordeal, and an Indian squaw took such good care of her that from then on she called her "Indian Mother."[15] Mrs. Burns and her baby, another pair of captives, were adopted by a chief and treated with such kindness by him that his wife became jealous. She treated Mrs. Burns with hostility and once almost tomahawked the child. Other Indian women protected them and they were taken to a place of safety.[16]

During the Revolutionary War, Mrs. Nealy, a captive, was given the choice of marrying the chief's son or being a slave to his oldest wife. She took the latter, and was very useful to her; the wife protected her after she tried to escape and failed. Mary Nealy told of being isolated when she got smallpox, and the help the Indian women gave her with food and special ointment. She spoke of the effort the women made to help other captives, not always successfully. One captive woman with a child just could not keep up the pace, "though assisted occasionally by kindhearted squaws."[17]

The devotion of Indian women to white men is probably best exemplified in the story of Dr. Muir and his wife. Accounts usually say that she dreamed of a white man who would unmoor her canoe and paddle it to her lodge; she recognized Dr. Muir as that man and proposed to him. "Her childlike simplicity, coupled with her beauty, innocence and devotion, made a deep impression on the tenderhearted Dr., and he married her." The stories vary somewhat, but all agree that after one child, he deserted her, some saying that it was because he could not stand the jeers of his fellow white men. All also agree that she took the child and followed him hundreds of miles through untracked wilderness until she found him. Such devotion prevailed and he returned with her to live in Galena, where they had three more children. She retained her Indian dress and presided over his table, respected by all who knew her.[18]

Legal marriages of Indian women to white men seem to have endured, many providing a bridge between the cultures. Half-breed children were plentiful, especially in the early French towns. This group intermarried with the later arrivals so that there were many who had some Indian blood and ties. There is no doubt that these ties were of advantage to the early whites, especially to the French, in helping forge amicable relations.

Many whites, however, did not legally marry their Indian wives and were free to leave or to take a white wife when they became more available. The Company of New France and the French kings frowned on such marriages and set up hurdles of red tape to discourage them. White women were shipped to the colonies, but the colonists, perhaps spoiled by the Indian women, complained about the quality.

The Church approved of legal mixed marriages; the children of such unions were accepted by the community. Illegitimate children, however, might be returned to the Indians; these half-breeds could make trouble. French civil authorities believed that any mixed unions degraded the white man to the level of the "savage" and produced children with the vices of both races. Finally, the French authorities forbade outright such marriages. In the French period, the mixed marriages contributed to the development of a class society, with the pure French on top. But since the French were more interested in the fur trade than in land, there was less of a clash between the two cultures than later under the British.[19]

In 1679, one of these mixed marriages took place in Kaskaskia, between Marie, daughter of Chief Rouensa, and one of the oldest settlers. Marie, an ardent convert to Catholicism, protested that she did not wish to marry but finally acquiesced in return for her father's conversion. When she became a widow with two sons, she married again, a captain of the militia, with whom she had six more children. She had done so much to help the Jesuits that when she died she was honored by being buried beneath her pew in the parish church.[20] In general the church was more successful with Indian women than with the men, as was the case with white women in frontier society.

Indian women seemed to have important status and roles other than just work, marriage and childbearing, but roles which were directly related to their feminine nature and to the form of their work. Since they planted and harvested the crops, it was understood that they owned the land. This is evident in treaty making sessions between Indians and whites. When Tecumseh came to Vincennes to prove his land claims to the Shawnee area of southern Illinois, he brought women with him to help prove his rights. In 1824, Blackhawk also tried to make this point. At the last meeting with General Gaines, a woman who said she was the granddaughter of a chief testified that "the men could not sell the cornfields because they belonged to the women." If the men had sold the land, they would have told the women, she continued. They had not done so; the cornfields were still theirs.[21] The tragedy of the Indians' effort to explain their ideas about landholding to the whites comes through in this effort of the women to back up the men.

Treaties also recognized the claims of Indian women to land. Archange Ouilmette, the Potawatomi wife of a French Canadian settler, was granted two sections of land along Lake Michigan by the Treaty of Prairie du Chien in 1829. She lived there until 1838 with her children—Wilmette is named after her. The Treaty of Tippicanoe of 1832 awarded land to Ganeer, an Indian woman, after whom Ganeer is named; to the half-breed daughter of Rancois Bourbonnois; and to the five daughters of Marie Lefevre, who also received two sections by another treaty in 1832. Monee is named after her Indian name.[22]

While the most competent Indian women joined the hunting parties to dress the meat, they do not seem to have joined the men in warfare. That this was not their role might be seen in the derogatory way in which the term "petticoat warrior" was used. Tecumseh once said in dismissing soldiers with whom he was disgusted, "Begone, you are unfit to command; go and put on petticoats."[23]

But the Indians recognized that since men were warriors, women could be more effective in making and keeping peace. The Shawnees, for instance, appointed female chiefs whose main duty was to prevent unnecessary bloodshed. If a war chief was bent on a war that other chiefs did not want, the woman peace chief could talk him out of it. She would appeal to his better nature, showing him what a war would mean to the women and children in pain and suffering. This was a last resort, but it "seldom fails."[24] Indian women apparently had real influence in tribal decision making.

Thus did the Indian women face the whites as the frontier moved west. At times these women were able to temper or even to ward off some of the hostility and cruelty of both white and Indian males. It has been suggested that this is one reason that the Indian women have found their way into white history.[25]

It is true that most information about these women relates to their involvement with the whites and not to their place in their own culture. But as Marion Gridley says, in her book *American Indian Women*, the Indian women "did not consider their lot in life a hard one. They did what had to be done for survival. They loved their children and were kind to them. Everyone from the oldest to the youngest in the camp circle was given some task to do, so all were secure in the thought that they were needed and wanted."[26]

CHAPTER 2

Women on the Illinois Frontier

"The hardest thing to bear in pioneer life: to sit in our little adobe or sod houses at night and listen to the wolves howl over the graves of our babies. For the howl of the wolf is like the cry of a child from the grave."

—A. H. Shaw, *Story of a Pioneer*

Since Emerson Hough wrote that the chief figure of the American West was the "sad-faced woman, sitting on the front seat of the wagon, following her lord where he might lead,"[1] little has been written about her contribution to the frontier. Men are given the credit for subduing the wilderness; it is their qualities which historians write about as characterizing that period of our history. Women have been given secondary credit for carrying out the "duties of a wife" and they have been called "brave," "mother of the frontier" and "worthy companion and counsellor of those noble and fearless men." There is little analysis of their actual contribution.

It is first necessary to define the frontier; the usual definition includes both an area with a population density of between three to five people per square mile,[2] and also the process which takes place as settlers adjust to new surroundings and conditions. In Illinois both these elements varied with time and place.

During the French occupation, from about 1690 to 1763, explorers and traders settled along the Mississippi in villages like Kaskaskia and Cahokia. Their fields spread out around the central town, and the women therefore did not experience the isolation prevalent on the later frontier. The Catholic Church and its priests came with the first settlers; there were also purely social and recreational gatherings in the towns.

There was a definite class structure wherein some of the women had leisure time. By the census of 1767, for instance, about 50 percent of Kaskaskia's population of 600 was black. Some women, therefore, had slaves who did much of the manual labor. Further, as the French government required the colonists to import cloth, women were spared the effort of preparing yarn and weaving; they wore silk and taffeta. These women were not living under the conditions which were experienced by the majority of the frontier women.[3]

A different kind of immigration began after the English and then the Americans took over. The first groups came from the South, many bringing slaves with them. They settled mostly in southern Illinois.

Later settlers arrived for the most part by way of the Ohio River and settled the central and northern parts of the state. From abroad came settlers such as the English at Albion, the Swedes at Bishop Hill and the Germans at Vandalia. They came to form communities; some came for religious purposes, others for the land and others for the developing industries and mining. Most settled along rivers in southern and east central Illinois. Then came New Englanders, called Yankees by the Southerners in Illinois, to the north by way of Chicago, as well as down the Ohio, to spread out across the prairie. Their industrious habits and way of life produced a conflict with some of their more easygoing southern neighbors. The struggle to decide whether Illinois would be slave or free intensified.

By 1830 many of the settlements along the waterways and in the southern parts of the state had ceased to have frontier conditions; yet Chicago at the same time had only Fort Dearborn and a dozen or so houses.[4] On the central prairies farther from waterways, the last to be settled, the frontier existed in some places as late as 1850.

During this period of settlement woman's work was never done; even social gatherings had a work purpose. "Laboring to the limit of her strength, in every waking hour, she was perpetually tired, and the fatigue was not lessened by a succession of children, born usually without benefit of a doctor. Her entire life was spent in a bare shack . . . . The work, the hard water, the heat, . . . combined to make her look old by thirty. For months she might not even see her closest neighbor. Little wonder that many a pioneer wife sat down and cried bitterly at the memory of her lost girlhood spent in the east."[5]

This seems to be a realistic picture of what women faced. They had left large families with many hands to lighten the load; they had left towns, neighbors and friends. Their former homes had some conveniences, at least water pumped in, and separate rooms for privacy. Furniture, utensils with which to work, dishes and cupboards—most had been left behind. Frontier life was an abrupt change; women had been suddenly cast into a new environment where they had to "make do" as best they could.

Frontier experience very often, therefore, was a shock; it was more so for women than for men. Fowler, in *Woman on the American Frontier*, quotes a woman pioneer as saying,

The husband goes to work in his old woods, and fields: tills the same soil . . . gazes on the same book of nature which he has read from his infancy and sees only a fresher and more glowing page . . . She has found 1000 differences which her rougher mate can scarcely be taught to feel as evils. She has been looking in vain for any of the cherished features of her old fireside.

Most tellingly, Fowler points out that "the sacrifices in moving west have been made largely by women."[6]

This lack of continuity for women included not just materials and methods used in their work, but the kinds of food they cooked and the clothes they wore. They even took on many chores which had not been considered women's work in the East. While the men plowed much the same way they had before and hunted using the same weapons with greater success, the women took on more work under greater difficulties. They made soap and candles, both long and tiring chores. They had to spin thread and weave cloth to make clothing and even worked at shoemaking. Care of animals often fell to them; they built fences, took care of the "kitchen garden" and helped in the fields—all this while pregnant about 30 percent of the time. Women's activities changed, increased and became far more difficult.

Moreover, women often had little choice about moving either to the frontier or moving on again after a year or two of settlement. The men made these decisions; wives or fiancees were expected to follow. Sometimes the men went on ahead to acquire land and perhaps to erect some kind of building, leaving the women behind to live with their family or to fend for themselves until the men returned.

Catherine Clark, a well educated New Yorker, visited her family for the last time before leaving for Illinois with her child and husband. Her father, fearing she was not sufficiently robust for frontier life, begged her husband not to take her. No one seems to have considered that she might stay or their plans be changed; her husband had the right to decide where they would live and therefore, at sixteen, she went. Eight children later, after the loss of two of them and her husband's year long illness, she died at 32, shortly after he had struck a lode of ore which made him one of the wealthiest men in the northwest. While some of her story is not typical, she shared the common experience of most women on the frontier—to be without choice and relegated to a life full of hardship.[7]

For immigrant women from England and Europe the change could be even more drastic. More than American women, they had little idea of what their new life would be like. Besides a new language, the women found the crudities jarring. Manners seemed lacking; the sight of tobacco juice on every floor appalled them. People were hospitable, but too boisterous or too glum. While immigrants might have joined others from their own country, they could not duplicate their old way of life nor had they any hope of ever seeing again those they had left behind. Some had been accustomed to servants, but even if they were available on the frontier they "did not know their place," might even expect to eat with the family and probably did not stay long as servants. Immigrants not only had to adjust to getting along without their former amenities but also had to adjust to new customs and people. The same experience often held for those "Yankees" who found themselves living among former Southerners.[8]

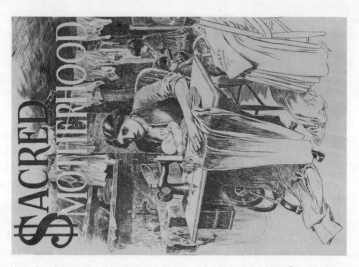

Sacred Motherhood; Luther Bradley cartoon from *Chicago Daily News* used as part of an "Exhibit to Dynamite Sweatshops" in 1908.

Black women had even less choice; a black woman's life differed substantially from that of a white. Even though Illinois was a "free" state—the question of slavery had been settled in 1824—blacks were subject to black codes controlling movement and requiring papers. Blacks found themselves threatened with kidnapping and a return to slavery. If indentured, they were subject for 30 to 40 years to the same kind of drudgery slaves experienced. The laws on indenture perpetuated many of the abuses they had endured while slaves.

Christiana Tillson, an educated New Englander who had come to Illinois in 1822, reluctantly purchased for $500 a black woman named Lucy for a term of 30 years. She also purchased Lucy's husband Caleb in return for some lumber. Tillson had often had to feed eight to ten men for days on end. When she had tried to hire a series of young women to help her in exchange for education, she had found their departures a relief. In spite of her conscience disapproving of the indenture laws, she accepted Lucy, a good cook and a good worker. For Lucy, the choice was indenture in Illinois or being shipped down the river to New Orleans where she would be worth more as a slave; she begged to stay. It was advantageous to both women.[9]

All black women were not as fortunate as Lucy. During the French period when most households had a slave and some had many, there is evidence that they were fairly well treated for the most part. An exception in 1748 may have been Marie Jeanne who dismembered her new born child and buried it. The local authorities avoided the issue of why she had done it and sent her to New Orleans for punishment.[10]

The statutes set up to maintain the indenture system may well have been the first non-discriminatory laws on the basis of sex; they applied with equal brutality to men and women alike. Depending on the offense, the law provided for a specific number of stripes on "his or her bare back." For being away without a pass, leaving without permission or assembling, both men and women were subject to the same punishment.[11]

As more New Englanders sifted down through the state, abolitionist societies increased their efforts to help blacks. Both men and women participated in these groups. Women formed their own Female Anti-Slavery Society in 1844, and in 1846 they undertook a state wide petition against the Black Codes.

In the late 1830s and 1840s Mary Brown Davis of Peoria, the mother of four sons, helped her husband edit the family newspaper. She wrote articles against slavery; she also wrote for temperance, prison reform and women's rights. She even defended dress reform.[12]

Women also participated in the underground railroad. One evening three prominent women of Quincy went down to the jail to take dinner to a slave who was being held there. Knowing them, the jailer let them enter the cell. As they left they blew out their candle and walked past the jailer. The next morning he found one of the women in the cell, and realized that the slave was well along on his way to Canada.[13]

Another active network was in Galesburg. One runaway they rescued was Sukey Richardson, who had left southern Illinois with two small children and a 17 year old son, only to be arrested when they arrived in Knoxville, near Galesburg. They were all out on bail, in different places, when their master arrived and found the two children. The best the abolitionists could do was to hide Sukey; they could not prevent the return of the others. Sukey lived on in Galesburg alone, "free," and helped others escape.[14]

The black woman had fewer choices; no matter what the choice she made, the risks were high.

The scarcity of women on the frontier also affected their situation. It was difficult for them to remain single. Girls as young as 10 were courted, and might marry at 13 or 14. Sidney Breese, a lawyer whose statue stands in the capitol, met his wife when she was 14, playing with her dolls in the courtyard of her wealthy father's home. She went from her father to her husband at that age and had 14 children.[15] Many brides were 16 and widows and women who would have been considered spinsters elsewhere married readily. Young women who went west to teach often did not teach long, marrying quickly. It became advisable to train more westerners.

Moreover, there are many indications that the reason for marriage was male convenience. The following are typical newspaper ads:

Wanted a WIFE, from 14 to 25 years of age. She must be of respectable
family, liberally educated, inclined to industry, so far as to look after
domestic affairs, capable of arranging a dinner table in the most modern
style, also of entering a drawing or ball room gracefully, edifying in
conversation, truly chaste, and partial to children.

. . . a good looking modest girl (under 25) who can and will spin and knit, and
by herself and not by deputy, attend to all the domestic affairs of the house .
. . . One who is fonder of spinning cotton, flax and woolen yarn than street
yarn.[16]

Another man sought a girl who possessed a "skillet and the ability
to make a hunting shirt." A well established widower married a
widow of 40 who had eight children, the eldest being established in
business and able to take care of the younger ones. He explained "I
will now say that I have entered into this marriage solely with a view
to the benefit of my children . . . . My children wanted a counsellor, a
guide, a mother. My duty to them required that in providing one I
should consult their good in preference to my own fancy, and I
believe I have conscientiously discharged this duty."[17]

Obviously frontier men needed wives for many reasons; love and
the welfare of the women did not always rank first. That the
arrangement may not have been beneficial to women may be seen in
that the newspapers also ran ads for runaway wives. A woman had
more choice on the frontier, but her marriage would probably be a
working arrangement.

Some historians claim that the lopsided ratio of men to women on
the frontier resulted in "deference" toward the women. They were
"sought after, venerated and pampered to a degree unrecognizable in
areas with more women in relation to men." Americans elevated
women to a pedestal, showered them with gadgets that would
relieve them of their rightful duties in the home and treated them
with a respect that struck masculine visitors as disgraceful."[18]
Scarcity of anything can increase it value and make it sought after,
but scarcity was not the only reason why frontier men found women
so attractive. Their contribution to the men's success went far
beyond their appearance. On the Illinois frontier "pampering,"
"deference" and "gadgetry" were far more apt to be exhibited by the
woman as she took care of the man, deferring to his needs and
making an incredible effort to keep him well fed and clothed.
Moreover, frontier conditions did not offer many opportunities for
"pampering" by anyone. Some historians say that the men and
women were partners, that they labored side by side in pursuit of
their goals. This was sometimes true; but only after success was
achieved was some pampering possible—and the man might be on

his third wife by that time. And then perhaps, as Harriet Martineau observed, "Indulgence is given her as a substitute for justice";[19] that is not deference.

While the frontier held great hazards for both sexes, these seem to have been harsher and more numerous for women. Their isolation was often one of the greatest harships, especially in the British and American periods when population density was low and farms spread out. When a man went off hunting or fishing, replenishing supplies or building his political fences, the woman and children were alone, sometimes for weeks at a time, and usually without even mail delivery. For someone who had been accustomed to friends and neighbors in close proximity, this was a dismal situation.

A well-educated daughter of an English merchant and her husband came to Chicago in 1816. They had a 20 foot cabin with a floor, luxury for the time and place; he felt the winter "glided pleasantly" as he frequently indulged his propensity for hunting. But his pregnant wife became so despondent that her sister, on a visit, had to nurse her until the child was born; both died.[20] Many women complained about such loneliness.

Indians and marauders were also hazards to women left alone. It was at such times that they were kidnapped or scalped. Many cabins were built with a crawl space beneath the floor boards for hiding. Women learned how to handle firearms; but often coolness was the best defense. One woman was in bed when a Indian arrived demanding whiskey with the threat of a knife; she pulled back the covers to show him an infant only a few days old. "White papoose," he whispered and tiptoed out.[21]

Prairie fires and wild animals were also frontier hazards. One minister's wife refused to live in the log structure built for them in Carlinville because the puncheons of the floor had been laid so green that they had warped and shrunk. At night wolves could be heard "shouldering underneath and sniffling at her young brood."[22]

Perhaps the ultimate hazard was that the man would not return. Nathan Olney had brought his wife and five children to Shawneetown in 1818; he left them while he went down the river to trade goods and reconnoiter. A storm took his life and goods; two months later his wife gave birth to twins. What does the mother of seven do in such circumstances? The record does not say how she managed. The eldest daughter married in 1818 at 15, which may have helped—or it may have been the daughter's way out.[23]

While not every absence brought tragedy, such separations did provide prolonged periods of anxiety and extra work. The women managed the farms, took in sewing, washing and boarders. When the mines opened in Galena, many men rushed to get in on the bonanza. Some spent their summers there and returned home only in the winter. When the California gold rush began, so many men departed that the wives left behind were called "California widows."

But the prolonged absence of husbands relieved the women of the production of children, even as it forced them into more unaccustomed roles as both mother and father.

The life span of both men and women was shorter on the frontier; but women were subjected to illness more frequently than men. A medical history lists the causes of poor health on the frontier to be the lack of cleanliness and sanitation, the high use of liquor, excitement—perhaps the violent religious enthusiasm at camp meetings, and in many cases early marriage.[24] Women were vulnerable to all these, with the exception of liquor; they may have been more prone to its use than the records indicate. Eliza Farnham, as well as other commentators, attributed the ill health of women to their mode of living. They were "always in the home, usually without shoes or stockings, and roasting themselves over large fires." They were the ones who worked in the kitchens in the hottest weather, who breathed in the smoke and soot and who alternated between too much and too little heat.[25] If there were not enough food to go around, the women took what was left. Pale, emaciated women, shivering with ague—the frontier fever, a type of malaria— were often described by travelers. The lack of dentists was particularly hard on pregnant women; most suffered from poor teeth, as well as from melancholia and depression.

Families were also larger on the frontier; statistics show about 10 percent more children under ten than in the East.[26] Travelers reported that they never saw a "cabin without a swarm of children." Eventually all those children might be extra help. In the meantime, however, the mother might die, leaving the oldest, hopefully a girl, in charge and burdened with tremendous responsibilities at an early age.

Because of the continual movement of the early frontiersmen, women might have their babies in several different places. One wife reported having had 12 children, with no two born in the same house.[27] It is no wonder that the mortality rate of women on the frontier, by most indications, was higher than that for men.[28]

The lack of churches and ministers on the frontier was more of a hardship for women than for men. Women made up the audiences, for the most part, of the circuit riding ministers and camp meetings, when they were available. Many criticized the low level of preaching and high level of emotionalism in the frontier camp meetings, but for women it was often the only diversion available to them. While the first ministers and missionaries in the West were men, women were active in providing church services. Mrs. Shadrach Bond of Kaskaskia held religious services in her home during the 1780s, and Sarah Marshall of Shawneetown had started its first Presbyterian church in her home.[29]

Frontier entertaining was another diversion which was more taxing for women than for men. Even social gatherings served an industrial function. The men might be raising a house or clearing land, in which case they brought their sharpened tools and probably had competition as they worked. The women's work was cooperative, as in quilting. But the women probably worked for days beforehand getting food ready and took unfinished handwork home afterwards to finish. When the men finished their work, they retired to the "sky parlor" to talk, while the women laid the tables until they groaned with food. If there were not enough room for them all to eat at once, the women served the men first. Afterwards they had all the cleaning up chores, with no paper plates, no running hot water and only themselves as dishwashers. These "frolics" ended with fiddle music and dancing,[30] and one just hopes the women were not too tired to enjoy it.

The frontier had a reputation for hospitality which depended on the work of women and which was not without its toll on them. Travelers counted on being able to stay in cabins overnight even though they might take pot luck of mush, milk and maple sugar. A cabin might already be wall-to-wall with travelers, forcing them to go on to the next one. People slept head to foot on puncheon floors, sometimes more than a dozen in a 14 by 16 foot cabin. Privacy was only for those fortunate enough to have a bed with a curtain around it.

The first woman to keep house in Springfield in the spring of 1819 found life "so hard, so much to do, so pitifully little to do with." She had five children and a houseful of men, with guests coming and going who often stayed for weeks. With little rest, but much "grinding, grueling work," she died in 1820.[31]

The importance of the availability of such housing may be shown from the choice of Springfield as the site for the temporary county seat of Sangamon in 1821. Eight of the men in the government lived within a radius of two miles. At no other place in the county could the circuit-riding lawyers and judges secure board and lodging, all thanks to the efforts of the wives of those eight men.[32]

The places where there was the warmest welcome were often those most isolated, where the sight of an adult face and someone for conversation made it worth all the effort. The Furgesons, who had put up a sod house for the winter with a floor of loose planks were an example of those who offered hospitality. There were seven of them, but Mr. Furgeson could not turn anyone away. When the number reached 13, Mrs. Furgeson went off into a corner and wept. In January they became fourteen when her next child was born. One guest was a midwife; she had plenty of help. Later Mrs. Furgeson remembered that winter as one of the high points of her frontier life.[33]

But Rebecca Burlend wrote that on their trips they found that the reputation of Americans for hospitality needed to be qualified. They were exceedingly hospitable to lone men making a tour, and to their

Lizzie Rogers, age two-weeks, with her mother, Master Workman Rogers at a Knights of Labor Convention in 1886.

(Photographer Mike Tropea)

Anne Marie Catania with her mother, Representative Susan Catania, in her office early in 1976.

own neighbors, but "when they saw a person really must trouble them, they appear to be aware that they are conferring a favor, and expect an equivalent." Apparently, 25 cents was the standard charge for a night's shelter and breakfast.[34]

Besides overcrowding and the work of feeding and housing guests, there was the problem of those who became ill. Nursing and even doctoring was the woman's work; women often traveled miles to help those who were ill. Ague was common in spring and fall, and newcomers were especially vulnerable. An extreme example was the wife of John Flowers who managed to take care of 12 sick people, even carrying water from a distant well. Thanks to her efforts all survived except the infant she was nursing at the time.[35]

Much useful information about herbs came from women doctors and from their contacts with Indian women. Dr. Anna Bixby of Hardin County is credited with finding the cause of "milksick," a disease which attacked both humans and animals, and which had caused the death of Lincoln's mother, Nancy Hanks. A Shawnee woman told Dr. Anna that the disease came from the white snake root plant which cattle sometimes ate, she was right.[36]

Midwives continued to enjoy popularity even after male doctors became more numerous. Mrs. Robertson of Chicago, called a "feminine Hippocrates," had a large practice in 1839.[37] Margaret Logsdon of Shawneetown earns the prize as the most available. She lived in a large house with six children, but she kept a horse ready and a boat at the landing so that she could go whenever needed. One night a man hallooed across from the Kentucky side of the river; when she went down to respond, her boat was missing. Undaunted she found a large log, with a branch still sticking up at one end, tied her dress to the branch, swam across pushing the log ahead of her. She donned her dry dress and delivered the baby.[38]

There is some evidence that women tried to avoid constant pregnancies. "Old wives' tales" tell of following the cycle of the moon or using button hooks for abortions. Indian women, who did not have large families as did many frontier women, recommended pennyroyal, sometimes called "squaw mint," because they used it to help suppressed menstruation. They believed that if they drank enough of it regularly, it prevented pregnancy.[39] There was widespread advertising in the mid-nineteenth century of ergot and other drugs to bring about "accidental miscarriages" and "to procure abortions."[40] Indian lore, however, was probably more available in rural areas. There were women who had only a few children; whether it was due to attempts to practice contraception, to husbands who were away much of the time or to other causes cannot now be determined.

The most crucial and unsung contribution of women was probably the support system they supplied the men; they made the men's success possible. Men and women worked together on the necessities for immediate survival; but then it was the woman who did all the domestic chores, freeing men to go hunting and fishing or to plan political campaigns and run for office.

The elegant figure of territorial governor Ninian Edwards, riding off to the seat of government in broadcloth with a ruffled white shirt, illustrates the amount of work done by women. There was no permanent press, no washing machine, no running hot water. The spotless shirt might be one item in a washing process that took a whole day of hard work, hauling water, making soap and finding a place for drying. Then would come the ironing, with wood for the stove and alternating irons on top of it to keep them just the right temperature with only a sizzle of water to tell whether it would scorch or press. No matter what the weather, this hot, time consuming job must be done if the governor were to maintain the look of the Virginia gentleman that he had been. The process in his household was done by a black woman but his wife would have to supervise the whole operation of which producing the proper linen was just one small part. She was in charge of a support system which not only turned out the apparel to make him so presentable, but maintained his status by providing all the essentials for elaborate entertaining. Moreover, this set the example for all other wives whose husbands aspired to high places; deference entered the picture as men were still voting for their "betters."[41]

Women took on additional work in emergencies. Often when a man was ill at harvest time, women and children had to do his job. Rebecca Burlend, who brought five children under ten from England, tells how during their second harvest, an accident incapacitated her husband. She and her ten year old son reaped and gathered three acres of wheat, winnowing it by hand. With a borrowed wagon and oxen, they hauled 50 bushels to the store, settled their account and had enough left over for two pairs of shoes, although she looked longingly at the calico. One bushel of wheat bought two pounds of coffee, and she had to buy seed for the next year's crop. She managed to get two tin milk bowls and bartered a china tea cup for chickens.[42]

When Graham's Drug Store burned down in Carlinville one night, Hannah Graham was out the next morning selling ginger cakes and bread to all who came to view the ruins; she continued until the store could be rebuilt.[43]

Few men could have been political or business successes without the help of women. Many women urged their husbands to buy land and helped them save money to pay for it. The profits from the cheeses made by Mrs. John Twist helped buy their first 80 acres.[44] Uniting money and ability in marriage is a time-tried method of achievement; David Davis married Sarah Walker, who started him on his way to wealth by bringing with her to Illinois a comfortable fortune.[45]

Mrs. John Edgar helped her husband in a most spectacular fashion. She had convinced him to leave the British navy and join the Americans during the Revolution. He was caught, however, helping others to desert. All their assets in Detroit were confiscated and he was sent in chains to Quebec. He escaped, joined the rebel army and ended up in Kaskaskia. Rachel Edgar had stayed in Detroit until with "rare sagacity" she managed to salvage $12,000. When she joined her husband, this money made him the richest man in Kaskaskia. She continued to provide him with assistance as he became the richest man in the state.[46]

Women also provided the civilizing function on the frontier. Education was started at home under the direction of the mother. At first, most teachers in formal schools were men, but as the female seminaries began to turn out graduates, they found positions with ease. Frances Brard Ellis was instrumental in establishing a female seminary. In 1832 she was boarding young women in her home to help them learn to teach and started a Ladies Education Society, the main purpose of which was to encourage young women to qualify for teaching. She and her two young children died in an epidemic in 1833, before she could see the incorporation in the Jacksonville Female Academy which grew from her efforts.[47]

In 1833, Eliza Chappel began what was probably the first Chicago school. In 1836, Frances Willard, (not the later WCTU president) directed a female seminary with an enrollment which grew from 17 to 57 in a few months. There were others, nonetheless, who found that education was wasted on women. Christiana Tillson suspected that nine-tenths of her neighbors felt that women had better things to do than to read books. But evidence shows that many women did not feel this way. When they had access to education, they took advantage of it and used their education to teach others.[48]

The manners and social amenities on the frontier were largely the responsibility of women. They were responsible for the calico in the windows of early cabins, for flowers in the garden, for what is called the "woman's touch." They were the ones who insisted on niceties such as spittoons and improvements in houses and barns. In the presence of "ladies," men were pressed to assume the role of "gentlemen."

Indian women had often tried to bring about peace on the frontier; at least one white woman did the same. Madame Le Compt, twice widowed and with a large family, had lived with Indians as a child, spoke their language and had no fear of them. In Cahokia with her third husband, she was able several times to prevent Indian attacks. She would be warned by the Indians of a pending attack so that she could save herself and her family. Instead she would walk alone to the Indian encampment and talk them out of the attack. She always averted bloodshed.[49]

But in indirect ways, the presence of women on the frontier encouraged war with the Indians. With families to be protected there was more effort to build forts and to make treaties, which often in themselves stirred up trouble. Women were active in some of the battles and learned how to defend themselves. Yet this influx of settlers roused the Indians to more resistance, which both fomented and eventually ended the warfare. Women's presence meant that the whites were not merely hunting for furs, but were settling on the land; this would lead to displacement and eventual destruction of the Indian culture.

The experience and presence of women affected life on the frontier and differed from that of the men. These episodes illustrate how much more difficult life was for women than for men; their contribution was indispensable. In addition to making life bearable, frontier women produced and nurtured new life. They helped people the frontier, producing our most valuable natural resource. They did it while they worked to help others survive.

Women provided this support system with courage, stamina and patience. These qualities carried over into the reform efforts in which they participated as the frontier days ended. As towns developed and the number of people per square mile increased, there was a change in the condition of women. Some frontier women saw improved living conditions during their lifetimes; certainly most of their daughters faced different circumstances. There was an overlapping of luxury and hardship as pianos, carpeting and other amenities, began to arrive from the East. Servants became more available as immigration increased, and middle class women found themselves with more time than they needed for absolute necessities. Since they had been conditioned to the service of others, it was natural for them to find new ways to be of assistance.

As early as the 1830s in Chicago, women, through their church organizations, put on "ladies' fairs," annual events for philanthropic purposes. Some women became active in movements for the abolition of slavery, for better prisons, and for temperance. They held meetings, circulated petitions, called on officials and wrote to the newspapers. Some used even more innovative methods to carry out their goals. Singing hymns in front of taverns was sometimes successful in closing them. One woman in Steeleville went farther; she measured the distance from the outside of the tavern's door to the location of the whiskey barrels. She then took an auger one dark night, and drilled holes in the outside wall directly into those barrels—a temporary expedient.[50] Women were taking direct action to accomplish their aims.

During and after the Civil War, the participation of women in these and other causes would increase, as women found opportunities to channel the energy they had used on the frontier to improve the quality of life in Illinois.

CHAPTER 3

Women Through the Civil War

"American women no longer followed in the dull beaten track of examples, but striking out into new and untried paths, lay their plans and execute their purpose with self poise and fearless of results. . . . War enabled her to rise to a measure of usefulness that was hitherto even by herself undreamed of."

—Stella Coatsworth

By the time of the Civil War, the most strenuous part of the frontier experience was over. Servants were easier to obtain; some women with prominent and successful husbands were spending a good deal of time as "gracious hostesses," bringing together important people and facilitating the exchange of views and arrangement of deals. Far less physically demanding than housekeeping on the frontier, this was, of course, far more enjoyable.

Some women also had time for new activities. Education for women had become more available; lower schools had increased in number and higher education was becoming established. Between 1830 and 1860, 27 seminaries for girls had been chartered in Illinois. The first one, Jacksonville Female Seminary, opened in 1835 and Monticello followed in 1838.[1] Catherine Beecher started a teachers' training school in Quincy in 1850. While the school itself did not survive, Beecher succeeded in encouraging teachers to come to Illinois from the East. This increased the number and quality of teachers, and also promoted the process of developing local teachers.[2]

Mt. Carroll Seminary opened in 1854 under Frances Wood (later Shimer) and Cinderella Gregory. It was an institution "built, controlled, managed architecturally, educationally and financially by the genius of women" writes a male historian.[3] In 1855, DuQuoin, Perry County, set up the first female seminary in the southern part of the state with Eliza Paine as its Eastern educated teacher. The next year she traveled East to raise money, returning with $3,000. During the depression of 1857, Mrs. Morrison of Collinsville saved the school from collapse with her financial contribution.[4] Thus women helped establish schools, financed them, staffed them and attended them—all of which prepared them for broader fields.

By 1856 Illinois had almost as many female as male teachers; as military duty drained off the men, women replaced them. By 1865, the number of women teachers had doubled. Male teachers were never to regain their superiority of numbers, possibly because their salaries averaged $28.82 to $38.89 a month, as compared to $18.80 to $24.89 for women.[5] Another effect of the war was to increase the number of women in college. Many schools were forced to accept women in order to stay open, as the men left to fight in the war.

With more education and time, women became more involved in reform movements—temperance, abolition, education, prisons— and even in suffrage and dress reform, the most radical of all. When men permitted, women cooperated; when men denied them participation or temporized, the women started their own organizations often more radical in action than the men's. The first local women's suffrage association, for instance, was organized in Earlville in 1855.

Women worked for temperance individually and in small groups, wearing the "white ribbon," as a symbol of the cause. In 1859, 700 women pressured the Rockford City Council into banning liquor sales and then set up vigilante committees to enforce the prohibition.[6] A few women even lectured in public. The famous temperance advocate Lucy Stone toured the state in 1853, visited Chicago and succeeded in gaining some support for suffrage in Springfield. Olive Stair Wait of Illinois lectured in southwestern Illinois in 1853 on women's rights, and in 1855 she talked in Springfield also.[7] Although many disapproved both of the subject and of women speaking in public, they seem to have listened.

Women in Chicago had the largest number of organizations even though they were not the most radical. In addition to those connected with churches, the Chicago Female Guardian Association was formed in 1853; it objectives included attempts to "reclaim abandoned females, to afford aid and protection to those exposed to temptation, and by all justifiable means to promote the cause of moral purity." The organization operated an asylum for "fallen women." During 1856, when Kansas was suffering from its civil war, Chicago women organized a Kansas Women's Aid and Liberty Association, with auxiliaries in other towns in northern Illinois, a forerunner of the kind of effort they would make during the war.[8]

Other women joined forces for civic betterment; those in Naperville, DuPage County, managed to have the proceeds from one of the first county fairs applied toward building sidewalkss[9] which they needed to cope with the mud, perhaps as a substitute for dress reform. The radical change to the "bloomer dress" which only a few had dared to display in public in the early 1850s had a brief revival in 1858. The Aurora *Beacon* favored it as a costume that would aid the wearer "in attaining that position side by side with man, . . . his co-worker in life and its duties, . . . and give a more correct idea of the natural proportions of the human form."[10] But most women favored the Paris inspired hoop skirts.

Women had come out of the home. They brought with them to

public affairs their morally uplifting influence and desire for improvement. Since men were accustomed to women in that role, their emergence into public life in a similar way was acceptable to many. Where it was not acceptable, the men managed to ignore it for the time being. But women were ready to bring their efforts to the outside world and, as if in response, the Civil War offered them new opportunities and challenges.

Men took the political and military steps which resulted in the conflict; women do not seem to have contributed directly to these decisions. Most did agree with the men in the ideas of honor and rights which had somehow made compromise impossible. Since women were on the fringe of the action and since many had been in both open and silent opposition to slavery for years, they were probably more surprised by the suddenness with which war descended upon them than were the men. But they were caught up in the same maelstrom; their lives were never to be exactly the same again.

Once again women's roles were largely supportive. They provided encouragement and cheered the men on. Some sent their men off to war while they stayed home to care for family and farm or business. Others tagged along, enlisted with their men or tried to stay with them as long as possible. Women supplied more and more support to their men as conditions became increasingly difficult.

Their recent organizing experiences proved an advantage; women's groups converted into aid societies which plunged into the making of bandages and other medical supplies. The women on the home front kept necessities flowing to the troops, from home cooked food and delicacies to clothing and medicine. This effort may have eased the burden of worry for those who were separated from families, perhaps not to hear from them for years.

While many families experienced separation when the father and sons went off to war, the splitting of families into sympathizers with either North or South caused even greater pain. Perhaps the most tragic example of this was Mary Lincoln. A Kentuckian brought up in a household with slaves, she had been visiting her sister, Mrs. Ninian Edwards, in Springfield. There she met and married the man destined to preside over the country as North fought South. Nothing in her background had prepared her to cope with housekeeping for this prairie lawyer, out riding the circuit much of the time, absentmindedly keeping irregular dinner hours, careless of dress, yet who was so kindly that her heart constantly forgave the aggravations. Neither did she know how to handle the kind of criticism to which they were subjected during the war. By that time she had borne four sons, had lost one, and had lived through the election campaign. She both enjoyed and despaired of filling the position of first lady. She had to watch her husband grow constantly more haggard as the battles waged both ways; she lost another son.

She was cut off completely from her own family, while three of her brothers died fighting for the Confederacy.

With all her grief, Mary Lincoln was subjected to nasty criticism from the press. When her sister, a war widow with three children, arrived at the White House to plead for permission to send her cotton through so that she could get desperately needed money, they had a sad reunion over the barrier of war. Her sister, Emilie Todd Helm, felt that it would be disloyal to her dead husband to take the oath of allegiance to the Union but without it no permission could be granted. Regardless of what the Lincolns did about her predicament, as far as the press was concerned, the White House had sheltered a traitor. "I seem to be the scapegoat for both North and South," said Mary Lincoln sorrowfully to Emilie.[11] And that she was. Unable to communicate with her own family, suffering from the loss of another child, almost everything she did was subject to negative comment. Then the worst of her fears materialized; she was with Lincoln when he was shot, another victim of the war.

Another woman whose family was divided by war was Mary Logan, wife of John Logan. She had travelled with her husband on his judicial circuit and joined him in Washington when he was elected to Congress. Before the war, John Logan had worked for the compromise solution; like many from southern Illinois, he was thought to have sympathies with the South. But as war broke out, Mary Logan is credited with keeping their community and his constituents loyal to the Union, even though her own brother had fled across the river to join the Confederacy. She also helped to sway many to the Union side to join her husband in enlisting. Like Mary Lincoln, Mary Logan experienced the anguish of having old friends refuse to speak to her; she experienced the reality of the divided loyalties of southern Illinois settlers who had their roots in the South.[12]

Julia Dent Grant, the wife of the well-known general, also had Southern roots. Raised with slaves in Missouri, she owned four all during the war, although she did not take them to Galena, where they lived before and after the war. She spent much of her time with Grant during the war, but when he left for battle, she would take her children to stay with relatives, often in slave states where they could not believe that their Julia was not in sympathy with the South. She said her husband had "offered his sword" to his country, she felt it was her duty to "take care of his little ones."[13]

How did the war experiences of men and women differ? The men too worried about their families' welfare while they were gone. On $10 a month pay there wasn't much they could do to help; many sent money home and others deserted in desperation to try to help.

Evidence shows that they were a communicating group as letters flowed back and forth; 45,000 letters went daily to the army on the Atlantic coast and an equally large number went back. Notes were put into food boxes to try to keep such items from being pilfered before they reached the soldiers.[14] While the men fought for their country and worried about their families, the women fought for and worried about their men—all in the name of patriotism. They made beautiful banners for regiments to carry into battle; they pulled lint, wrapped bandages, stitched shirts and knit socks; they worked in the newly opened munitions plants and in the manufacturing of clothing. But aside from the fact that the men were bent on taking the lives of others while women were trying to save lives, there was an even more fundamental difference between the activities of men and those of the women.

Men went off to war, as men have gone for centuries, to act in a way that had meaning and form for them, a way that could lead to glory, death or both. The pathway to becoming a hero was strewn with adventure, uniforms, bands, all the military hoopla and civilians' cheers. It could even lead to a brilliant political future. When the men arrived in camp, places had usually been set up for them; tents and blankets were provided, a routine established with drills, mess and orders. They were expected to obey commands and there were definite standards of soldierly conduct for them to follow, along with such extra inducements as opportunities for gambling, plenty of liquor and "loose" women. They were relieved of the chores and the decisions they had to make; they were offered opportunities to enjoy pleasures which they could not indulge in at home. They often did not consider the horrors of war; these were thrust upon them.

The women had nothing to compare with this experience. A few "daughters of the regiment" went legitimately along with the troops when they could be properly chaperoned. Some of this group became heroines and they received a most favorable press. Most of the women who went with their men were considered "camp followers." They served in the same capacity they had served at home. They wanted to be with their men, perhaps to check up on them or they may have heard they were wounded and needed care. Others may have been looking for excitement, or trying to get away from loneliness. Whatever their reasons, they were carrying on under very difficult conditions. If they were officers' wives, the government provided for them when possible. Wives of soldiers had to fend for themselves, find housing and facilities for cooking and laundering. Often they fought their way into hospitals where they were not wanted to serve as nurses. Many in this group were inevitably called prostitutes; many were probably a nuisance to the military authorities trying to fight a war, especially in the beginning. Some women camouflaged themselves as soldiers and enlisted in efforts to both serve their country and to be with the men.[15] Regardless of how or why, these women were in many ways repeating the experience women had had on the frontier. They were expected to provide sustenance, using whatever equipment might be available. They were often called upon to do "men's" work. Those who became nurses proved themselves so ingenious and hard working that they eventually achieved recognition. They certainly brought about lasting changes in the conditions of war.

Women's efforts, however, began on the home front. When the man left, the woman's first responsibility was to herself and to her family. There are indications that not all the women were at all times pleased with their husbands' departures. One war correspondent saw a crowd of women, some with children in their arms, standing in front of a large house where men were being processed, looking up angrily at the windows, shaking their fists. He found that they were "wives, mothers, sisters, and daughters of volunteers who had gone off and left them destitute."[16] Enlisting for a bonus and glory must sometimes have been a form of escapism. For whatever reason the men went, the women were left to struggle with family care.

Most of the home front efforts were directed toward the soldiers, not to the families they had left behind. The government made no provision for soldiers' families, letting local and private philanthropy take over the responsiblility of caring for them. Mary Livermore cites eight cases of destitute women, starving themselves to feed their children, until they came in desperation to the Sanitary Commission for aid.[17] Many women could not reach such aid; while neighbors and relatives helped, many had to move. To manage, they taught school, sewed, took in boarders and laundry—which was considered respectable only when absolutely necessary. Few women had money they could call their own, and earning it, especially in the southern part of the state, brought a woman pity or contempt.

The farmers' wives may have had the heaviest burden. The crops of 1859 had been the largest in the history of the country. Yet the production of wheat in 1859 was surpassed every year of the war, as was the annual production of wool. Labor saving machinery, such as the reaper, is usually given credit for making this possible but woman power was a major factor. Young women went into the fields, and usually received relatively high wages. A popular song went,

> Just take your gun and go;
> For Ruth can drive the oxen, John,
> And I can use the hoe.[18]

The experience of taking over the operation of the farm was not unusual for women. The magazine *Prairie Farmer* told stories of the accomplishments of the "female farmers"; it listened to their woes and answered their questions. In June of 1863, the Decatur *Magnet* wrote of a "young woman about 19 years old, who takes the lead at agricultural labor. One of her brothers is in the army, one . . . sent home a cripple, and the father is also disabled, so she has gone into the fields and about three weeks ago, covered 1,050 hills of corn in five hours. She was draging [sic] oats when last heard from."[19] By 1864 the Carthage *Republican* wrote that a grown man in the field was "a rare sight."[20]

Members of the hundreds of women's organizations, meeting almost daily, probably provided the most noticeable war assistance. The help of these "stay-at-homes" was crucial. From a group in Galena who decided to uniform their first company of soldiers—and in a few days subscribed the money, bought the material, had tailors cut it and then sewed the uniforms themselves—to the final Sanitary Fair in Chicago which netted $358,070, women were the major organizers of money and relief.

The Sanitary Commission, a national organization, was charged with coordinating the efforts of volunteers to help the medical department of the army get the supplies to where they were needed. Men had succeeded in pressuring a reluctant government into granting official authorization; women, who had participated in the planning, comprised the majority of the workers.[22]

Eliza Porter, head of the Chicago Headquarters, with Mary Livermore and Jane Hoge developed an organization comprised of hundreds of aid societies all over the northwestern part of the state with a membership of thousands. Porter later traveled and wrote about her experiences; Mary Livermore also wrote about her experiences during the war, and became active afterwards in the suffrage movement. By 1863, they had proved that they could get supplies coordinated and shipped; all they lacked was money. The idea for the first Sanitary Fair began with Mary Livermore and Jane Hoge. They planned to raise $25,000. Men, underestimating the determination and ability of these women, scoffed at the possibility until nearly the end when the tremendous response from all over the north and east produced a bandwagon effect. The Commission staged an extravanganza in Bryan Hall and six other Chicago buildings which lasted from the inaugural procession on October 28th to the closing dinner for 800 Camp Douglas soldiers two weeks later. They raised over $70,000. Lincoln contributed the original copy of the Emancipation Proclamation, auctioned for $3,000—which earned him a gold watch donated by a jeweler as the prize for the gift which brought the largest price.[23]

Another outstanding woman active in the Sanitary Commission's work was Myra Bradwell. After the war she studied law with her husband, a lawyer and judge, and was to become most influential in the cause of women's legal rights. She was not able to be as active as others in the early years of the Commission; her oldest daughter died in 1861, and her fourth child, a two year old boy, died in 1864. In the 1865 Fair, however, Myra Bradwell was director of the Committee on Arms, Trophies and Curiosities; the exhibit was the major attraction of the Fair.[24]

All the aid societies sponsored money raising projects. These projects might be just an ice cream and cake social, such as one in Decatur which cleared $33, or an state wide fair, such as was held in Decatur in 1864.[25] Each town had aid societies many of which cut across class and denominational lines. Some had imaginative names, like the "Needle Pickets" of Quincy who made needle books for soldiers.[26]

Some groups like the Good Samaritans of Quincy included men in their membership. But nothing that men thought was "peculiar to their own methods" was lacking in the plans of the women—they showed great aptitude for business. Perhaps this was because they were "clearer and more united than the men, because their moral feelings and political instincts were not so much affected by selfishness and business or party considerations."[27] They represented a display of real executive ability by any standard.

The most attention has been paid to the efforts of women as nurses during the Civil War, possibly because women at the front made better publicity. While few had previous training, the legend of Florence Nightingale in the Crimean War was an example to follow. They did not wait for the government to act nor did they listen to the generals who did not want them. Their men needed care of the "tender and loving" variety and they turned out to see that they got it.

Elizabeth Blackwell started a nurses training program in New York in April of 1861. In July of the same year, Dorothea Dix was appointed Superintendent of Women Nurses. She insisted that all her appointments be over 30, plain in appearance, willing to wear dark, hoopless dress. One pretty outcast exploded, "Dragon Dix . . . won't accept any pretty nurses . . . . Just think of putting such an old thing over everyone else. Some fool man did it, so . . . his sex must suffer from it."[28] The government paid nurses 40 cents a day plus subsistence; many went as volunteers, privately supported, or managing somehow, simply because they wanted to be of service.

Mary Ann Bickerdyke of Galesburg was one of the first to arrive and stayed to become one of the greatest. A widow with experience in "botanic" medicine, she volunteered to help shortly after the war began when her pastor described to the congregation the appalling conditions among the new recruits at the Cairo camp. Leaving her two sons in the care of others, financed partially by church funds and later by the Sanitary Commission, she spent four years covering 19 battlefields and gaining a reputation equal to that of Grant or Sherman. Called a "cyclone in calico"—and many other less flattering names—she commandeered what she needed, had no patience with shirking or corruption, and did not hesitate to say what she thought in rough language. Of course she made some enemies, but she made many more friends among the soldiers. After the war men kept in touch with "Mother Bickerdyke" and helped in her future efforts.

The hospitals where she took over became models of what wartime hospitals should be. She used every means to stop the pilfering of Sanitary Commission supplies. A ward-master she caught wearing gifts meant for the men was stripped of his shirt, socks and slippers—much to the delight of the watching soldiers. When she suspected the kitchen help of taking delicacies, she added an emetic to stewed peaches; she told the suffering thieves that the next time it would be "ratsbane." Her complaints to Chicago brought her a large refrigerator with a padlock, where she stored all the special items and locked it in the presence of the cook. When the lock was broken that night, she linked the thievery to the cook; she went at once to the provost marshall and told her story so well that the cook was in the guardhouse and a guard assigned to the kitchen before most of the camp was up. She made her charges stick; she not only got rid of that cook but many others who were also guilty, including a surgeon who was derelict in his duty. Everyone knew by both her reputation and prestige that not only was she incorruptible but she would not tolerate corruption. When a surgeon once questioned her authority, she replied, "On the authority of the Lord God Almighty. Have you anything that outranks that?" General Sherman, responding to a similar complaint, remarked, "If it was she, I can't help you. She has more power than I—she ranks me."

After a battle, Mother Bickerdyke would return to the field after dark with a lantern to search for the living among the bodies. She would even comb the bushes looking for anyone with a breath of life.

Mother Bickerdyke usually had supplies when she needed them, either through the Sanitary Commission or her own efforts. When there were not enough eggs or milk to meet the demand of the Memphis hospitals, she went on leave in Illinois. She procured cows and enough chickens to turn the Chicago Sanitary Commission office into a hennery. Twenty days later she was in Memphis followed by almost 100 cows and over 1,000 hens.[27]

Mary Ann Bickerdyke was a magnificent worker, with heart and head but crude manners and explosive tirades—always for the benefit of the soldiers. Her co-workers were often her opposites in temperament. When she arrived in Cairo, the first June of the war, the community rallied around to help, finding her a room and the supplies she needed. One of the first to help was Mary Safford, called the Angel of Cairo, who had already been delivering the food and supplies donated by her banker brother to the hospitals in the area. Frail in comparison to the robust Mother Bickerdyke, Mary Safford was a perfect complement. She spoke both German and French; she had a quiet poise and dignity which smoothed over difficult situations. She broke down after working hours on a hospital ship without rest, ending her wartime career; but her medical career had just started. She went on to medical school, practicing in Chicago for a time. She performed the first ovariotomy ever done by a woman.[30]

Eliza Chappell Porter, wife of a minister and a school mistress, became a director of the Sanitary Commission in Chicago. She led a group of women to join Bickerdyke in 1862. Mother Bickerdyke called the tiny, auburn-haired woman "little brown bird." She too had a moderating influence on the rough and ready nurse from Galesburg. They worked together through several of Sherman's battles, one of which saw her eldest son in the thick of action. She wrote about her experiences and the efforts of the nurses in these battles, helping the public to understand the work of the Sanitary Commission.[31]

Mary Newcomb of Effingham joined the Cairo group after her husband enlisted, and did without complaint the dirtiest jobs which were necessary to keep the hospital running for the benefit of the soldiers. In writing of her experiences later, she tells of a Southerner who saw her doing such work. He said that he had five daughters, but would rather shoot them than let them do what she was doing—that kind of work was for slaves.[32]

Stella Coatsworth of Chicago left for the front when she received word that her husband was dying. After an arduous and dangerous trip, she found him barely alive and the doctors without hope. She saved his life, only to see him fight again. The second time he was wounded she could not reach him in time; he died at the age of 32. She continued to work as a nurse, and wrote in criticism of some doctors and officials and in praise of many nurses.[33]

Mary Livermore and Jane Hoge, while traveling for the Sanitary Commission, pitched in to help at the hospitals they visited Mother Sturgis and Aunt Lizzie Aiken of Peoria were two more who became favorites of the soldiers.[34]

Emely Gear Hobbs, of Galena, and her doctor husband were an unusual couple. When he enlisted, refusing a commission as a surgeon, she joined him, sending her three children to stay with an aunt in Joliet. She worked alongside him throughout the war, living on soldiers' rations and pay, coping with diseases from small pox to typhoid as well as battle casualties. She too wrote of her experiences for her grandchildren, describing the bravery and ingenuity demanded of women at the front.[34]

Along with the independent women, financed privately or by the government, Catholic nuns contributed greatly to the nursing effort. Mary Livermore reported some prejudice against many Protestant nurses. One surgeon told her, "Your Protestant nurses are always finding some mare's nest or other that they can't let alone. They all write for the papers and the story finds its way into print and directly we are in hot water. Now the Sisters never see anything they ought not to see, nor hear anything they ought not to hear and they never write for the papers . . . . And the result is that we get along comfortably."[35]

Many sisters received high praise and not only for their discretion. Colonel Mulligan and his Irish Brigade from Chicago wanted Sisters of Mercy as nurses. They called on Mother Frances and her assistant to be with them. The Sisters of Mercy took charge of a hospital in Jefferson City and also the hospital ship Empress, along with Marian Mulligan, wife of the Colonel.[36]

Mother Angela Gillespie, who founded the Sisters of the Holy Cross and made it one of the best teaching orders in the country, set up a hospital in a row of old warehouses in Mound City, where 1,500 patients could be cared for. Mary Livermore called it "the best military hospital in the United States." Eighty Sisters of the Holy Cross served as nurses during the war.[37]

All women of course were not capable of such work. After watching one who fled at the sight of a wounded man, Stella Coatsworth wrote that only those women could function as nurses who had "good judgment and self control, a fine organization, lively sensibilities, a gentle voice, soft touch, and quiet step; magnetic and mesmeric power and an intuition that silently understands and forestalls the wants of the patient."[38]

It was quite an order but many were tested and not found wanting. At first the surgeons made it as difficult for them as possible, demanding long hours, the scrubbing of floors, windows and kitchens—chores that many of the men who demanded them would not have permitted their wives and daughters to do. But these women had come down off their pedestals; with no previous experience, they pushed themselves almost beyond the limits of human endurance, proving that if men have to fight wars, they can do it better and with less agony if they are joined by women.

Not all the officers' wives dedicated themselves to the welfare of the wounded. Some may have been more like Julia Dent Grant, who stopped attending after a few aid society meetings, when she found she was unable to do proficiently many of the projects upon which they were working. When in camp she tried nursing in the hospital. But when she returned with the inevitable request for Grant to sign to release a soldier, he exploded and forbid her to spend any more time at the hospital. He had to deal with such things all day and he had her with him for "rest and sunshine."

Grant, like Lincoln, had a difficult time refusing requests for leniency. Once Julia let a woman pleading for the life of a deserter see him and he granted her plea. Mary Livermore once was able to pass all the guards between Grant and civilians to obtain discharges for 21 sick soldiers.[39] Many nurses felt the wounded needed this kind of attention, but it took connections such as Julia Grant's commanding attention, but it took connections such as Julia Grant's or a commanding presence like Mary Livermore's to reach such a solution.

(Newberry Library)

Mother Bickerdyke, Civil War nurse, checking the battlefield after dark to bring help to a wounded man whose life might be saved.

Where there was the best nursing, there were fewer deaths. These women brought cleanliness, good nursing care and high standards of performance which obviously raised the level of care for all. Supplies were made available at the front lines almost as soon as they were needed. Bandages, candles and hot soup would arrive right after a battle, often to the surprise of the commanding officers. This helped the surgeons and nurses start care of the wounded immediately, which saved lives and made recuperation faster and easier.

The efforts of these women saved both lives and suffering, but no one kept track of this; body counts were only for the dead. The men who were doing the killing had time to keep track of exactly how

(Illinois State Historical Libary)

Jenny Hodges, who fought during Civil War as
Albert Cashier, and who kept up her masquerade
as a male longer than any other woman veteran.

many were killed—that is the aim of warfare. We have no way of knowing how many thousands lived, perhaps just to fight again and die, because of the dedicated efforts of these nurses.

Women also made life easier for those recuperating. Women read to them, wrote letters for them and furnished them with books. They acted as messengers to families, sometimes being able to arrange furloughs or discharges for badly wounded men when surgeons refused—because it might make their record look bad. These women earned the names of "angel" or "mother" by soothing, singing to and praying with those confined to hospitals.

These women also saved large amounts of government money. Old buildings were made functional, they solved the bug problem, made old clothes reusable by setting up laundries. Before they arrived much soiled clothing had simply been discarded. They cut food waste and introduced the kind of methodical, efficient management such women had practiced at home.

The Civil War was marked by its informality. Wives could go to nurse husbands; women by the wagonload tagged along as camp followers, officers sent for wives, children and nurses. Women could dress up as men and enlist. One estimate is that about 400 did so, but Mary Livermore, who covered much territory during the war, believed there were many more.[40] Some of them were not unmasked until they had served two or three years. The record is held by Jennie Hodgers of Illinois, who had posed as Albert Cashier, fought honorably for four years and received a pension in 1899. She was not unmasked until an auto accident in 1911 sent "him" to a veteran's hospital.[41] Another, who took the name "Frank Miller," was Frances Hook of Chicago who enlisted with her brother. She served ten months, was mustered out when discovered and reenlisted. She was not exposed until captured by the Confederates, who shot her in the leg when she tried to escape. Jefferson Davis offered her a commission, which she refused, and he returned her to the North. She said she had assisted in the burying of three female soldiers at different times, whose sex no one else knew.

Dr. Mary Walker, an army physician, argued that Frances Hook should be commissioned, that "patriotism has no sex."[42] Many women, however, disapproved of women soldiers, agreeing with Mary Livermore that it was not women's place to take lives; they should be healing wounds, not making them.[43]

There were diverse factors motivating this type of enlistment. Many probably simply had no place else to go. As one woman said, "I have only my husband in all this world. When he enlisted I promised that I should go with him, and that was why I put on his clothes and enlisted in the same regiment, and go with him I will in spite of everybody."[44] Others may have gone for what they thought would be excitement or for the plentiful supply of single men. Patriotism certainly was concocted of a mixture of emotions and not confined to one sex; the so-called glory of war had its attractions for women too.

Nadine Turchin, a Russian who had been with her husband in the Crimean War, joined him when he came to the United States and was commissioned a colonel by Illinois Gov. Richard Yates. She was very popular with the men whom she nursed and befriended. Once when her husband was ill, she led his regiment in battle and faced the fire as well as the men—while riding sidesaddle! The men followed her "cheerfully." When her husband was to be court-martialed, she went to Washington and returned in the nick of time with an order voiding it; he was promoted instead. She was indeed a resourceful woman.[45]

Belle Reynolds of Peoria was another extraordinary officer's wife. She joined her husband when he enlisted and stayed to help in any way she could. When the captain of a hospital ship was trying to keep a mob from boarding, she stood on the top deck with two pistols, ordered to shoot when he gave the word. While it was not necessary, she acquired such a reputation that Governor Yates commissioned her as a major, which made her outrank her husband. After the war she studied medicine in Chicago, and became the resident physician at the Home for the Friendless.[46]

Unfortunately we have no way of knowing more about some of these women who served so gallantly, either with their husbands or as enlistees. It seems obvious that there was cooperation between soldiers of both sexes, for how else could so many of the female soldiers remain undiscovered for years? Conceivably they added spice to camp life, and there must have been at least tacit agreement that what officers didn't know, they couldn't spoil. The accounts reflect the women's in circumventing regulations, their mastery of manipulation achieved during centuries of subjugation. While as Dr. Walker said, "patriotism has no sex," sometimes sex can masquerade as patriotism.

One of the problems facing the North during the Civil War was the Confederate sympathizers in the army. Illinois had many from its southern counties, and many of the deserters were from that area. Between June and October of 1863, 2,000 deserters were arrested in the four southern counties. When enrollment officials tried to enlist men, sporadic rioting broke out. In Boone County women threw eggs at them, and in June of 1863 a mob of 300 to 400 men and women attacked a deputy U.S. marshall and his assistants because they had arrested two men for refusing to give their names to the enrollment officials.[47] Some women were involved in hiding deserters, others may have helped to expose them.

One of the major scares concerning Confederate efforts in the North resulted from the uncovering of a plot to free the prisoners who were held at Camp Douglas in Chicago during November of 1864. One of the Confederate plotters was said to have hidden inside the box springs of a bed where a woman pretended to be very ill.

Later he was helped to get past the guards outside by escorting a woman who had come to call. Mary B. Morris was arrested and imprisoned in connection with the conspiracy; though she was not tried, she was sent o her parents in Kentucky for the rest of the war.[48] Such episodes demonstrate that where men's opposition to the war involved them in anti-governmental activities, they had the support and assistance of women.

The problem of refugees, both black and white, loomed large in the southern part of the state. They pilfered, got in the way of legitimate operations and were a general nuisance. Southern white girls who might have worked, for there was much to be done, were prevented by their men who would say, "my gals ain't no nigger."[49] It took strong management and understanding of ex-slaves to get the contrabands to work, and to find enough projects they could handle without too much additional training. Many nurses complained about them; Mother Bickerdyke seems to have been the most successful in using them to advantage. One historian said that it was the women who saw that slavery must go and who demanded that the ex-slaves be used for hard work instead of their husbands and sons, many of whom were breaking down from their unaccustomed army service. The women felt that the ex-slaves could do their part too.[50]

Women during the Civil War contributed a tremendous amount of labor and understanding, taking repeated tragedy in their stride as they kept on working. They found themselves capable of many things they had never dreamed they could do and they gained self assurance they would never lose. Those who lost men, or whose men returned crippled, had to carry on after the war as well. They needed all the reassurance they could get. Many of the leaders had discovered how capable women were and how much they needed more opportunities to prove it. Stella Coatsworth said that "American women no longer followed in the full beaten track of example, but striking out into new and untried paths, lay their plans and execute their purpose with self poise and fearless of results . . . . War . . . enabled her to rise to a measure of usefulness that was hitherto even by herself undreamed of."[51] Many of these women who rose to these heights continued their careers after the war.

Women proved during the war—to themselves and to men—that they could accomplish great tasks. After the war they were to turn their energy and their new found assurance to many areas of life in need of reform. These new efforts came from both their experiences during the war and from the organizations they had founded to serve wartime purposes.

But the history of women, like that of most groups with minority status is cyclical; they rise, only to fall back. They would have to prove themselves over and over again as capable, resourceful and strong.

CHAPTER 4
Women and Change
1870 - 1920

"If a woman is a good housekeeper in her own home, she will be able to do well that larger housekeeping."

"Good Government means clean alleys and clean streets; it means safety on the streets and in the home; it means health and happiness for women workers; it means fine schools and wholesome recreation; it means a well ordered community life that leads to the national well-being."

Louise deKoven Bowen

With the end of the Civil War, women, who had dropped their efforts for their own rights to concentrate on the war and the cause of the slaves, expected to have their wrongs redressed along with those of the blacks. They were to be bitterly disappointed. The men who had supported women's right to vote limited the fourteenth amendment by inserting the word "male" into the Constitution for the first time. They carried the insult farther in the fifteenth amendment by making it unconstitutional to deny the vote on the basis of "race, color and previous conditon of servitude," refusing to add the word "sex" to that list. Most women were not then concerned about the issues of equal rights and suffrage. But many who had been active during the war and who had become accustomed to organizing and administering to protect the public welfare also began to realize the effect of legal and political discrimination on their own lives and on their ability to help the larger community.

In the years following the Civil War, Mary Livermore, Myra Bradwell, Catherine Waite and others began to activate the state wide network of women, who had been associated with the Sanitary Commission, for the cause of women's rights. This movement involved more than suffrage; it included the rights of women as human beings and their role in community affairs. While there was an overlap between these concerns, some women focused their energies on suffrage, others on equal rights, which was as radical then as women's liberation today, and still others on humanitarian and cultural improvements.

Beginning in the years after the Civil War, there were a series of steps in the progress of women's rights. One of the most effective leaders was Myra Bradwell, who had also worked with the Chicago Sanitary Commission. Her career illustrates the contradictions between a woman's role and the legal discrimination against her. Bradwell had continued her work after the war by supporting projects to help crippled soldiers and by establishing a sewing exchange to teach needy immigrants a way to earn a living. In 1868 she redirected her efforts toward legal reforms.

Having studied law under her judge husband, she decided to start a weekly legal newspaper, the *Chicago Legal News*. The Bradwells had sufficient influence in Springfield to have Myra Bradwell named president by special charter of both the *News* and the publishing company—inspite of the fact that under law her married status prevented her from obtaining a notary public's license.

The state legilsature declared the newspaper a valid source of information on Illinois laws. It soon became the most important such publication west of the Alleghenies, cited constantly by male lawyers. It carried columns devoted to reforming the courts, the profession and the law; it also carried a regular column on the legal status and problems of women. For example, the paper reported a case where the wages of a woman had been garnisheed to pay her husband's saloon bill. The publicity helped arouse public interest; in 1869 a bill drafted by Bradwell to give women the right to control their own earnings was then lobbied through the legislature with the help of Judge Charles Waite, Catherine Waite and Mary Livermore. Another bill giving widows an interest in their husband's estates in all cases was also passed.[1]

Myra Bradwell also had passed her bar examination and had applied for admission to the Illinois Bar. But in 1869, the Illinois Supreme Court held her ineligible as a married woman to practice law, using the words, "by reason of the disability imposed by your condition." She carried the case to the United States Supreme Court, which after a two year delay, decided that the matter was a state issue. But the court did say that the "Laws of the Creator" placed limits on the functions of womanhood. In a similar case, the Supreme Court clearly stated its philosophy:

It is a public policy . . . not to tempt women from the proper duties of their sex by offering the duties peculiar to ours. The peculiar qualities of womanhood, its gentle graces, its tender susceptibility, its purity, its delicacy, its emotional impulses, its subordination of hard reason to sympathetic feeling are surely not qualifications for forensic strife. Nature has tempered woman as little for juridical conflicts of the courtroom as for the physical conflicts of the battlefield. Woman is moulded for gentler and better things, and it is not the saints of the world who chiefly give employment to our profession.[2]

Although barred from practicing law herself, Bradwell supported the efforts of Alta Hulett. Hulett had studied in a law office in Rockford and passed the bar examination at age 18. When denied admission to the bar, she prepared a bill to bar discrimination in employment. She was joined by many others, including Bradwell and Ada Kepley of Effingham. Kepley, the first woman in the United States to graduate from law school, had also been denied the right to use her degree.

They lobbied the bill through the legislature; it became law and went into effect in July 1872. The law was the first in the country to prohbibit discrimination against women in employment. It stated that "no person shall be precluded or debarred from any occupation, profession or employment (except military) on account of sex." It did exempt women from jury service, work on roads and streets, and elective office.[3] Alta Hulett became the first woman in Illinois to be admitted to the bar, on her nineteenth birthday in 1873. Other women did enter the legal profession, including Bradwell's daughter, Bessie, who was valedictorian of her class at Union College of Law, now part of Northwestern University.[4]

The state legislature, following the logic of this anti-discriminatory bill, began to remove other limits to women's professional activities. In the same year a law was passed granting all women over 21, married or single, the right "to hold any office under the general or special school laws in this state." Nine women were immediately chosen as County Superintendents of Schools; the best known was Mary Ellen West of Galesburg.[5]

In 1875, the legislature removed another limit when women gained the right to become notary publics. Annie Fitzhugh Ousley along with six others from Cook County were immediately commissioned.[6] If women could become lawyers, that is, serve as officials of the court, it had become absurd to bar them from this legal function.

The improvement of women's legal and economic position made it easier to gain, in 1873, a right long desired by the women's movement—equal guardianship of children after divorce. In comparison with other states, Illinois had liberal divorce laws. Between 1857 and 1886 the courts granted 36,072 divorces, leading the nation.[7] Illinois had also in the past shown great consideration to divorced women; since 1859 women had been allowed to take back their maiden names.[11]

The existence at the same time of a well organized suffrage organization around the state may in part account for the success of equal rights legislation. The leaders of the suffrage group were usually among the most vocal and effective lobbyists. Many also had politically influential husbands who supported their cause. But equal rights laws proved easier to promote than suffrage, probably because in reality they affected only a few persons. Suffrage, of course, would involve half the population and thus threatened to transform the whole structure of public decision-making. Certainly those who opposed suffrage feared this, but the prospect also accounted for the energy many of the leaders put into the cause.

Before the war, Mary Livermore, as the wife of a minister, had involved herself in charity work, the temperance movement and in numerous other good causes. She also helped her husband edit the Universalist monthly, *The Covenant*. Her wartime experience broadened her vision, providing her with contacts around the state and training in the art of organization and public speaking. Like many others, Mary Livermore believed that women were spiritually superior to men and that it was their duty to fight against such evils as poverty, drunkenness and prostitution. Until the war, however, she did not support suffrage. After her experiences and travels, she came to the realization that the only way women could be effective was to become involved in politics.[9]

In 1868, Livermore organized the first women's suffrage convention in Illinois, becoming president of the Illinois Woman Suffrage Association, with Myra Bradwell as its secretary. To facilitate communication, she also started a newspaper, *The Agitator.* By the time the State Constitutional Convention met in 1870, suffrage groups had been formed in all major towns and were ready to bring pressure on the convention. They met in Springfield to prepare a petition to have the issue of women's voting placed on the ballot. While many influential men gave their support, the only organized group to endorse their cause was the Irish Republican Convention[10] By this time women were voting in Utah and Wyoming; these Illinois women wanted to be third.

Four of the nine members of the Committee on Suffrage of the Constitutional Convention, led by Elijah Haines of Lake County, were willing to present the issue to the voters. In April the Convention voted 40 to 21 submit the question, along with the constitution, to the voters. But in May, they reversed themselves and struck out the provision. One reason for this change of mind was the number of protests from various parts of the state as opponents organized against it. A petition from women in Peoria, bearing over 1,300 signatures, said in part

fearing that a small minority of their country women by their boldness and misdirected zeal may succeed in carrying a measure which we believe to be prejudicial to the highest interest of our sex if not in direct opposition to both divine and national laws . . . [we declare] that we are unalterably opposed to any action on your part which shall confer upon the women of this state the right of suffrage.

The petition continued with resolutions which stated that

While we admit the necessity of expansive reform both in the political and social relations of life, we deny that the bestowal of the right of suffrage on women would in any way hasten reform. . . . That women's sphere of duty is distinct from man's and is well defined; and that as going to the polls forms no part of it, we will strenuously oppose this movement as an invasion of our right not to do man's work. . . . Therefore, that we are the true advocates of women's rights and that those of our sex who are clamoring for suffrage should call themselves the 'man's rights party' since they are grasping after duties, powers, and privileges that naturally belong to the stronger sex.[11]

Another reason for the reversal may have been the hostility generated by reports that some suffragists had said that "men are out of their places in the legislative halls and on the judicial bench—that these places should be wholly given over to women and the men go into the fields and workshops."[12] In 1871 suffragists tried to press the issue all over the country by appearing at the polls to vote. Among these was Catherine V. Waite of Chicago; her husband tried to overturn the refusal to permit her to vote with court action which failed[13]

The point of view of the opponents of suffrage as presented in the Peoria petition was, in the context of its time, almost as much of a declaration of woman's independence as that of the suffragists. In the pre-industrial era and in the more recent frontier period, women had worked alongside men, as hard as men, yet had had little status or identity separate from that of their fathers or husbands. The rapid development of a commercial and industrial economy had led increasingly to division of labor by sex and to the separation of the home and the work place. As woman's work became defined more narrowly in terms of maintaining the home and child rearing, her actual decision making power increased. She no longer was simply an auxiliary to her husband; within the home, and on issues dealing with the home and child rearing, men informally abdicated decision making. The cult of true womanhood—that is, placing the woman on a pedestal—produced a cultural perspective in which middle class men and women came to define women as spiritually superior to men. Through child rearing, education and church work, women could express their desire to reform. In the eyes of many women, the suffrage movement threatened their new found status which rested on a clear separation of spheres, a view which the Peoria petition seems to articulate so well.

Middle class women, unlike working class women, had the luxury of staying at home and concentrating on children, the luxury of creating a small utopian world free from the ugliness and compromises of the business world. But over the 20 years following their first few steps forward on the legal front, women would in increasing numbers leave the home to participate in a variety of community and humanitarian activities in large measure directed towards improving or protecting the home and its environment. For many, fate or some great crisis would lead them into a more active life. For others it would be the search for companionship or mutual enlightenment which life within the confines of an isolated household did not provide. Whatever the reasons, by the turn of the twentieth century, the life style which had formerly appeared to be a utopian solution for increasing numbers of women would take on the characteristics of a prison. The participation of women in various reform movements, not just in suffrage, prefigured this new vision of women.

The Chicago Fire was a crisis which changed the lives of many and produced a number of leaders of future reform movements. The Fire left women of all classes homeless and forced them to think of others outside their immediate families. It fostered a communitarian spirit. Every home located far enough away to be safe was crowded with refugees, both friends and strangers. Others camped on the prairies until relief in various forms could be organized.

As the relief and aid societies which had functioned during the Civil War sprang into action, women proved once more their organizing and administrative skills. Halls, church basements and homes were used both to shelter refugees and to be turned into factories where clothing and bedding could be made. An umbrella organization of women's groups kept track of people and their needs, obtained sewing machines and tried to take care of both present and future. Supplies poured in from all over the country and were distributed; more than 150,000 people were helped.[14] Aurelia King, whose husband was chairman of the Relief and Aid Society, went daily into the city from Elmhurst to give out the items sent directly to her. She wrote, "I can never resume the even tenor of my way. . . . I feel as if my life were beginning again."[15] The diaries, letters and memoirs of many testify to similar feelings. As one woman said, "I never enjoyed anything so much in my life. It seems terible to say it, when so many people were suffering, but I felt important and useful."[16]

Many women who later became leaders in reform activities had their first taste of helping others in the aftermath of the Fire. Mary

McDowell and Louise deKoven Bowen, later active in settlement houses, helped distribute supplies. Bertha Palmer, the new bride of Potter Palmer, opened her house to refugees. Harriet Hubbard Ayer, whose baby died the night of the fire in the flight from the flames, left for Europe shortly afterward to overcome severe depression. She was to find both herself and a formula for face cream which she later used to establish a cosmetic company. Frances Willard, president of the Evanston College for Ladies at the time of the Fire, found that the future of that institution was curtailed because all available funds went to rebuild Chicago. When her college became part of Northwestern University, she found her future with the Women's Christian Temperance Union.[6]

Bessie Bradwell, Myra's daughter, rescued the subscription list of the *Chicago Legal News,* the only thing the 13 year old could save. Myra took the list to Milwaukee, where she continued to publish the *News.* She appealed to lawyers all over the country for help in rebuilding the destroyed law libraries; she was also instrumental in the passing of the Burnt Records Act, which covered proof of real estate titles after the Fire.[17]

At the other end of the scale was Mother Jones, a working class woman with a successful dressmaking business who began her life anew as a labor organizer at the age of 40. The Fire took her home and business, leaving her penniless. She joined the crowd which found shelter in Old St. Mary's Church. While helping other refugees, she spent her evenings nearby at meetings of the Knights of Labor. This rekindled old memories from her life in Memphis before a yellow fever epidemic had taken in one week the lives of her four children and her active union husband. After the Chicago Fire, she devoted the next 50 years of her life to the union struggle, moving from one town to the next, from one strike to the next, organizing workers and their wives, fighting injustice wherever she found it with everything from broomsticks to propaganda. She fought not for suffrage, but for higher wages and better conditions for workers so that their wives could have the opportunity to stay home from the mills and raise their children. She is buried in the miners' cemetery in Mt. Olive, Illinois, with a special monument.[18]

After the Fire, many women became more involved in group efforts. They joined all varieties of clubs, giving impetus to the movement which would grow rapidly through the turn of the century. The major causes of this phenomenon, which swept both men and women into organizations segregated by sex, were the social forces set loose by industrialization and urbanization. But certainly the Fire, like the Civil War, played a significant part. Women had become conscious of their loneliness and boredom.

They also began to realize that the home and community could not be fully separated; the community constantly impinged upon and threatened the security and well-being of the home. They could not improve society—which they saw as the responsibility of women—

(Chicago Historical Society)

Executive committee of the Candy Dippers deciding whether to strike.

(Midwest Women's Historical Collection, University of Ill. at Chicago Circle)

Garment workers strike, 1915.

by staying home; neither could they isolate the home from an unreformed society. Jennie June Croly, the initiator of women's clubs in the East, explained the need for such clubs in these terms:" It is one of the paradoxes in human nature that women, while being responsible for social conditions, have been condemned to individual isolation."[19]

Church societies which traditionally had provided women with opportunities to socialize and to perform socially useful services to others no longer seemed sufficient. They divided women within the community into separate religious groups. They limited the expression of a woman's own identity and her ability to work out her own destiny. Church societies also tended to be under the control of a male hierarchy.

Women were yearning to realize more fully their culturally assigned roles beyond the confines of the home and missionary sphere. To extend themselves to this out-side world demanded that they gain greater knowledge of themselves, of their values and of the larger society; this knowledge had been denied them as unnecessary to their function in the home. They had had little opportunity to develop the knowledge and skills needed to provide a spiritually and culturally uplifting environment within the home—the role that had been increasingly relegated to them—to say nothing of carrying on such a function outside the home.

Many of the first clubs formed in the 1860s and 1870s, therefore, began with concentration on self-improvement. Women joined such groups to study everything from history to art and literature and also to carry out their own ideas through their own activities. They were considered radical at the time and often met with derision; yet women increasingly gathered for such purposes. Club women found themselves becoming more concerned with matters of public affairs which were considered men's sphere. As they studied and discussed the world at large, they also learned a host of new skills—how to debate and speak before an audience, how to do research, how to run a meeting with parliamentary procedures, how to raise funds and how to administer institutions larger than the home.

These early clubs were criticized because they took women outside the home, which would, it was widely believed, cause delinquent children and the dissolution of the family. Louise deKoven Bowen remembered her father forbidding her to associate with her neighbor, Kate Doggett, who had gained his disapproval because she both wore her hair short and belonged to a woman's club.[20] Kate Doggett was the founder of the famous Fortnightly in Chicago in 1873, and went on to support such radical reform as suffrage.

The desire for self-improvement was not limited to women of leisure in cities like Chicago. As early as 1866 women in Quincy formed what was probably the first such group in Illinois, the Friends in Council, aimed at attracting those "who valued the world of thought and who were zealous for self-improvement." Their motto, "Neglect not the gift that is in thee," symbolized their major purpose. One woman, later president of the group, remembered that when a member called on her and asked her to join, "an offer of a seat in the Cabinet of the United States would have surprised me less: . . . I remember regretting that I should happen to be wearing an apron at such a momentous hour."[21]

Self-improvement and community improvement in the areas of culture and knowledge soon fused. In many places women's efforts were crucial to the establishment of the first libraries. In 1867, Decatur began a Ladies Library Association and opened a library three days a week. When a law was passed in 1872 permitting a tax levy for libraries, the women urged the city council to take over the project. When the mayor, who was in favor of.doing so, was absent from the meeting, Jane Martin Johns drove her buggy through mud and rain to persuade him to return with her. He cast the deciding vote for the town supported library.[22] In Cairo the Woman's Club and Library Association had its own building provided by Anna Safford in memory of her husband, used as a library and a club house.[23] In many more towns, women's efforts were responsible for the first libraries.

Women also helped promote the Chautauqua plan for home study and lectures. There were about 675 circles in 425 localities, more than 60 of them in tiny villages. These were for both men and women, but much of the support came from women; many of the featured speakers were also women.[24] Women were also concerned with the preservation of the cultural inheritance in rapidly changing communities. The saving of local records and landmarks was an important activity of the Daughters of the American Revolution, which by 1902 had three chapters in Illinois. The Dames of the Loyal Legion collected Civil War memorabilia.[25]

Women's groups also formed to promote art and music. The first was the Jacksonville Art Association, formed in 1873, but within a few years similar groups were formed in Lincoln, Champaign, Springfield, Decatur and Bloomington. They fostered an interest in the arts, held exhibitions and presented speakers.[26] Chicago had a number of such societies; the Palette, formerly the Bohemian Club, was the first, but was joined in the 1880s by the Altrua, Arché, Municipal Art League, the Niké, the Society for Decorative Arts and the Public School Art Society[27]

While the cultural activities of women's clubs served as substitutes for higher education, they also deepened women's appreciation of formal schooling. College graduates were active in women's clubs, which provided a congenial social environment. They also were a self-conscious group, with their own associations concerned with the advancement of women in higher education. Since the 1850s the Ladies Education Society of Jacksonville had been helping indigent young women acquire an education and become teachers. With the club movement flourishing, others joined them. PEO started as a college sorority in 1869, but changed toward the end of the century into community oriented groups while retaining its name. It became involved in helping women go on to higher education, even starting its own junior college. In 1883 college graduates in Illinois formed the Western Association of University Women. Their efforts also went toward helping more women gain more education through scholarships and fellowship awards for advanced study. After Marion Talbot came to Chicago in 1892 to be the country's first dean of women at the University of Chicago, she increased both the scope of activities of the AAUW.[28]

In 1873 club women, educators and others involved in the struggle for suffrage organized the Association for the Advancement of Women. The association was originally sponsored by the New York Sorosis, the first New York women's club, founded by Jennie June Croly. Chicagoans, such as Ellen Mitchell, the first woman on the school board, were active in the national movement. Mary Livermore was elected its first president, with Frances Willard as vice president. The group sought to promote the image of women as thinkers and to also provide a voice for moderate feminism at a time when many felt that the two branches of the suffrage movement were too radical and eccentric. The second meeting of the Association was held in Chicago; in 1878 Chicagoan Kate Doggett was elected its president.[29]

One of the most famous and important national organizations was the Women's Christian Temperance Union. The WCTU, which still has its national headquarters in Evanston, Illinois, grew out of the Women's Crusade Against Alcoholism which swept the Midwest in the 1870s. Praying bands of women began spontaneously closing saloons throughout the Midwest. The groups took organizational form in 1874 at a convention in Bloomington. Frances Willard became its secretary; within a few years she was president of the national organization.

The WCTU, so different in its constituency and style from other women's reform groups, reflected the same broad notions about women as a social force for good that inspired the club movement, the suffrage movement and the Association for the Advancement of Women. However, the WCTU more closely tied this vision to the home. As a result it grew into the largest woman's organization on the local, state and national level. In their view, saloons and dance halls supported a moral environment which undermined society's cultural values and family life and which promoted prostitution and poverty. Temperance societies were not new and generally in the past had included both men and women. The sudden and disproportionate concern of women with temperance during this period transformed it into a woman's issue of first magnitude.

Under Willard's leadership, the religiously inspired WCTU extended its vision and diversified its activities, as she used it as an instrument to promote feminism among traditionally conservative women. Very early in her own life she had determined not only to expand her own intellectual capacities and interests, but to devote her life to a career of service "among the class that I have always loved and that had loved me always—the girls of my native land and my times."[30] Born in 1839 in upstate New York, she grew up on a farm and taught school after receiving a degree from Northwestern Female College in Evanston. She became the president of the college in 1871. Her hopes for the future of the college were soon dashed after the Chicago Fire when it became a part of Northwestern University. Although Willard had stayed on as dean of women and a professor of English, she resigned in a dispute with her former fiance, then president of the university, over the status of women's education.

In 1876, the Illinois WCTU, swayed by her eloquence, adopted a resolution looking forward to "that day when the mothers and daughters of America shall have a voice in the decision by which . . . the rum-shop is opened or shut beside their homes." But Annie Wittenmeyer, president of the national organization, declared that "we do not propose to trail our skirts through the mire of politics." The national did not change its position until Willard became president in 1878.[31]

She thought of the WCTU as a school to interest women in life beyond the family circle so that they might take a more active and useful part in society. To encourage the timid, she tied her cause and organization to the home. Step by step she led her followers into the peace and arbitration movement, labor reform, the "social purity" movement concerned with prostitution, health and hygiene, city welfare work, prison reform and the advocacy of police matrons. Saloons, in her mind, were the symbol of separatism and of all that was corrupting in society. In Evanston, the dry town where she lived, she noted that "the absence of saloons and bars reduced to a minimum the separatist conditions between men and women with which most places are cursed."[32] More money, she observed, was spent in saloons than on schools. Under her leadership Chicago women gathered 14,000 signatures to enforce a Sunday tavern closing ordinance which had been ignored for years. When they presented their petition to Chicago's common council, however, it was tabled. The irate mob outside—with no police protection for the petitioners—made it necessary for them to leave by a side door to avoid violence.[33] It was the first and last time that the women went before the common council on this cause, but it helped strengthen their convictions on women's suffrage.

Frances Willard dreamed of an inclusive reform movement and to this end she brought her organization into closer relationship with others. For a few years after 1886, the WCTU and the Knights of Labor exchanged fraternal delegates at their conventions. In 1888, Willard participated in the formation of the International Council of

Women, an organization designed to draw together representatives of a wide variety of organizations. She served as first president of its national council. The following year she helped in the formation of the General Federation of Women's Clubs. Her most controversial action was leading the WCTU into supporting the Prohibition Party. But by stressing familiar themes—home, family and temperance—Frances Willard captured the confidence of a generation of conservative women, many of them indifferent to other reforms, and led them into new areas of public activity. By early 1900 Illinois had 475 WCTU groups and thousands of women proudly wore the "white ribbon." Frances Willard's statue stands today in the national capitol, sent there by the state of Illinois as a testimonial to the importance of her career.[34]

Most women's clubs followed the same path, starting with narrow goals and diversifying as they grew. The Union of Bohemian Women illustrates this process. Founded in Chicago during the Civil War as a protective society by women to help each other in case of illness or death, it grew and diversified in the decades following the war. By 1898 it had become the largest woman's literary society in Illinois with 2,300 members scattered throughout the city in both poor and middle class neighborhoods. It then extended its concerns from self-protection and self-improvement to the protection of women and children in poor neighborhoods, and sponsored such legislation as parental schools where truants could be sent.[35]

The Chicago Woman's Club, whose organizational structure became a model for women's clubs around the nation, including the WCTU, differed only in the sense that it was originally organized to satisfy the desire of a group of women to be socially useful. Its founders, active in the Fortnightly, wanted to discuss current problems rather than the classic course of study the club had chosen for 1875 and 1876. In 1876, Caroline Brown called together a group from both within and without the society for the purpose of forming a new type of club. They originated the idea of departments, which would become typical of the structue of women's clubs. At first they only had four departments: home, education, philanthropy and reform. Soon they added art and literature, and philosophy and science.

The department structure was meant to meet different interests and to attract various types into one club. As stated later in the annals of the club, "timid souls who feared that women might get outside their sphere could surely not object to serving in the interest of the home. Mothers would all take a lively interest in education; all good church workers might lend a hand to philanthropy, and the unterrified would gravitate toward reform, which looked more formidable then than now."[36] Every member was required to serve in at least one of the departments.

Nine hundred club members paid entrance fees of $15 and annual dues of $10 which were used to carry out numerous projects and to start reform activities. The club sponsored the appointment of a woman to the Chicago Board of Education, the appointment of a woman physician to the Cook County Insane Asylum, the installment of kindergartens in public schools (first at private and then at public expense), financial support for a school in jail for boys and support for an industrial school. The Woman's Club also supported the Women and Children's Protective Agency, the Chicago Political Equality League and the Women's Trade Union League. The club spawned numerous specialized associations to carry out work that they could not do themselves, sending representatives to these associations to keep informed. The club had committees to watch over the activities of public and private charitable institutions and to collect data on matters of interest to its departments. Despite its emphasis on action, the Woman's Club remained essentially an educational experience, providing its members through lectures and reports a common body of information and ideas to help shape the perceptions of those not active. It also bound together in common causes the housewife and the professional.[37]

By the late 1880s there were so many clubs supporting the same philanthropic endeavors that the leaders, who kept crossing each others' paths, decided that it would be more efficient if they collaborated. Groups working for the betterment of conditions for women and children formed an umbrella organization, the Illinois Woman's Alliance. Under its auspices were joined suffrage, medical, temperance, ethical and labor organizations plus the order of the Eastern Star and a Christian Science Association.

Women's clubs came together in the General Federation of Women's Clubs in 1889 in New York; their second convention was held in Chicago in 1892. By 1894 members of 77 Illinois women's clubs met in Chicago and set up a state federation whose first president was Isabella Candee of Cairo. By 1903 the state federation had 24,000 women from 246 clubs with 19 standing committees. There were possibly twice that number of clubs in the state, but most of the strongest became federated. These state and national federations were important in giving women from different locations a common outlook and set of causes; but they were more important as organized and extensive pressure groups which made it more difficult for those in power to disregard their demands.[38]

Middle class housewives and professionals of town and city were not alone in their passion for organization during this period. Farm women were admitted on an equal basis with men into the Granges. Not fewer than four of the thirteen persons needed to begin a Grange had to be women and some rose to positions of leadership. Farmer's Institutes, which furnished adult education, included women among their speakers and women formed auxiliaries known as Domestic Science Associations. By 1906, 55 counties in Illinois had active chapters which held state wide women's institutes. They studied the value and cost of food, hygiene and sanitation, diet and other subjects of interest. Unlike other women's organizations, those among farm women were supported by an act of Congress. In 1914 money was appropriated for extension work in home economics and agriculture. This provided professional leadership in helping farm women meet and study together. While farm women did not have access to the variety of groups open to urban women, they had organizations designed to meet their own particular needs. The programs, moreover, included the whole family, leading to more "togetherness" in these women's club experience.[39]

Clubs also gave women the experience in business enterprises necessary to become experts in the art of financing and management. When in 1889 the Decatur Woman's Club decided to build its own club house, they organized a stock company with a capital of $6,000 with shares of $10 each sold only to women. They built a building which gave them rental income as well as a meeting place. Many other clubs followed their example, the most ambitious project being that of the National Headquarters of the WCTU. Matilda Carse, the WCTU's chief financial officer, raised almost $1 million for the Woman's Temple in Chicago. The depression of 1893, however, spoiled its money making possibilities.

Many clubs had their own newsletters and magazines. One of the best known was the WCTU's weekly journal, *The Signal,* which is still being published. Another business service was providing a place for women to sell their handiwork. Women's exchanges became the place to buy handmade objects and at the same time give maximum return to the women workers.[40]

Some club businesses were conducted as philanthropic endeavors. The Klio Associations's Noonday Rest served lunch and offered a library, the services of a physician and evening classes for working women while giving work to the volunteer members who staffed it.[41] The Young Women's Christian Association, the YWCA, set up an employment bureau, a dispensary and a boarding home. By 1880, however, they had stopped placing women in domestic service because they wanted to upgrade their applicants; they concentrated on clerks, nurses, teachers, bookkeepers, governesses and dressmakers.[42] It is ironic that women consistently downgraded the work which was considered part of their own sphere, paid the least to those who did it and rated it as menial and unskilled. It is particularly ironic since the availability of women to do housework was essential to the middle and upperclass woman's participation in clubs and settlement work.

By the 1890s the club movement had reached out to more women and extended its range of activities through networks on the local, state and national level. But it had also become a dynamic force in what is now known as the progressive reform movement. Greater involvement in civic reform distinguished the clubs' efforts from those of their earlier period and reflected a new self-confidence of women in their own values and their own abilities. This self-consciousness and assurance was not only the result of years of self-improvement and of practical social service in organizations. It also came from the national exposure provided by the 1893 World Columbian Exposition in Chicago.

The Exposition marked the beginning of women's collaboration with men in large scale civic projects during peactime. In 1890, a presidential order created a Board of Lady Managers for the Fair, chaired by Bertha Palmer, with Ellen Henrotin as vice chairman and with representatives from every state. The board gave elaborate receptions for glamorous foreign visitors and established boarding houses where women from out of town could stay safely and cheaply. A more lasting effect was its participation in the organization of congresses which provided women with a platform. The board was in charge of a special Women's Building designed by Sophia Hayden with a mural by the famous artist, Mary Cassatt. The Women's Building provided a center for women visitors and for exhibits by women from other countries, displaying their progress and their problems. Bertha Palmer, dubbed the "In—Keeper's Wife"by the Spanish Infanta, presided over the opening ceremonies of the building. Her speech received extensive coverage by the press.

Bertha Palmer had always been lavishly supported by father and husband; she looked every inch the queen of Chicago society that she was. But her speech reflected the new consciousness of women—that being on a pedestal for most women was neither completely satisfying nor a true picture of their life. She protested the dependence and helplessness of women, condemning their poor pay, their lack of education and the other handicaps which kept women out of lucrative industrial enterprises and high positions. "Freedom and justice for all are infinitely more to be desired than pedestals for a few," she said. Bertha Palmer would not go as far as many of the activists of the time; she refused to work for suffrage and withdrew her support of Hull House when they permitted anarchists to speak. At the time of the Fair, however, she used her position with tact and diplomacy to promote the progress of all women.[43]

The feminist character of the Fair was in large part a product of the activities of Ellen Martin Henrotin, vice chairman of the Board of Lady Managers and a member of numerous elite social clubs and reform associations. She took over the management of the Women's Branch of the Congress Auxiliary. Her efforts ensured that women were added to many of the formerly all male committees. Of the 5,977 speakers at the Fair, 25 percent were women.

The Women's Congress presented speeches on such topics as "The Civil and Social Evolution of Women," "The Ethics of Dress" and "Women's Place in the Legitimate Drama." The first day drew so many that an overflow session had to be arranged. Both men and women attended a fashion show, designed to demonstrate improvements in women's dress; while immediate change did not result, it was due more to a lack of patterns than to women's lack of interest in the new styles. The meetings on women's right to vote pulled the biggest crowds, with more than 10,000 attending.[44] The Congresses demonstrated not only women's ability to organize on a large scale, but their ability to articulate ideas intelligently and in a scholarly manner.

The World's Parliament of Religions directed attention to women as ministers, as well as to women's perception of the significance of religion for them. Augusta Chapin, a Universalist minister from Oak Park, and chairman of the Woman's General Committee, spoke twice. Lombard University of Galesburg awarded her the first honorary Doctor of Divinity degree given a woman. Fannie Barrier Williams, a woman active in club work and philanthropy who later became the first woman and the first black on the Chicago Library Board, gave two speeches, one entitled, "What Can Religion Do To Further Advance the Cause of the American Negro?"[45]Henrietta Szold of San Francisco discussed "What Judaism Has Done for Women," and Josphine Lazarus spoke on "The Outlook for Judaism."[46]

By bringing women from organizations around the country together in a stimulating environment, the Fair fostered the organization of a number of new state and national groups. Among these was the Household Economic Association organized by Mrs. John Wilkinson. She considered it a waste of time and energy to arrange for such a conference just for the Fair; she made the work permanent with a national organization which worked through seven committees.[47] Since 1893 was a depression year, the Fair also became a center for discussing welfare problems. It helped to revive the clearing house for charities in Chicago which grew into the Associated Charities, having 325 member organizations in 1911.[48] Other groups saw the need for collaboration, resulting the following year in the Illinois Federation of Women's Clubs.

But the Fair also exposed and encouraged a tendency for women to divide by ethnicity, religion and race. Hannah Solomon, whose sister had been the first and only Jewish president of the Chicago's Woman's Club, was asked to organize the Jewish Women's Congress, out of which grew the National Council of Jewish Women. This organization sought to unite women interested in the work of religion, philanthropy and education. Hannah Solomon and her sister, Henriette Greenebaum Frank, who both became presidents of the Council, would continue particpating in the activities promoted by the Chicago women's clubs, but their social relationships and positions of leadership would increasingly be with Jewish women's organizations. One of their most significant activities was the formation of a Bureau of Personal Service to help new Jewish immigrants.[49]

The exclusion of black women from the Fair's committees was further evidence of the segregation of races which neither a common feminine identity nor common class could overcome in the 1890s. The result was the creation of the first black women's club in Chicago in 1894, the Ida B. Wells Club. Wells, a militant crusader against lynching and other injustices, used her lecturing and journalism to expose and correct wrongs. Born in 1862 into a slave family, she became a teacher in Memphis after a high school education. Protesting the conditions in schools for black children cost her the teaching job; protesting lynching cost her a press and a newspaper. She came to Chicago because Ferdinand Barnett, also a fighter for civil rights, lived there. At the time of the Exposition, she was in England, but when she returned in 1893, she helped bring black women together. The first club in Illinois had been the Autumn Leaf Club of Galesburg, started in 1890. By 1899 there were seven different groups in Chicago which consolidated and joined the National Association of Colored Women's Clubs, inviting that group to hold its next convention in Chicago.

Unlike white women's clubs, black women's clubs were less preoccupied with the issue of self-improvement than with the issue of uplifting the race and changing the distorted images of black women held by white society. Where white women had been placed on a pedestal and viewed as pure and sexually passive, letters written to newspapers and circulated in that way around the nation described black women in reverse terms, calling them "morally depraved," and suggesting they were the basis of the black man's problems.

This was an additional concern reflected in the formation of the Phyllis Wheatley Club in 1896, with Elizabeth Lindsay Davis as president. This club later opened a home for respectable young women who came to the city for work. They were not only excluded from boarding homes run by white organizations but had more difficulty finding cheap and safe housing because of real estate practices and the location of the red light district in the black ghetto. The Phyllis Wheatley Club had also fought saloons next to schools, started nurseries and taught newcomers how to live in the city. Other black women's clubs fostered kindergartens for their children, supported the work of juvenile courts, ran orphanages and homes for the elderly. The Amanda Smith Home for Children had been started by a slave whose father had purchased his family's freedom. Amanda Smith had become a temperance lecturer and preacher who invested her life's savings of $10,000 in the orphanage which she operated.

Still the color line was very much in the open when in 1916, after much pressure, the YWCA added a "colored" branch. The Y had set up a separate dining room at their boarding home for colored employees; they now hired a director for the branch and gave it $50 a month for expenses. The same kind of activities were offered that the other YWCAs provided. During 1916, out of 230 applications for for jobs, 100 women were placed, a lower percentage than that of white applicants.[50] Nothing is recorded about what kind of jobs the black applicants obtained. In an investigation done by the Juvenile Protective Association in 1913, Louise deKoven Bowen wrote of the hopelessness with which educated blacks looked for work because the skilled jobs were seldom open to them. For black women, who might find it easier to get work than black men since there were more openings for unskilled in housework, scrubbing and laundering, it is probable that as high as 80 percent worked in domestic service. They also went to the more undesirable neighborhoods where white women would not go. Most of the maids employed in houses of prostitution were black; if agencies sent white girls who later became prostitutes, the agency could have been charged with pandering.

Black women's clubs had many of the same aims as other women's clubs—to take care of their own, to provide social services associated with the domestic environment. As Fannie B. Williams described them, they were "a new intelligence against an old ignorance." Moreover, black women's clubs faced a more difficult funding problem since their members had fewer sources for money and less time to devote to such activities. Their members showed great ingenuity, pride and willingness to work. They had many effective leaders—Ida B. Wells, Elizabeth Lindsey Davis, Fannie Williams, Amanda Smith and Mary Church Terrell. By 1920 there were 60 black women's clubs in Illinois.[51]

As women's clubs became centers for community action and lessened their emphasis on study, the interest in self-improvement for women did not diminish. Entrepreneurs now saw a market for those who wanted to continue their education and who would spend money for the privilege. In 1910, the Delphian Society was incorporated in Illinois as a national profit-making organization to furnish home study courses for women. These Delphian Societies soon became "self-functioning" groups who were furnished with organized text material for a three year course on "Patterns of Modern Living." Everyone participated; women acquired public speaking skills and assurance. Many took more active parts in other clubs because of their experience in the expanding Delphian Societies.[52] Women's clubs had achieved a certain status when they went from objects of derision to a money making business for men.

Women's clubs and the Exposition had provided women a stimulus for action and further participation in the community. The settlement house movement was much more important, although the membership of the two groups overlapped to a significant extent. The leading settlement workers were active in women's clubs and depended on them for both moral and financial support.

The settlement houses served as stable centers where men and women of different social backgrounds and intellectual orientations could not only discuss new ideas in a congenial environment, but also carry on experimental programs. In examining the civic and humanitarian organizations flourshing after 1890—as the women's rights, suffrage, reform and peace movements—the critical role of the settlement house workers in stimulating progressive social reform becomes obvious.

Both the founding and the expansion of the activities of Hull House, the model for American settlements, demonstrate the changes taking place in women's perceptions of themselves and their roles. Jane Addams and Ellen Gates Starr, the founders of Hull House, and Julia Lathrop, who soon joined them, all came from rural Illinois families with a tradition of participation in idealistic movements.

Jane Addams grew up in Cedarville and attended Rockford College. After graduation she found herself with little to do except to pursue culture, travel and be a maiden aunt. Her health had forced her to drop plans to become a doctor, and she suffered from periods of despondency. Toynbee Hall, an English settlement house, provided an example of a way to direct her humanitarian ideals. Yet she vacillated until the enthusiasm of Ellen Starr, a friend from her Rockford days who had been teaching in Chicago, persuaded her to take Hull House. In the fall of 1889, they moved into the old house in the 19th ward on Chicago's West Side, an area through which many different groups of immigrants passed—Irish, Italian, Russians, Greeks, Germans. Their needs were great and Hull House was to develop one solution after another for particular ills. It should be stressed, however, that Addams also perceived Hull House as a vehicle to provide society ladies with an outlet for their energies and a sense of accomplishment. Too many women at the time seemed to suffer from melancholia and hysteria for which doctors prescribed rest and isolation. The sense of purpose settlement house work offered proved a better cure. Jane Addams emphasized that "one gets as much as she gives."[53]

Hull House became a prototype for settlements around the country. By 1893, Hull House provided space and leadership for some "forty clubs, functions and activities, including a day nursery, gymnasium, dispensary and playground, cooking and sewing courses and a cooperative boarding house for working girls; 2000 people each week were crossing its threshold." By the early 1900s there were 16 more houses in Chicago, many of them founded and staffed by former Hull House workers. The first settlement house for blacks, the Frederick Douglass Center, at 3032 South Wabash, was set up in 1905 by Celia Woolley, a Unitarian minister, and her husband, to try to meet the needs of blacks who were arriving in Chicago in greater numbers and who had no access to the YMCA,

YWCA or other establishments. The Woolleys lived at the center, which was then on the fringe of the black section. Volunteers of both races helped form recreational groups and provide programs. A woman's club was part of it, with a white woman as president and Ida B. Wells as vice president. But no matter how well meaning this group, they did not meet the needs of the poor blacks who needed them most and who lived too far away or who were not interested in the discussions and teas. In 1910 Ida B. Wells raised funds to start another center to meet these more basic needs. She set up the Negro Fellowship League on South State Street to provide lodging and recreational facilities. When financial support failed a few years later, she moved to less desirable quarters where she kept the League going by accepting an appointment as a probation officer for $150 a month. For ten years her probationers reported to her at the league headquarters before she finally had to close it.[54]

Like Jews and blacks, Catholic women at the Chicago Columbian Exposition banded together to form the Catholic Women's League. Their purpose was to improve and expand the range of family services. Catholic parish houses, staffed primarily by religious and lay women which provided the traditional services of charitable societies had long dotted the neighborhoods of Chicago. The new League, however, concentrated on developing settlement type programs. They organized the St. Elizabeth's Day Nursery, St. Mary's Settlement and Day Nursery in 1893, St. Anne's Nursery the next year, and provided probation officers to the Juvenile Court. In 1910, like their female counterparts in other social groups, they organized a complete traveler's aid program for women.[55]

Hull House, however, differed in the breadth of its vision from most of the smaller settlements, missionary houses and institutional churches which provided recreational, educational and health services to neighborhoods. The goal of Hull House was not the creation of more private settlements here and there, but rather the provision of uniform social services through the transferring to government agencies the responsibility to carry out successful experimental programs. The leaders of Hull House linked the integration and expansion of such services to urban social reform. Towards this end they expended much energy in collecting and publicizing statistical data and other information.

The inner city neighborhoods were examples of the continuing failure of urban municipal policy to make the city a viable environment for family life according to American ideals and standards. Hull House itself stood as a symbol of the failure of schemes to resolve social conflict through a policy of suburban retreat. It was a stately mansion which had been built outside the crowded sections of Chicago in 1850; by 1880 it was in the heart of a slum, subdivided and used as rental property by the time Jane Addams took it over.

Among those associated with Hull House who would rise to national prominence in the field of social work and reform was Julia Lathrop. She was instrumental in the establishment of the first Juvenile Court in the United States in 1899 and was later to be appointed by President Taft to head the Children's Bureau, created by Congress in 1912. Associated with her in this effort was Louise deKoven Bowen, a society lady seeking an outlet for her energies. After presiding over the Hull House Women's Club, Bowen went on to be a leader in many other women's groups. She provided money to support recreational facilities at Hull House and a summer camp; she went on to organize the Juvenile Court Committee, the Juvenile Protective Association and the Juvenile Psychopathic Institute, all of which were concerned with helping delinquents and preventing the conditions which led to delinquency. The Juvenile Protective Association collected and published vital statistics and descriptions of the conditions undermining family life among ethnics and blacks, directing attention to the problems of employment as well as those of the physical environment.[56]

Florence Kelley, another Hull House resident, concentrated not on social work but on reforming the conditions of work for women and children. She, too, came from a tradition of reformers. Refused entrance to a law school, she studied abroad where she met and married a Russian medical student and socialist. They lived in New York for five years, but in 1891 she left him and arrived at Hull House with her children. She quickly became involved in child labor protests, investigated sweat shops and worked for legislation to correct the abuses. In 1893 Governor Altgeld appointed Kelley the first chief factory inspector in Illinois. She went on to study law and obained her degree.[57]

Grace Abbott, another woman who went on to state and national fame, was born into a politically conscious and idealistic family from a small town in Nebraska. With a master's degree in political science, she became attracted to settlement house life. With Sophonisba Breckinridge, a lawyer and the first woman to receive a Ph D. in political science, she organized the Immigrant's Protective League in 1908. Its main purpose was to combat the hordes of unscrupulous cab drivers, lawyers, travel agents, "white slavers," operators of fraudulent "savings banks" and "employment agencies" who preyed upon the confused and frightened immigrants from the countryside and abroad. Abbott followed Julia Lathrop as head of the Federal Children's Bureau, becoming one of the most effective administrators in promoting the abolition of child labor and creating centers for prenatal care and child health. In 1934 she retired from public affairs to become a professor of public welfare at the University of Chicago's School of Social Administration, where her equally famous sister, Edith, was dean.[58]

Hull House also attracted, inspired and facilitated the work of a number of women doctors. Dr. Alice Hamilton, who arrived in Chicago in 1898 with a medical degree from Johns Hopkins to teach pathology at Northwestern University, turned her attention to industrial diseases as a result of her experiences at Hull House. Dr. Cornelia De Bey, in private practice, became involved in public school affairs. Dr. Rachelle Yarros, a Russian immigrant, lived for 20 years at Hull House, practicing among the poor of its neighborhood.[59]

Hull House became a clearing house of reform activity; Jane Addams was a cultural heroine until World War I, when her pacifist views turned many against her. She acted as a mother protector for activists of various persuasions whose style and background often generated hostility from others. She had a unique ability to harmonize diverse groups and individuals around common goals.

Mary McDowell, head resident of the University of Chicago's Back-of-the-Yards Settlement House, was in many ways similar to Jane Addams. She too came from a background of reformers in a small community and believed in self-help and democratic participation in group decision making. Unlike Addams, she remained close to her neighborhood groups. She was more open and vocal in her support of trade unionism which she saw as central to improving the social and economic opportunities of the working class. Like Jane Addams she directed attention to the problem of garbage collection and for her efforts to clean up the neighborhood would become known as the "Garbage Lady."

Jane Addams had become a garbage inspector of the 19th ward at $1,000 a year. She rose at six to see that the men were at work, forcing improved collection practices on reluctant contractors. McDowell, whose neighborhood was ringed by open garbage pits and Bubbly Creek, an open sewer, used a different approach. She first trained the local residents in organizing a petition to the city council. When the council refused to stop dumping garbage, she turned to her fellow members of the Woman's City Club, who launched a major campaign on a citywide level. They sent her to Germany in 1911 to investigate European methods and she returned to report on the use of reduction plants. After women received the vote in 1913, she was appointed chairman of a commission which installed a reduction plant for Chicago. She acted as Assistant Commissioner of Sanitation and later as Commissioner of Public Welfare; she established a Bureau of Employment and a Bureau of Social Surveys which carried on research on migratory labor, women offenders and housing. McDowell's concern with social harmony led her to organize in 1919 an Interracial Cooperative Committee composed of representatives of 80 white and black women's clubs and to become a member of both the NAACP and the Urban League.[60]

Mary McDowell never attempted to organize political opposition to the established ward bosses. This may be because she had learned from watching Jane Addams' attempt. Addams, like other settlement workers, had realized from her experiences that voluntary services provided by the settlement houses could never reach a scale sufficient to deal with the magnitude of the problems city neighborhoods faced. Settlement houses and other philanthropic associations promoted by women's clubs and religious institutions could provide playgrounds, kindergartens, day care, medical services, training in home economics—but not for all who needed them. Ultimately they recognized that their programs must become urban services and that they should be administered efficiently and economically. Such a view brought them into conflict with the machine and into confrontation with political corruption.

In 1895, Addams decided that the only way to get clean streets and good schools was to take on the local ward boss, Johnny Powers, by opposing his candidate for alderman. They successfully ran a man from Hull House's Men's Club, but he became co-opted by Powers, known as the top "boodler" on the city council. In 1896 and 1898 Hull House ran candidates against him but lost each time.

Addams therefore turned away from grass roots organizing, but she wrote articles explaining why such ward bosses gained popular support and power. Political science treatises ever since have repeated in essence her views to explain the success of the machine and repeated failures of reformers. Ward bosses did personal favors, found jobs and used their political pull in the courts in ways that their constituents considered beneficial. The machine, it became clear to settlement house workers, understood well the immediate need of the man of the household, who was expected to make money, but not the needs of family life which were the particular concern of women. The importance of woman suffragè would become clearer, and the struggle for it more intense, as a result of women's experience in seeking ways to civilize society.[61]

The rising demand for social and civic reform in the last quarter of the nineteenth century came not alone from women of the more fortunate classes; the demand grew directly out of the experiences and activities of working class women. The ethnic groups strongly believed that woman's place was in the home, bringing up children, but for those in the working class, reality did not permit them this luxury. Wages were too low, men worked only part of the year and husbands and fathers often died young from industrial accidents, leaving widows solely responsible for the family. The most striking expression of these women's devotion to their families was their preference for garment labor which they could take home, but which added to the unsanitary and unhealthy conditions of the tenements. It was also the lowest paid labor. Women also supplemented the family income while staying at home by taking in boarders, doing laundry or peddling. It is ironic that middle class women, deeply concerned about the breakdown of the family in the slums, would direct much of their reforming zeal to abolishing tenement house labor and boarding, which they saw, correctly, as detrimental to privacy and health. But they did not realize that they were economic institutions which enabled mothers both to work and to stay home with their children.

The least desirable job from the perspective of laboring women was domestic service even though it paid more than factory labor. Living with another family isolated them and limited their personal autonomy. After 1900 black women would increasingly replace immigrant women, who had replaced native farm girls. The servant problem would be much discussed in women's clubs, but without much insight by those who hired them as to why so many women would do anything rather than work for them.

Census data reveal these patterns and trends in woman's work in Illinois. In 1890, 46.4 percent of the female labor force was in "domestic and personal service," a classification which also included waitresses, nurses and midwives. By 1920 this had dropped drastically to 23 percent, and "nurses professional" had its own category. The number of women in "manufacturing and mechanical" pursuits, which had provided an outlet for departing domestics, had declined slightly while the number in clerical positions had increased. The percentage of women doing farm work, who were included in the census, had decreased from 6.4 to 2 percent between 1890 and 1920.[62]

Another trend of great importance was the increased number of working women, both married and single. In 1890 only 14.3 percent of all females over ten were engaged in what the census called "gainful occupations." By 1920 this had risen to 21.3 percent. While in 1890 only 6.8 percent of working women were married, by 1920 this figure had almost tripled.[63]

In Chicago these shifts were even more pronounced. Not only were 30 percent of all women working in 1920, but they were one quarter of the entire labor force of the city. Employment in domestic service declined from almost 30 percent of working women to less than 20 percent, but in clerical occupations it increased from less than 20 percent to 31.6 percent between 1910 and 1920. Probably the most significant change in the area of industrial employment was the entrance of women into slaughtering and meatpacking and into electrical apparatus and supplies. Once these had been exclusive male preserves, but in 1920 they ranked third and fifth in terms of the percentages of women employed.

Census figures for Illinois and its largest city show that women in 1920 had a greater range of opportunities in large part because they would work for lower wages than men. Moreover, fewer women were leaving the work force after marrying. For those who felt that women should stay at home with the children, the disturbing reality was that among these working married women, 67 percent were in the age category from 25 to 44; 39 percent were between 25 and 34 -

early child rearing years.[64]

Moreover, the thousands of women who worked with husbands and fathers on farms and in small businesses were not included in the census, which did not consider them "gainfully employed." Yet these women also were working both inside and outside the home.

Prostitution is the another form of female labor on which we have no good statistics, but which inspired much reform activity. Those trying to stop it called it the "white slave trade." Women at the top of this business could make a fortune, although their expenses in the form of political protection and clothing were extremely high.[65] By the turn of the century the most elaborate and famous house of prostitution in Chicago was run by the Everleigh sisters, Minna and Ada. It had gold faucets, chandeliers, real silver and china. Most prostitutes, however, did not live in such lavish surroundings but rather in "cribs" or moved from house to house. Reformers were always trying to save women from this terrible fate by legislation to improve the conditions of work in more acceptable trades and by providing guidance and shelter to migrants through such organizations as the YWCA, Traveller's Aid and working girls' homes, Reformers believed that standing in a store for ten hours a day for low wages or the conditions of sweat shop labor were responsible for driving women into prostitution. While this may have been true in many cases, the evidence available suggests that the problem was more comples. A survey conducted in 1880 counted 302 houses and 1,097 prostitutes in Chicago. Interviews with 557 of the women showed that almost one-third went directly from the home into prostitution, about 30 percent came from domestic service in homes and hotels, while fewer than 15 percent came from the ranks of seamstresses (the remaining 22 percent are unaccounted for).[66]

Nonetheless, the economics of city life seem to have played a major role. A *Chicago Tribune* editorial in 1885 attacking the white slave traffic cited cases of girls who worked and lived with a man in order to get better clothes.[67] More recently it has been suggested that it was an effective way to accumulate a dowry. The Vice Commission of 1910 reported 1,020 resorts, operated by 1,1880 keepers and madams and housing at least 4,000 prostitutes, most of these in the segregated district in the first ward. The commission estimated that hundreds of women, besides those accounted regular professionals, "were ruined" by the system. It blamed this situation on organized crime, corrupt politics and the economic system.[68]

Whatever the reason for women turning to prostitution one fact is clear; women *were* concentrated in unskilled work with few means to change the situation. Unionizing for higher wages was extremely difficult. Those who most needed unions did not make enough to pay the 50 cents a month minimum in dues considered necessary to maintain a union. Social attitudes about women increased the organizational problems. The myth that women's work was only temporary—until marriage—kept many from joining to protest their exploitation.[69] The American Federation of Labor provided little encouragement to the unionization of women, except to protect the wages of men or to eliminate women from the work force by making it expensive to hire them. The editor or the *American Federationist*, their national organ, wrote:

We believe that the man should be provided with a fair wage in order to keep his female relatives from going to work. . . . Respect for women is apt to decrease when they are compelled to work in the factory or the store. . . .If women labor in factories and similar institutions they bring forth weak children who are not educated to become strong and good citizens.[70]

John Fitzpatrick, organizer of the Chicago Federation of Labor, however, did encourage women to organize separate unions and respected their toughness and executive ability.

The responsibility for union organizing and for improving the working conditions of women, for the most part, fell to women themselves. One of the earliest leaders in the movement was Elizabeth Flynn Rodgers, who organized the Chicago Working Woman's Union in the mid-1870s. She then went on to make women's presence in the Knights of Labor more visible. She became head of the all woman Local Assembly 1789, served as a delegate from 1880 to 1887 to the State Trades Assembly of Chicago and as Master Workman of District Assembly 24. She attended the national convention in 1886 with 16 other women and her two week old son. He was presented with a silver spoon and cup by the delegates. Rogers declined the nomination for general treasurer because being the mother of ten took too much time. When the Knights of Labor deteriorated, she left the field of organizing and became a partner in a printing firm. Later she helped organize the Women's Catholic Order of Foresters, a life insurance company, of which she became the High Chief Ranger, or president.[71]

Elizabeth Flynn Rodgers had been a housewife who identified with unions. But most union leaders after the 1890s came from the ranks of the workers. They had diverse ethnic backgrounds; some were Yankees, other German, Swedish, Scottish, Irish, Jewish and English. Female trade union leaders did share common social characteristics; they were almost without exception, unmarried and without exception totally dedicated to the union cause. Chicago women workers had a long history of union activity. According to a 1903 article in *Leslie's Monthly*, "Trades-Unions in Petticoats," women in Chicago were well organized, unlike their apathetic sisters in the industrial Eastern states.

Of most of the hard working organizers on the local level we know little. There was Mary McDermott, walking delegate of the Scrubwomen's Union and Janitor's Protective Association; Josie Schroeder of the Amalgamated Association of Miscellaneous Restaurant and Hotel Employees; Anna Schofield, president of the Candy Dippers' Local 329; Lily Harkins of the Lady Core-Makers;

and Kittie Schultz, Secretary of Local 222 of the Retail Lady Clerks Union.[72]

Others, associated with settlement houses, the Women's Trade Union League or radical movements also rose to local and national prominence. At 13, Alzina Stevens went to work in a textile mill in Maine. Moving to Chicago in 1872 she took a job as a typesetter and joined the Typographical Union. In 1877 she started the Working Woman's Union #1 of which she became president. By 1892 she was living at Hull House and helping their members understand the needs of working women. She became a factory inspector under Florence Kelley in 1893, and was the first probation officer of the new Juvenile Court in 1899. Within a few months she had a staff of six under her.[73]

Mary Kenney O'Sullivan was one of the most influential of the early trade union leaders; she was a tall, attractive, red haired woman, who organized the bookbinders. After she dined at Hull House, Jane Addams asked how she could help. The bookbinders then held meetings there and Hull House paid for printing and helped distribute their circulars. Soon half a dozen union groups were meeting at Hull House and listening to speakers like Clarence Darrow and Henry Demarest Lloyd. From her contacts with Addams and Hull House grew the Jane Club, a cooperative living arrangement for which Hull House found and furnished apartments. Mary Kenney located working women who needed a place to live. For $3 a week, each had shelter, food and a congenial social life. Within a year they had filled six apartments and had become a prototype followed later by the Eleanor Clubs and many other small groups.

Samuel Gompers appointed Mary Kenney the first woman organizer for the American Federation of Labor but she only lasted a few months. By 1893 she was back at Hull House, helping lobby for the first factory law and becoming a deputy factory inspector under Florence Kelley when the law passed. Later, as Mary Kenney O'Sullivan, she moved to Boston, but she too had helped open the eyes of many in Chicago to the conditions under which women worked.[74]

Agnes Nestor, a glove cutter, led one of the first successful women's strikes. Arriving in Chicago with her family in 1897, she started to work at 17 in a glove factory, ten hours a day, six days a week. By spring she was no longer able to accept the tyrannies of the situation—buying her own needles, renting the machine she used, responding to speedups. She led her fellow workers out on strike; ten days on the picket line brought them victory. Nestor dedicated the rest of her life to the organization of women workers and became one of the most effective. She helped organize and later became president of the International Glove Workers Union as well as the Chicago Women's Trade Union League. She was active in union drives in the stockyards, garment industries and among waitresses, dressmakers, milliners, nurses and teachers. In Illinois she was best known as a lobbyist for protective legislation for women and child workers, later serving on a number of state and federal commissions.[75]

The Back-of-the-Yards, where Mary McDowell had a settlement house, became a center for union organizings. The "petticoat butchers," as the young women doing what had once been men's work were called, were slower to organize than men. But the conditions—and the encouragement of McDowell—soon led them to realize that women too had to organize to improve life in the district. Women, first largely of Irish and German-American descent and then Slovak and black, worked sewing up "babs" for hams. After the men's 1894 strike, women were hired in the previously all male departments of can stuffing, sausage linking and meat trimming, but at lower wages. Both women and men never knew when they left home whether they would work one or sixteen hours, nor could they be sure how much they would be making under the piece work system. Those who worked fastest made the most, but as they speeded up to earn more, the rate would decline; it would be necessary to work faster just to stay the same.

In March 1900 an unorganized band of young Irish women under Hannah O'Day decided they could no longer work under these conditions. Tying a red handkerchief to a stick, they walked out of the packing house. Southern European women were employed to break the strike, leaders Hannah O'Day and Maggie Congdon were blacklisted, but they went on to form the Maud Gonne Pleasure Club in 1901.

Within a year, with the aid of McDowell and union organizer Michael Donnelley, the club became a local of the Amalgamated Meat Cutters and Butcher Workmen of North America. Soon they had 1,200 members, including black women. In 1904, these "petticoat butchers" were among the 22,000 workers who went on strike; Mary McDowell joined the picket line and raised relief funds from her wealthy friends at the Woman's Club. She and Dr. Cornelia De Bey, associated with Hull House, helped mediate the strike. The strikers did get better wages and working conditions. But they failed to gain union recognition, which they saw as central to future gains. The Slavic women immigrants, as they entered the work force, refused to join the union, which led to its dissolution. When the union was reconstituted in 1917, however, these women were the first to join.[76]

The opening years of the twentieth century saw rapid progress in union organizing among women. They were becoming less timid and more conscious of their oppression; in the process of organizing to overcome this oppression they developed among their ranks women of remarkable executive ability.

The 1903 Labor Day Parade in Chicago reflected the new sense of camaraderie among workers from different trades, as well as their growing articulateness. Hundreds of women marched, not knowing whether they would have jobs the next day. There were two wagons filled with women dressed in white with banners from the Amalgamated Meat Cutters and Butcher Workmen of North America, who sang labor songs as the crowd along the line of march cheered. The parade included garment workers, sausage girls, lady cracker packers, waitresses, public school teachers, candy dippers; decorated buses and floats and women marshalls on horseback filled the parade. The scrub women sang,

> With love united may they not
>   Have power almost divine?
> Shall idle drones still live like queens
>   On labor not their own?
> Shall women starve while thieves and rings
>   Reap where they have not sown?[77]

Yet this was not, of course, the first time that women had come ut in large numbers in a parade. On May 1, 1886, many women paraded in the great May Day march led by Albert and Lucy Parsons, which saw an estimated 80,000 strikers and sympathizers march for the eight hour day. Marches of this sort took place simultaneously throughout the state and nation. On May 2, Lizzie Holmes who had organized the garment workers led a march of sweat shop workers through the Chicago Loop. On the night of May 4, Lucy Parsons and Holmes left a meeting of garment workers to attend the demonstration at Haymarket Square to protest police brutality against strikers at the McCormick Harvester plant. A bomb exploded among the police, who opened fire into the crowd; the red scare which followed set back both union organizing and the eight hour day movement for nearly a decade. History remembers Albert Parsons, an anarchist hanged on inadequate evidence for instigating mob violence. But few remember his equally articulate and active wife Lucy, "a dark faced woman of mixed blood," Indian, black and white, who protested the plight of labor before and after Haymarket, despite police harrassment.

Parsons joined with Mother Jones at the founding of the Industrial Workers of the World. In 1915, after the European embargo depressed the American economy, she led the unemployed on a hunger march from Hull House, demanding union wages instead of charity. Jane Addams; who like most members of the middle class, disapproved of militant tactics, bailed Parsons and five others out of jail. A week later Parsons was leading another demonstration to test the court injunction. She was a woman of principle, always reminding Americans that democracy was an inclusive concept, not one limited to one class or race. She had a large following during a period when socialist oriented groups were far more popular then they are today.[78]

Although women tended to be less visible in the large and famous strikes such as the Pullman strike, they were often there, either as strikers or as auxiliaries to their husbands. But in the Chicago garment strike of 1910, which included men and women from nine ethnic groups, they were not only visible, they were initiators. On September 22, 1910 Hannah Shapiro, who had informally acted as spokeswoman for women in her shop in their grievances, persuaded fifteen others to march out with her to protest a wage cut at Hart, Schaffner and Marx. Within three weeks the strike spread to the rest of this largely unorganized industry, as an estimated 40,000 workers joined the walkout.

Working women of diverse ethnic backgrounds found an opportunity in this strike to exercise their talent for leadership. Bessie Abramovitch Hillman, a Russian Jewish immigrant who had arrived in America in 1905, began her career as a labor organizer during this strike at the age of 21. One of the few women to rise to a policy making position in a mixed union, she later served on the executive board and as vice president of the Amalgamated Clothing Workers of America (ACWA). Sidney Hillman, whom she met during the strike, was the first president of this union, formed in 1914 from a nucleus at Hart, Schaffner and Marx.

Another effective organizer on the shop level was Ellen Lindstrom, whose background differed greatly from Bessie Hillman's. Before coming to America, Lindstrom had taught school in Sweden, had served as governess in a Danish noble family and had planned a literary career. In Chicago; however, she sewed pants and turned her mind to the issue of inequality. As early as 1903 she was known in labor circles as one of the most effective organizers.[79]

The garment strikers had numerous allies who helped in the process of organizing and fund raising. The Women's Trade Union League, drawing on the philanthropic experience of some of its members, established commissary stores to serve the families of strikers and appealed for public support. Its literature emphasized the family orientation of the strikers. The League also participated in the task of organizing by sending in professional union organizers, among them Agnes Nestor of the Glovecutters, and Mary Anderson, president of Stitchers Local 94 of the International Boot and Shoe Workers. In 1920 Anderson was appointed head of the Woman's Bureau of the U.S. Department of Labor.

On January 14, 1911 the workers at Hart, Schaffner and Marx broke ranks and ratified an agreement with their employers which established a committee of arbitration to handle grievances and to work out regular procedures for the future. On March 13 this committee, composed of the prominent lawyer, Clarence Darrow, who represented labor, and Carl Meyer, who represented Hart, Schaffner and Marx, drew up a code which became a model for constructive labor relations. It provided for better sanitary conditions in the shops, equal division of work during the slack season, a 54 hour week with overtime pay at the rate of time and a half, a minimum wage and a uniform ten percent wage increase. It also set up a permanent grievance machinery. This agreement, however, affected only the 8,000 workers at Hart, Schaffner and Marx. Strikers at other shops who stayed out a month longer, gained nothing and remained unorganized for many years.[80]

The following years saw numerous strikes. One of the most famous was that of waitresses against Henrici's restaurant over the eight hour day. This strike, which began in January 1914, lasted a year and a half and spread to other restaurants. Mrs. Medill McCormick, Ellen Gates Starr and other prominent women joined the picketers in an effort to curb police brutality—a major feature of this strike as it had been of the garment strike. The strike of waitresses, like so many others, would in the end be broken by court injunctions and police harrassment. Not only the waitresses suffered. George Knab, who was forced to sell many of his restaurants to hold out, later said that the strike taught him that "there was no use fighting women."

Elizabeth Maloney, who had organized the waitresses' union in 1902, linked the goals of unionization to a vision of feminine purity inspired by Catholicism. She demanded that waitresses be treated with the same respect given to ladies. Union contracts stipulated that "waitress shall not be reprimanded in the presence of guests" and that" no profane language shall be used." She saw the eight hour day in the same terms. For years she fought unsuccessfully for the passage of a bill which would, in a single stroke, give women time to enjoy the benefits of civilization. Working women need shorter hours, she argued, because the physical strain has "evil effects that often last for life. The girl's normal resistance to tempting baits is weakened by her weariness." They also needed time to pursue culture. "What is the good of all the store of beauty, of books and pictures and music that this world contains if one is to be always too tired to enjoy it." In 1917, Maloney, who was also on the executive board of the Women's Trade Union League, was appointed to the Illinois Industrial Survey Commission which was charged with making a complete study of all industries in which women were engaged and with recommending legislation on hours and health.[81]

Certainly one of the most striking features of this period of civic and social reform was the way women of different social classes, of different ethnic backgrounds, of different political persuasions, united around causes relating to the well-being of women, children and the family. This does not mean that there were not tensions and misunderstandings as middle class activists strove to uplift and Americanize those below. Workers often resented the reformers' "maternalism." This was to be expected. The extent to which a common feminine identity and outlook had emerged is remarkable; women were able to at least partially cut across class lines in an era that was very conscious of social distances

In 1903 the National Women's Trade Union League was formed in the East with Jane Addams as vice president. In 1904 the first meeting of the Illinois branch was held at Hull House. Mary McDowell became the first president and Ellen Martin Henrotin the treasurer. Henrotin represented the club women and had the highest social credentials.[82] From a wealthy family, she had lived and attended schools abroad. Her husband was a banker and later president of the Chicago Stock Exchange. From 1874 when she joined the intellectually oriented Fortnightly, she expanded her interests step by step until she became one of the most active seekers of solutions to social problems. As vice president of the "Women's Branch" of the Congress Auxiliary at the Columbian Exposition, she has been credited with its "strong feminist emphasis." As Henrotin became active in education, she was elected a trustee of the University of Illinois in 1912. She also helped the Park Ridge School for Dependent Girls and the Amanda Smith Home. Henrotin also espoused the teaching of sex hygiene in the public schools.

During four years as president of the General Federation of Women's Clubs, Henrotin not only saw the tremendous increase in clubs and membership, but also brought them to support many reforms for women, both in education and labor. When she became president of the National Women's Trade Union League, she worked to encourage unionization, as well as to acquaint the public with the grievances of workers. Henrotin helped publicize the need for reform through such means as a "Chicago Industrial Exhibit" which displayed the worst aspects of sweatshops, child labor and the hazards of industry. When her concern turned to the problem of prostitution, she became a member of a vice commission which investigated and reported on the problem, and continued her efforts as a director of a private anti-vice organization. Like many other women, she actively supported the efforts of suffragists to fight for reform.[83] Once again she represented a link between rich and poor.

Another helpful member of the group was Alice Henry of Australia. Successful as a journalist and lecturer on reform topics, she came to the United States in 1906 to lecture on suffrage. Accepting an invitation to become office secretary of the Chicago Women's Trade Union League, she edited *Life and Labor*, which became one of the most readable of labor magazines.[84] The journal supplemented labor news with articles on international affairs, woman's suffrage, home making advice and stories. It reflected the club woman's concern with improving social and cultural conditions.

Margaret Dreier Robins also came from a background of wealthy and socially concerned people. She sought satisfaction in helping others and therefore became involved with the Women's Trade Union League in New York. Arriving in Chicago with her husband, she joined in helping the Chicago Women's Trade Union League become a success.

Although at the beginning, women from the leisure class dominated the leadership of the Trade Union League, by 1907 most of the board members and officers were union leaders. Among these were Agnes Nestor of the Glove Cutters Union, Elizabeth Maloney of the waitresses, Mary Anderson, Mary Kenney O'Sullivan and Josephine Casey of the Elevated Railway Employees' Union. The League collected money, provided organizers to help women form unions, found meeting places, provided relief for strikers and furnished bail and lawyers. Wealthy women sometimes walked the picket lines and patrolled the streets to limit police brutality during a strike. They also helped spread information to other club women who were in a position to put pressure on husbands and friends in the employing class.

Women could also use confrontation tactics when they felt it necessary. Mary Wilmarth was a strong supporter of Hull House and many welfare causes. She had a country estate on Lake Geneva and had founded the Lake Geneva Fresh Air Association to give poor women and children a summer experience away from the city. Once when she felt the Cook County Board of Commissioners were not giving adequate support to facilities for the care of abandoned children, she took a baby from a shelter, strode into the meeting of the commissioners and deposited the infant on their conference table. She left without a word; she also got them to act.[85]

The question must be asked as to why club women put so much emphasis on the importance of unionizing as well as on protective legislation. Mary McDowell, for one, had found from her experiences living in Packingtown that the issues of wages and conditions of work could not be disentangled from those of community harmony and development. She had also found that unions tended to break down the ethnic barriers dividing people and to unite them in working for common goals.[86] She could explain this to club women.

Many allies, as club women were called, saw trade unionism also as an educational process, in the same way that clubs had been for middle class women. At a union meeting, Agnes Nestor wrote, young women gathered and discussed the many questions that arose, learned to conduct meetings, to debate and to vote intelligently on important matters. Finally, unions served a social function for the lonely and poor young woman in a new work place who had difficulty finding friends and proper place to relax.[87] The League's cultural and social activities for union women paralleled those promoted by middle class philanthropic organizations.

Union leaders also gained from their participation in the Women's Trade Union League the opportunity to demonstrate their executive abilities in a way not possible within the larger American Federation of Labor or their own national unions. Although dedicated and able, they found themselves excluded from leadership. The men were hostile to women working and helped in organizing them only when their own interests were threatened. In the Women's Trade Union League the wealthy allies encouraged women to take over their own unions, and created training classes to help them do so. The numerous female trade union leaders who eventually served in various federal and state officers were promoted through the League. In time, just as the allies had come to conclude that community betterment could not be disentangled from trade unionism, so female union leaders would come to conclude that their particular bread and butter issues could not be disentangled from community issues, particularly the issues of child labor, hours legislation, safety, public education, sanitation and health.

But the Women's Trade Union League and the settlements were not the only links between working class groups and voluntary associations composed of middle class women. As early as 1888, the socialist Elizabeth Morgan, who was a master workman for the Knights of Labor, formed the Ladies Federated Labor Union, soon to include 23 craft unions. She then helped form the Illinois Women's Alliance which included both union and women's groups interested in child welfare, suffrage and other problems. They worked for an enforced truancy law and a compulsory education law, both of which passed in 1889. The law increased the number of truant officers, some of whom were women. Morgan also investigated sweat shops; in 1891 she wrote what Florence Kelley called a "trail blazing report," which helped to bring on a formal investigation. The Factory Act of 1893, the first attempt to regulate child labor and restrict the working hours of women and children to eight a day, was passed in large part through her efforts.[88]

Industry united against the Factory Act. Despite the efforts of Florence Kelley and her deputies to have the act enforced, the Supreme Court found the section that restricted hours of work unconstitutional. Mary Anderson, a Swedish immigrant who started at $1.50 a week and worked up to $14.00, remembered that after working from 7:30 a.m. to 6:00 p.m. with a half hour for lunch, she worked one day for just eight hours. What a delight! And then the court decision sent her back to the old hours.[89]

Another umbrella organization concerned with child labor, women's wages and working conditions was the National Consumers' League, organized in 1899, with Florence Kelley as its executive secretary. The league sought to organize boycotts against companies which exploited women and children. It recommended to women, particularly club women who shopped in department stores, that they only buy goods with a union label or shop in "standard" stores which obeyed child labor laws, gave women equal pay with men and paid an adequate weekly wage, provided seats for women clerks and paid overtime after six. The Chicago Woman's Club published an exposé of the big stores during the pre-Christmas rush. All women's groups focused increasingly on both the need for better law enforcement and better laws.[90]

The 1903 child labor law, for example, was drawn up by the industrial committee of the State Federation of Women's Clubs. In large measure, it was a product of women's pressures from the marchers in the Labor Day parade, the women's clubs around the state and the women's labor unions. If the Chicago leaders tended to be more visible, it must be stressed that this and other legislation of benefit to women could not have been achieved without the support of women's clubs throughout the smaller towns and cities. If such women had been either passive or opposed, the efforts of those in Chicago would have been fruitless. Legislative successes rested on the innumerable downstate women who were equally effective organizational leaders within their communities.

But women found they could not influence the process of governmental administration and the courts, where the absence of women as voters and administrators proved critical. The fate of the Factory Act was an important lesson. Repeated examples of this kind would lead women in highly different organizations to come to the conclusion that if women were to be able to protect themselves and to improve their communities, they would have to have the vote.

Continued pressure by women brought a 1904 law prohibiting child labor in mines; Florence Kelley said that Illinois had surpassed Massachusetts in leading the field of enlightened labor legislation. In 1909, the ten hour law, which covered work in factories, mechanical establishments and laundries was held constitutional by the Illinois Supreme Court. That same year brought the tragedy in Cherry, Illinois, when a fire in the mine killed 259 miners and left their families destitute. Although the company did provide some support money, the extent of the tragedy helped prompt the Mothers' Pension Law of 1911, the first in the nation, and an appropriation for the care of dependent and neglected children.[91]

The story of Margaret Haley, Catherine Goggins and the Chicago Teachers' Federation illustrates the process by which women in this era, outside the middle class, became militant social feminists. The Chicago Teachers' Federation both became an instrument for feminism and also played a prominent role in civic reform in the attempts of progressive women to create a child oriented education system.

From 1894 when the elementary teachers joined together, with the help of the Woman's Club, to fight for the creation of a pension system, to 1906 when the Chicago Teachers' Federation campaigned for the election of Mayor Edward Dunne, the female elementary school teachers had moved from a traditional perception of themselves and their role to become the cutting edge of urban progressive reform. In the process they had learned the significance of unionization, the intricacies of pressure group politics and governmental organization. They also learned that their most immediate personal needs—pensions, salaries and tenure—could not be separated from broader goals of community welfare.

In 1897 the attempt to suspend the pension system led the most vulnerable group, the elementary teachers, into a union. In 1898 the withdrawal of the first salary raise for these teachers, whose pay had not risen since 1877 and who earned half what their male counterparts made, led the new teachers' union to investigate the issue of school financing and taxation. Two Irish school teachers, Catherine Goggins, from upstate New York, and Margaret Haley, born near Peoria, became the "gatekeepers" of the Teachers' Federation. Haley, who led the investigation, wrote that when she began, such terms as "Board of Equalization," "capital stock" and "franchises," were Greek to her. But she studied the statutes and learned how to determine taxes. As she poured over assessment records, she discovered why the Board of Education could not pay promised salaries: the large and powerful corporations were not paying their legally required franchise taxes to the city. The Teachers's Federation instituted a taxpayers' suit which forced the government to collect from the utilities resulting in over $500,000 worth of new money for the city in 1901. The beneficiaries of this windfall were not the women teachers, however. The firemen, policemen and coal contractors, as well as the school maintenance men, were thought more important by the city and the school board. The women teachers did not vote or act as political organizers; they had to go to to court again to get their raises. Margaret Haley later resigned her teaching position to become a full time paid business agent for the Federation.[92]

The teachers, who had paid for court action and brought the issue of utility taxation to the front pages of newspapers, were not only back in court but also affiliated with the Chicago Federation of Labor. The 200,000 members of the male union, with children in the public schools, would give the teachers the political clout they lacked. They also became deeply involved in the movement for muncipal ownership of mass transit companies and utilities as a means of ending corruption and providing the city with better service at a better price. They worked for the referendum as a means of putting school issues before the public and for making the Board of Education an elective office; the goal was to make the schools more subject to community influence.

These issues led the teachers to support suffrage and the Political Equality League. They did not limit themselves to bread and butter issues, but became involved in many reforms: child welfare, protective legislation for women workers, civic reform and the organization and quality of education. Frustrated by the failure of the city council to respond to public opinion as expressed in referenda, they entered the mayoralty contest to elect a man who had been sympathetic to their cause, Judge Edward Dunne. Dunne became a reform mayor in 1905 and later governor of Illinois. The teachers became adept at organizing petitions to send home with children to arouse parents and to arouse male unions to action. Such circulars show how the various issues were entwined. One read:

What Chicago gives TO TAX DODGING CORPORATIONS: A gift of ten million dollars a year in the free use of the public streets.
TO HER CHILDREN: Half day schooling; overcrowded, unsanitary school rooms, factory system of education.
TO HER TEACHERS: Overwork in crowded school rooms, decreased pay.[93]

Later Haley's union exposed how the Board of Education gave valuable school property to newspapers for almost nothing. They publicized the close personal and social connections between the Board and corporate lawyers and leaders. In retaliation the Board in 1915 passed the "Loeb Resolution" which prohibited elementary teachers from joining unions; the resolution could not stop them from working for educational reform.

The teachers were supported by the Women's Trade Union League, to which they belonged until the passage of the "Loeb Rule,"

(Courtesy of Cody Hofmann)

Women of the 1890's in non-traditional role and dress: Dr. Ellen Flower Hancock, starting out on her evening rounds.

(permission of Ruth Aley)

Harriet Hubbard Ayer, cosmetic company founder, displaying a daring costume for business women in 1897.

the Chicago Woman's Club and the Chicago Federation of Labor. The Teachers' Federation was as much a feminist organization as it was a labor union and civic association. At the heart of their continuing battle with the Board of Education was a feminist professional democratic vision—teacher involvement in the making of curriculum and the determining of school policies through teachers' councils. Otherwise, they argued, teachers would continue to be mere "factory hands" and certainly poor models for the young. They were, therefore, in conflict with male superintendents who wanted autonomous control in shaping the educational system.

Women workers today in
non-traditional role and dress:

Judge Margaret O'Malley of Cook County Circuit Court in her robes between sessions.

Policewoman
(Photographer Mike Tropea)

(Courtesy of Wheaton-Glen Ellyn AAUW)
Truckdriver

Margaret Haley, known as the "Lady Labor Slugger," bridged the gap between the professional concerns of the new educators and teachers and those of the workers and neighborhood groups. She was also instrumental in helping change the National Education Association, whose leadership was comprised of male college presidents, professors and superintendents, but whose membership was primarily classroom teachers. The members were so passive that in 1901 Haley was the first female elementary school teacher to speak from the floor of an NEA Convention. Over the next few years, as the state organizations began to demand more representation, she forced the national group to begin considering problems of salaries, tenure and pensions which had traditionally been viewed as distinct from problems of policy and administration.

Haley helped organize the National Teachers' Federation which threatened to draw membership from the NEA and to undermine their status as sole representative of the profession. When a move was made to have the NEA nominating committee appointed by the president, she denounced it as an attempt to create a "self-perpetuating machine" which would "keep out the women who form nine-tenths of the membership."[94] As a result of the new activism she helped stimulate among the members, she was able in 1910 to engineer the election to the presidency of the NEA of Ella Flagg Young, the new superintendent of Schools in Chicago. By then the NEA was studying the issues of salaries and had even created a department of class room teachers.

The opposition of the Teachers' Federation to centralization of administration under superintendents has most often been viewed as resistance to professionalization. Certainly the social and educational background of teachers at the time and their educational problems viewed from the perspective of today could make that a natural conclusion. However, from their perspective and in the context of the period, these teachers were seeking professionalization; their devotion to Ella Flagg Young makes this clear. Primary school teachers were essentially considered potential mothers performing traditional duties within a public context under the guidance of professional superintendents. The teachers' efforts to become participants in the making of policy and in the development of the teaching process was professional. Only the union and an elected Board of Education could help them achieve their goals. The great innovators in education—John Dewey and Francis Parker—were pointing to the same goals as Ella Flagg Young's classic study, *Isolation in the School*, of 1900.

Young, who became superintendent of schools in Chicago in 1909, reflected in her career the changing ideas of women towards teaching. Born in upstate New York in 1848, she came to Chicago as a young girl. She attended grammar school and at 15 entered Chicago Normal School, graduating in 1862. She was one of the few teachers ith specialized training at the time when Chicago's new superintendent was trying to modernize public education by introducing a graded system with a graded curriculum and teacher training. With her talent and energy, she easily attracted attention; at the age of 29 she became principal of the practice school of Chicago Normal, later closed by politicians who considered it unnecessary. She then became a high school teacher, grammar school principal and in 1887 an assistant superintendent in Chicago. Although always diplomatic, she rose through her professional associations, not through politics; she always felt hostile to political control of the schools, But she believed even more strongly in teacher training and participation in planning.

As assistant superintendent she helped broaden the curriculum by introducing drawing, commercial subjects, manual arts and home economics into the elementary and secondary schools. She helped organize teachers' councils as an effective voice in administrative decisions and brought such noted educators as William James and John Dewey as speakers. When political changes threatened the teachers' councils, she resigned. She entered the University of Chicago, worked for her doctorate, and then stayed as a professor. A colleague, John Dewey, wrote of Young, "What I chiefly got from Mrs. Young was . . . the translation of philosophic conceptions into their empirical equivalents."[95]

Young moved on to become principal of the new Chicago Normal School and finally the first woman superintendent of Chicago schools. She had the loyalty and admiration of the Chicago Woman's Club, the Teachers' Federation and the professional educators. However, the politically oriented Board of Education constantly opposed her. She survived until 1915 only because of the total support she received from the women members of the Board, the newly enfranchised women voters, club women and teachers. Part of the opposition was based on her stand for women deans in high schools and the inclusion of sex education in the curriculum, which nonetheless had the support of Ellen Henrotin, the Woman's Club and women physicians.[96]

Other women also served in top educational positions. In fact, since education was considered a natural extension of the home, women had greater opportunities to demonstrate their talents and rise to the top then than today. Mary Ellen West of Galesburg, for example, was elected County Superintendent of Schools for Cook County in 1873. At 13, she had passed the examinations for Knox Female Seminary, and then taught two years until she was old enough to enter. After her higher education, she taught and administered, gaining such a reputation as a "lady of grit, grace and gumption" that in spite of her refusal to run for the office of superintendent, she was elected. As superintendent she did not condone any practices she considered wrong or slipshod, even refusing teaching certificates to otherwise qualified men who drank. She was reelected in 1877. Active in organizations such as the

WCTU and the Soldiers' Aid Society, she also wrote articles and a book. *Childhood: Its Care and Culture* was a treatise on how to raise children by a woman who have given much of her life to their education and welfare without having children of her own.[97]

It took longer to recognize women's natural qualifications to serve on school boards. In 1877 the Chicago Woman's Club sent a formal petition to the mayor requesting the appointment of two of its members to vacancies on the school board, a petition which was also signed by many influential men. It was eleven years, four petitions and three mayors later before Ellen Mitchell was appointed in 1888. By then some women had been elected to suburban school boards. Ellen Mitchell suggested reforms which resulted in the Chicago Manual Training School. Lucy Flower, who replaced her, helped introduce more reforms.[98]

Women also pioneered the development of kindergartens in public schools. Alice Whiting Putnam opened a kindergarten in her home in 1874; she went on to supervise a training school which by 1910 had prepared over 800 for kindergarten teaching. These women and club groups first persuaded the Board of Education to permit private kindergartens to operate in public schools; public ones were established through their efforts in 1892. Elizabeth Harrison, active in this movement, helped found the Chicago Kindergarten College in 1887 which became the National College of Education in 1930. Anna Bryan also worked with Francis Parker and John Dewey in instituting new ideas on kindergarten education. Through the chairmanship of the Child Study Committe of the International Kindergarten Union, she helped shape childhood education.[99] Again these developments were a natural extension of women's role in the home, but they became institutionalized and accepted through the executive ability of the women who promoted them.

The spread of libraries in the late nineteenth century, like kindergartens, became closely associated with the extension of public education. Women and women's clubs, in the community building stage of town development, had been deeply involved in the promotion of libraries. Even after municipal and state governments assumed responsibility for this service, the State Federation of Women's Clubs continued to work in close cooperation with professionally concerned organizations, such as the State Teachers' Association and the American Library Association, to make libraries more available and to increase the services they provided. In a tax conscious society, however, the spread of libraries and the quality of service rested on the fact that women provided the bulk of the labor force, either as volunteers or as professionals. Justin Winsor, in 1877, explained why American libraries preferred women in these terms: "They soften our atmosphere, they lighten our labor, they are equal to our work, and for the money they cost—if we must gauge such labor by such rules—they are infinitely better than equivalent salaries will produce of the other sex."[100]

Just as women, through the public school art association and teachers's organizations, sought to make the school more closely resemble the home rather than the factory, so women librarians designed the environment of the library to reflect the warmth of the well ordered home. The reader, like the visitor to the home, was given kind and individual attention, treated with tact and gentle manners. Reading rooms often had carpets, rocking chairs and attractive pictures. To women involved in library work, the library was seen as a major force in "moulding public opinion," educating all to the "higher possibilities of human thought and action."[101]

Katherine Lucinda Sharp, from Elgin, Illinois, advanced the development of libraries by organizing library schools. Sharp, a woman with a broad liberal education, developed an interest in the library profession after taking a position as assistant librarian at the Scoville Institute in Oak Park, now the public library. Seeing the need for specialized training, she left this post in 1890 to enter the pioneering library school in Albany directed by Melvil Dewey. After graduating she organized libraries in Wheaton, Illinois, and in Xenia, Ohio. She prepared the Comparative Library Exhibit for the 1893 World Columbian Exposition. The attention she attracted led to her appointment as librarian of the newly established Armour Institute of Technology and as head of its department of library economy. This was the first library school in the Midwest. Here she trained some of the future leaders of the profession, among them Alice S. Tyler, who had developed her professional interest while working at the Decatur Public Library, also started through the efforts of women's clubs.

Sharp's school developed such a reputation that in 1897 the University of Illinois suggested she move the school to their campus and enlarge it. Here she built one of the foremost schools in the nation and transformed the university library into a research library by expanding and systematizing the collections. A bronze bas relief portrait of her, by the sculptor Lorado Taft, commemorates her central role in an emerging profession, whose services became central not only to the cultural life of towns, but to public schools, universities and business organizations.[102]

Home economics was also a natural area for women's activity. They were responsible for having it accepted as part of public school curricula and of college studies. Isabel Bevier came to the University of Illinois in 1900 as a pioneer in food chemistry after study at MIT. The department was called Household Science to emphasize her goal of making home economics more scientific rather than just utilitarian. She originated the use of the thermometer in cooking meat. In 1908 she set up a house on campus as a laboratory for study, the first such in the United States.[103] Women with degrees from universities were often interested in the more scientific development of the subject. But while it raised the level of housework, it accentuated woman's role as wife and housekeeper.

Marion Talbot, who also had a degree from MIT and who had collaborated with Ellen Richards in editing *Home Sanitation: A Manual for Housekeepers,* came to the University of Chicago in 1892 as dean of women and assistant professor in sanitary science, then a part of the social science and anthropology department. By 1895 she was a professor in the new department of household administration. Sophonisba Breckinridge was also a member of the department even though she had a PhD in political science. With a law degree in 1904, Breckinridge taught courses on the economic and legal aspects of family life. She was one of the foremost social reformers of the period, residing part of the time at Hull House, writing and researching. She became dean of the Chicago School of Civics and Philanthropy. later part of the University of Chicago. Breckinridge linked the reforms in which. she was involved—settlement houses, home economics, immigrant and juvenile protection—to the development of social work as a profession.

Women were also presidents of colleges, improving the quality of education offered. Harriet Haskell took over Monticello in Godfrey in 1867, and made it into a highly respected institution. When it burned to the ground in 1889, she was the only woman on the Board of Trustees. She was the key person in planning a temporary structure and in raising money for it. Within eight weeks, she had the pupils back at work; the senior class graduated in June as usual. Monticello's future was due to her.[104]

Rockford College had a sound start under Anna Peck Sill, president from 1849 to 1884. Martha Hillard, the president until she married Andrew MacLeish and moved to Chicago in 1888, broadened its curriculum. But when Julia Gulliver took over in 1902, the college was at low ebb. She believed women should be "breadwinners" instead of "social parasites." She introduced more new subjects, such as home economics and secretarial studies. Bringing in new professors, she put rigor into scholastic studies until the preparatory department could be eliminated. She banned sororities, raised money and gained national accreditation for Rockford during her 17 years of administration.[105]

Women also became involved in business education. Pauline D. Summers who headed Summers College of Commerce, established in the 1890s, developed a successful system of individualized instruction. By the 1920s her school had an enrollment of about 450.[106] Women were shaping the colleges and the colleges were shaping the "new woman."

Many women were principals of grade and high schools. Obviously this was a field where women had always been acceptable, partly because they could be paid so much less than men. Yet at all levels they were leading innovators in the process of modernizing and improving educational theory. It is of great importance that women did *not* assume, as so many men did, that their biological ability to be mothers was sufficient qualification. They insisted on the need for developing specialized training and access to a broad liberal education.

By the turn of the century 8 percent of the faculty of the University of Chicago were women. They specialized in the area of civics and philanthropy which today is social service and education. In 1920, 16 percent of those who received PhDs were women. It is interesting to note that the ratio of women to men at graduate and at administrative levels in education was higher then than today.[107]

Women of the nineteenth and early twentieth century entered the profession of medicine in large numbers. Just as education had been seen as an extension of the home, medicine seemed to extend the traditional nursing functions of women. But, as in education, the advent of professionalism tended to deprive women of an opportunity to pursue a career. Women who had been midwives, and who as nurses were often the only medical care on the frontier, were harshly affected as medicine became professionalized. Men—who could attend medical schools—took over formerly female functions; women were excluded from qualifying and relegated to the position of nurse. Yet unlike law and business which were considered man's sphere from the beginning, the concept of a separate woman's sphere of the home provided an opening through which women could enter the world of medicine. When turned down by medical schools, they formed their own; when they could not have their patients admitted to hospitals, they opened their own. They had to create their own opportunities, and they did so.

By the Civil War in Illinois, women were practicing medicine only in the more remote areas. *The Medical History of Illinois* mentions only two from 1840 until after the war: the intrepid Margaret Logsdon of Shawneetown and Dr. Charlotte Stringer of Aurora. Stringer studied in the East,[108] where with Elizabeth Blackwell as an example, a few women had forced their way into medicine and set up their own schools. Cloe Buckel, a product of one of these, came to Chicago in 1859 and set up a dispensary for women and children which she ran until she left for the war in 1862. She may have paved the way for Mary Harris Thompson who also came from the East in 1863 to work for the Sanitary Commission. Convinced of the need for a hospital for women and children, Thompson started the Chicago Hospital for Women and children in 1865, with the help of Reverend William H. Ryder and a committee.[109]

Illinois was slow to either allow or help women become qualified as doctors, though Hahnemann Homeopathic College became coed in 1869. Nonetheless, homeopathy, until after the 1880s, was viewed by the established medical societies, including the American Medical Association, as a form of quackery.[110]

Rush Medical College, in 1869, permitted Mary Thompson and two other women to attend for one year, after which Thompson received a diploma and the other two were left hanging. The administration decided the experiment had failed because the men could not get an education in the presence of women. Denying the two women a chance to continue was a blessing in disguise as it forced them to seek an alternative. With the aid of Dr. William Byford and Dr. and Mrs. Dyas, and a few other sympathetic people, the Women's Hospital opened its Medical College in 1870. Both were burned by the Chicago Fire and reopened. The first 17 students even had trouble finding rooms as some boarding houses refused to take such outcasts. These women pioneers had to be strong, capable, dedicated and work twice as hard as men to gain acceptance. Praise is due to the few male physicians who assisted them, earning ridicule and even losing financially as patients left them for doctors less radical.

By 1879, the school had become the Women's Medical College and its seniors were allowed to take the examination for interning at Cook County Hospital. This too took great courage. They were hissed; at their first attempt no one was accepted. Yet they did prove that they were adequately prepared in the fields where the teaching had been done properly. Gradually acceptance came. Dr. Mary Bates passed the next examination for Cook County Hospital and became an intern there in spite of condemnation. Within a few years, several other women were accepted.

By 1890 the College had a four story building with two amphitheaters. It became a part of Northwestern University in 1891. Dr. Marie Mergler and Dr. Bertha Van Hoosen were on the faculty; a pathological laboratory had been set up under Dr. Veta Latham. By 1894 there were 350 alumnae. Cook County in the same year had over 225 women practicing as physicians,[111] probably about 10 percent of the total number.

In 1882, Julia Porter, the wife of a clergyman, founded the Maurice Porter Memorial Hospital for Children in memory of their 13 year old son. At first with room for only seven or eight patients, it grew to be the Children's Memorial Hospital, with room for 50 patients by 1903.[112]

The doors of the medical establishment cracked open when Dr. Sarah Stevenson was appointed a delegate to the American Medical Association's meeting in Philadelphia in 1876. Only her initials had been sent in with her name so her arrival was a shock. A motion to refer names of women delegates to the Judicial Council was tabled and she became the first woman accepted by that body. The Illinois Medical Society was also ready to use women's talents; two were put on the Committee for Diseases of Children and one on the Committee on Obstetrics, typically woman's place in medicine. Dr. Stevenson continued to break down barriers; she became the first woman on the staff of Cook County Hospital and the first to be a member of the State Board of Health.[113]

By 1902, women's acceptance in medical schools was such that Northwestern closed down its Women's Medical College for lack of students.[114] The *Medical Standard* which had fought against women in medicine, finally admitted that women are "peculiarly at home in the sick room, both as doctor and patient."[115] Women still had a long way to go, but such grudging acceptance was evidence of progress.

Women's contribution to medicine and public health care also emerged in their efforts to develop nursing training. Women had first become involved in such work on a large scale during the Civil War through their efforts to improve the chaotic and unsanitary military hospitals. Nursing, unlike medicine, posed no discrimination problems. But it did place nurses in a subordinate status to the doctors, many of whom too often preferred to think of nurses as "a sort of servant." Women, nevertheless, sought to develop this area and organized training schools to provide nurses for hospitals, dispensaries, schools, infant welfare stations and to make visits to patients in their homes. The creative possibilities of nursing and its importance to preventive medicine is seen most clearly in the early twentieth century through the association of nursing with social work.[116]

In 1880 the Illinois Training School for Nurses had been started by a group of women which included Lucy Flower, Dr. Sarah Stevenson and Sarah Peck Wright. In spite of the opposition of the county commissioners, they brought Mary E. Brown from New York as superintendent for $800 a year. Requirements for admission to the training course at Cook County Hospital were strict; by the second year remuneration was increased to $8 a month. In ten years the school had grown from 8 pupils to 90, expanding to also use Presbyterian Hospital. The school was supported in part by an association whose members paid $10 a year in dues. A major advance was made when Isabel Robb of New York came as the new superintendent in 1886. She was only 26, but her charm and force of character helped her make changes. In three years, she had established the first graded course of study for nurses in the United States. She inspired the establishment of the American Society of Superintendents of Training Schools for Nurses.[117]

Fannie Barrier Williams, outstanding at the Exposition and in club work, helped organize the first black hospital, Provident, with the Provident Hospital Training School for Nurses, in 1891. The *Daily Inter Ocean* gave the graduation of the first four nurses in 1897 a full column, with sketches of each graduate and quotes from the speeches of the presiding dignitaries.[118]

The first physicians, like Dr. Mary Thompson, were often so involved with their work that they did not have time for other activities; but many of the first generation of women doctors were involved in club activities and social reform. Dr. Thompson had favored suffrage for women, but her active club work was professional. She was director of the Physicians' Fellowship Club and president of the Chicago Health Officers Association. Many who followed her nonetheless showed an interest in a wide variety of movements and issues.

It is difficult to account for this. It may be, as Christopher Lasch suggests, that at the time pursuing a career was for a woman such a "burning social issue that it made indifference to related issues impossible." Or it may have stemmed from the same cultural perspective which inspired club women to undertake humanitarian endeavors and which inspired union women more than union men to seek improvment of the physical and social environment as well as better wages. Women, it must be emphasized, were socialized differently; that is, they were taught not to pursue their selfish interest but to think of helping others, whether it was their immediate family or the sick and unfortunate in their community. Career oriented men often found it difficult psychologically to place the interests of others ahead of their pursuit of individual success. Women were often the ones most concerned with correcting societal abuses.

The career of Dr. Rachelle Yarros illustrates this phenomenon. Born in Russia in 1869, she was forced to flee to the United States because of membership in a subversive society. Although she came from a well-to-do family, she began working in a sweat shop in New York. She managed to get a medical education in the East, encouraged by a fellow countryman Victor Yarros, a journalist, lawyer and philosophic anarchist whom she married. Finishing her degree at Michael Reese Hospital in Chicago, she began an obstetrical and gynecological practice in 1859. She volunteered and taught part time at a branch of the medical school of the University of Illinois, became a director of Chicago Lying-In Hospital and directed an obstetrical dispensary on Chicago's West Side to serve the poor.

Living with her husband at Hull House after 1907 probably broadened her perspectives; she became increasingly convinced that the physical problems of the women she treated in the neighborhood stemmed from their environment, from too many children and from not enough education. The social hygiene movement which she joined worked to eliminate veneral disease and prostitution. Yarros helped found the American Social Hygiene Association in 1914, becoming vice president of the Illinois organization the next year. She helped direct the programs of the Chicago Health Department and the Illinois Board of Health. The University of Illinois Medical School created a special chair in social hygiene for Dr. Yarros. To involve club women, she lectured and also headed a Social Hygiene Committee of the General Federation of Women's Club to set up a Birth Control Committee; with the Illinois Birth Control league, she opened the second birth control clinic in the United States in 1923.

Understanding the need for more knowledge to change attitudes, Yarros published in 1933 *Modern Woman and Sex*. More than most she recognized the links between the specific problems of the poor and their environmental conditions and problems; she also saw the solution to the problems in the broad participation of many groups. She wrote:

the physician is also a citizen [and] should not be ignorant of economics, of political science, of history, of philosophical ethics, of literature . . . [and should] sympathize with labor, with victims of exploitation and industrial autocracy, with the juvenile, and adult delinquents—products of the slums.[119]

This was a similar perspective to that which led Dr. Alice Hamilton to develop the field of industrial medicine and later to become the first woman professor of medicine at Harvard.

Dr. Julia Holmes Smith also joined organizations outside her field to work for social change. Married at 19 but soon widowed with a son to support, she became a drama critic and literary success. Marrying again, she was in medical school in Boston at the start of the 1873 depression. Her husband was sent to Chicago, where she finished her medical training. While practicing as a physician she became active in clubs, from the Fortnightly to the Chicago Woman's Club. The Illinois Women's Press Association was organized at a meeting at her home. Governor Altgeld appointed her as the first woman trustee of the University of Illinois. Organizer and first president of the Women's Medical Association, she did not retire from practice until she was 72.[120]

Women also pioneered in medical research. Dr. Lydia De Witt, a pathologist, joined the staff of Otho S.A. Sprague Memorial Institute of the University of Chicago in 1912. Her careful laboratory work in the chemical treatment of tuberculosis became a model for later investigators. Dr. George and Dr. Gladys Dick did famous studies on scarlet fever at the McCormick Institute for Infectious Diseases.[121]

Doctors from other parts of the state came to Chicago for their training and returned home to practice. Dr. Naomi Pierce Collins began her medical practice in Griggsville; in 1886 she moved to Decatur, where she had three patients the first day her office was opened. She too was active in reform groups, was secretary of the Equal Suffrage Association, helped select women for the school board and belonged to the WCTU.[122] When Dr. Josephine Milligan began practicing in Jacksonville in 1890, she experienced the hardships facing the first woman physician. Dr. Grace Dewey, who became her associate in pediatrics, led the fight for improvement in maternal and child health. She worked at Hull House and also founded the League of Women Voters in Morgan County.[123]

Women's role as guardians of the moral and spiritual values of the home would lead some into the ministry and many more into missionary work. A "good woman" provided the kind of influence from her pedestal that every home should have. More women than men participated in religious services, both at camp meetings and at the churches whose organization women had encouraged. Women naturally turned to leading religious ceremonies, though those who did were exceptional; churches were very often reluctant to ordain women. Illinois in 1893 had 334 women physicians, 23 lawyers, and even 16 dentists; but there were only 12 ministers.[124] Most women worked in church organizations or missionary societies. Women who wished to go overseas to convert the heathen were given official sanction, but few churchmen approved designating women officially to minister to local "heathen" or Christians.

One of the earliest chuches in Illinois to provide an outlet for women's efforts was the Church of the Latter Day Saints. Mormons made it possible for women to have meaningful activities and to feel they had an important part in the salvation of their families even though they had no part in the church hierarchy. Emma Smith, wife of the church's founder, Joseph Smith, was with him in Ohio, Missouri and Illinois through all their persecution by outsiders. She was president of the Female Relief Society, the woman's organization through which Mormon women contributed to the welfare of the whole church.[125] She also edited an important Mormon hymnbook.

A few women were actually preaching to groups before the Civil War. Madison County had two: Mrs. Hubbard was allowed to speak in the Baptist church after the men conferred and decided to hear her since their "curiosity was stronger than their objections," and Lily Henry was a regular and magnetic speaker.[126]

After the war, Maggie Newton Van Cott, a popular speaker, claimed to be the first woman licensed to preach by the Methodist Episcopal Church. Weighing over 200 pounds with a dramatic delivery, she conducted as many as three to four meetings a day. She also carried on her husband's business as a travelling salesman after his death. One wintry night she arrived in a town about 11:30 p.m. and had to walk to the only hotel down a deserted and unlighted street. The only other person kept to the street and left her the one sidewalk. The next morning he called the hotel, asking who the woman was who arrived on the late train, saying "Never did my heart so ache for a lady. I did not dare speak to her for I knew how frightened she was by the trembling of her voice—and I shall never forget the hymn she sang."[127] But Van Cott and others were only licensed to preach; they were not ordained as ministers.

The Universalist Church was one of the first to ordain women; there were women pastors at some of its smaller churches. Florence Kollock led the Englewood Church from 1879 to 1891. Augusta Chapin, who had been ordained in 1863, officiated in Blue Island from 1876 to 1888, moving to Aurora and later to Oak Park.[128]

Young women who felt called to help others find their religion became evangelists, perhaps as a way to combine adventure with an activity which gave their life purpose. The regular churches did not condone such practices, since such preachers were not licensed; at times they were even arrested. Sadie Cryer was part of such a group called "The Band" for 13 years. With a high school education and a teaching certificate, she chose at 17 to become an evangelist. Beginning in 1890 in Pekin she and those who joined her traveled the

Midwest, holding meetings wherever they could find a place, from halls to cornfields, and usually staying two to three weeks in one place. She was licensed in 1896 by the Free Methodist Church; after 13 years of evangelism, she married a minister, and filled the role of minister's wife. Later she studied theology and was ordained. Her second husband was also a minister; but Cryer had also presided over her own pastorates on the death of each husband.[129]

During this period the number of Catholic convents, schools and hospitals also grew. Mother Cabrini, who in 1946 became the first American to be canonized, opened a school in the Church of the Assumption parish in Chicago in 1899. She later started Columbus Hospital. Before she died in 1917, her authority extended over 65 religious houses and about 1,500 women.[130]

Unlike Mother Cabrini, the Sisters of Mercy were more closely tied to the history of Illinois, particularly to Chicago. When they arrived in 1846, Chicago was a frontier town with almost no medical or educational facilities. They established a hospital, taking over the burden of nursing and visiting the sick. At the same time they set up an academy for young ladies to help pay for a free school and an orphanage. To insure proper medical care, the Sisters leased a part of the hospital grounds to the Chicago Medical College. Its faculty provided medical and surgical attendance for the privilege of holding clinics. Sister Mary Gabriee and Sister Mary Ignatius Feeney worked in the drug room; upon transfer to St. Xavier Academy in 1883, they established a laboratory. Mercy Hospital in 1889 organized a Hospital School for Nurses which in 1901 extended its course of study from two to three years.

Almost every sister, among her many duties, served the sick. But besides running two female academies and a large hospital, the Sisters of Mercy also taught in the parish schools. Not only in Chicago, but in other towns of Illinois as well as other states, they were important in providing necessary community services.[131] Through such sisterhoods the Catholic Church provided the means for many women to achieve positions of leadership and women responded. The schools and hospitals they ran have a well deserved reputation for excellence.

Practical pursuits, especially making money, have long been considered to be the province of men with women in the encouraging and supporting role. Yet there have been successful business women. Many inherited the opportunity, managing farms or businesses after the death of a husband or father. Nettie Fowler McCormick is an example of a woman who had been in close touch with her husband's business. She encouraged him to rebuild after the Chicago Fire. When he died, she became "virtual president" of the company. She worked for the consolidation for the farm implement companies which became the International Harvester Company. Retiring from the business world after this success, she spent the rest of her life as a philanthropist giving money to many religious institutions and helping political candidates.[132]

Harriet Hubbard Ayer started her own cosmetic company after the Fire. Others built candy or breadmaking, all natural pursuits for a woman, into money-making propositions. Another business considered a natural for a woman was managing bordellos. Ada and Minna Everleigh were the most famous of these "madams"; they parlayed an inheritance of $35,000 into more than $1 million during the decade they operated the most lavish and popular house in Chicago.[133] Businesswomen also proved themselves capable in times of emergency, as during the Chicago Fire when Myra Bradwell managed to publish her *Legal News* and Margaret O'Toole was the first merchant to reopen for business in the burnt-out area, selling chestnuts on Lake Street.[134]

It was assumed that women were the moral custodians of society; they were therefore entrusted with the care and preservation of culture. It had been left to them to civilize and domesticate the frontier, to transmit the values of the past, and to create an attractive environment with suitable forms of entertainment to restore the frayed nerves of those of the world of commerce and production. The well bred lady read poetry to her family, played a musical instrument and decorated her home with arts and crafts of her own making. The Victorian home with its paintings, embroidery and sculptures often looks to the modern eye like an overcrowded museum. Culture was not viewed as a business enterprise but linked to the more spiritual faculties; it was, therefore, associated with femininity. Women could promote and pursue creative endeavors without breaking social sanctions.

Illinois produced three well known artists: Lucy Hartrath, Annie C. Shaw and Alice Kellogg.[135] Within the women's club movement, art and music were favorite subjects for study and practice. The Palette Club displayed the works of its members annually at the Art Institute. The Arché Club in Chicago offered prizes for sculpture. Club women saw artistic creations as spiritually uplifting in an almost religious sense. They fostered placing statues in parks They sought to improve the life of the poor in the 1890s by covering the drab and bare walls of public schools with paintings. By the 1890s they formed the Public School Art Society for this purpose. Other departments of women's clubs were active in promoting in the schools what later were called "fads and frills" by tax-conscious citizens—the teaching of music, singing and drawing.[136]

Musical evenings with orchestras, choruses and soloists, operas and operettas, became increasingly popular. Emma Abbot of Peoria, herself an opera singer, started her own company; between 1878 and 1890 she opened 35 new opera houses. Black women were instrumental in forming a black orchestra in Chicago. Music schools were established, for instance by Miss Wythe in 1834. Mrs. H. Huefner-Harken, a concert musician, joined the Chicago Music College in 1883. In 1890 Fannie Bloomfield Zeisler, perhaps the most famous woman musician and teacher, delivered a paper, "Women in Music," to the male dominated Music Teachers National Association.[137]

Many talented women were drawn to a career in music, despite its being considered scandalous by some. Their number is so large that it is only possible to list a few. Sara Hershey-Eddy taught piano and voice and helped organize the Lady Quartette in 1875. Maud Powell, a violin prodigy, toured with the Chicago Ladies Quartette until she formed her own. In the 1890s she devoted herself to spreading music to smaller cities and towns and worked with the Music Service League to provide prisons and institutions with recorded music.[138]

Helen Morgan of Danville, a cabaret dancer who later worked on Broadway in countless musicals, was best known for her blues style rendering of "Why Was I Born?" and "My Bill." Loie Fuller of Hinsdale wrote and produced plays. Later she opened a theatre in Paris where she helped launch the career of Isadora Duncan. Fuller was noted for innovative use of colored lights in conjunction with dance.[139]

Women were equally active and numerous on the literary scene. Harriet Monroe, a Chicago poet, encouraged the spread of poetry and provided young writers with an outlet by starting the journal *Poetry: A Magazine of Verse,* the first of its kind. *Poetry* gave out annual awards and, perhaps more important, paid for poems it published. Monroe's first major effort had been the "Columbian Ode" for the Chicago Exposition which was set to music and sung by a large chorus. Many great poets were first published as unknowns in her journal.[140]

Margaret Anderson started the *Little Review,* which became famous for its willingness to publish the ideas of the radical Emma Goldman. Its opposition to the execution of labor martyr Joe Hill, and other radical actions, made the financing of the review extremely difficult. One year, Anderson staved off bill collectors by living from spring to fall in a tent on the lake shore with her children, sister and cook.[141]

All over the state women's clubs sponsored dramatic performances; the play "The New Woman" for instance, appeared in the tiny town of Elsah in 1896.[142] Anna Morgan, a forerunner and inspiration for the little theatre movement, formed her own studio dedicated to educational and cultural work, specializing in interpretative reading and study of literature. From 1890 to 1920 she brought outstanding performers to Chicago and directed numerous productions. In 1902 she produced Shaw's *Caesar and Cleopatra* with a female cast.[143]

Women from Illinois were also playwrights. Rachel Crothers of Bloomington wrote plays that often were about women and their problems—*Nora, He and She,* and *Susan and God.* Margaret Cameron Kilvert of Ottawa wrote plays, stories and travel books, such as *The Involuntary Chaperon,* which appeared in 1909.[144]

Women were naturally among the foremost writers of juvenile literature. Cornelia Meigs began in 1916 with *The Steadfast Princess*, and continued for over 40 years. Lucy Fitch Perkins wrote *The Dutch Twins* in 1911, and went on to write 26 more. A visit to Ellis Island had shown her the need for understanding between people of different cultures; the "Twin" books were the result. *The Little Corporal*, a children's magazine, was edited by Emily Clark Huntington Miller, who also wrote stories. Her religious involvement led her first to missionary societies, then into education and the temperance crusade. She helped found the Evanston College for Ladies of which Frances Willard was president.[145]

In a society devoted to change, women writers helped to preserve the past through autobiographies, histories and historical romances. As early as 1853, Sara Marshall of Shawneetown published her diary, *Early Experiences*. In 1856, Juliette Kinzie's *Wau-Bun* appeared, drawing a picture of frontier life as she had known it.[146] Mary Hunter Austin of Carlinville, published her autobiography, *Earth Horizon*, which described growing up in the 1860s and 1870s in Illinois; Maud Rittenhouse's *Maud* described life in Cairo in the 1870s. Julia Dent Grant and Mary Logan wrote about their lives with their famous husbands.

Other authors presented history in novel form. Mary Hartwell Catherwood, who taught at Danville and Hooperston, wrote historical romances, among then *The Spirit of an Illinois Town* and *The Queen of the Swamp*. Mary Hastings Bradley covered the period of 1812 to 1893 in *Stories of Old Chicago*. Edith Wyatt, considered by William Dean Howells to be one of the best writers of the Chicago School, wrote such classics as *True Love, A Comedy of Affections*, and *Every One His Own Way*. Florence Finch Kelly of Girard, Neith Boyce Hapgood and Katherine Holland Brown of Quincy were also successful novelists of the period.[147]

Women with a talent for writing and time could find careers and outlets for what was called "scribbling" by writing and editing magazines. But women had more difficulty in being accepted into newspaper journalism which, it was often held, dealt with matters not properly within women's sphere. Some women, nonetheless, were able to become journalists during the Progressive Era. Most focused on areas of interest to women. Amy Leslie pursued a career in light opera until the death of her son. After her husband left her, she became drama critic for the *Chicago Daily News*.[148] Another newspaper woman, the first to be elected to office in the National Editorial Association, was Caroline Alden Huling. Arriving in Chicago in 1884, she edited the *Bookseller* and was active in women's rights groups. Both women also wrote books.[149]

The varied activities which brought women out of their isolated homes into social clubs, professional careers, humanitarian and community activities had the effect of making them self-conscious as a social group and at the same time developed their skills of leadership. By the turn of the century, many women no longer felt that the home was a large enough arena to satisfy their personal and social goals—to improve themselves and the corrupt society which surrounded them and often undermined their efforts. Active participation in voluntary associations had made them aware and knowledgeable; participation had also intensified their desire to make the community more closely resemble their moral and aesthetic home environment. Working within organized groups had also made them conscious of their potential power. In the process of trying to achieve specific goals—temperance, better schools, improved sanitation, parks, the protection of women and children against exploitation—they increasingly found that their political disability, the absence of suffrage, limited their ability to achieve these goals.

Even professional women who were striving for individual success, to prove that women could do as well in the professions as men, came to feel that woman suffrage was extremely important, if not absolutely essential, to expand opportunities for women. The first generation of women professionals was unlike the larger part of career oriented men; they fused social improvement of the community with their personal career aims. They also relied on the moral support and encouragement of women's groups to help them overcome the anxieties associated with being an alien in male occupational structures.

Women's clubs helped professional and union women to set up their own structures when it was the only way they could take part in their field. One of the most striking features of women's clubs, as has been noted, was the way in which they united the home maker, the humanitarian, and the professional. Within the women's clubs, the professionals often did committee work, exposing the homemaker to the facts and problems of the working world of which she had little personal knowledge. Mary McDowell, for instance, translated her Packingtown experiences into personal terms for the club lady; she made larger social problems more comprehensible and inspired such women to broader activities. Agnes Nestor, and other union leaders, spoke at club meetings.

It was not, however, the career women who would lead the suffrage movement which reached a crescendo in the early twentieth century; the community conscious women and humanitarians, who had all along been practicing the arts of politics and administration through their club activities, were to be the most active and successful.

Before suffrage, women seeking reforms relied heavily on personal influence with men in power or with access to power. They had experts write bills and then they descended upon Springfield to lobby for them. When the socially elite Louise deKoven Bowen, president of the Juvenile Protective Association, wanted to shift the cost of Juvenile Court probation officers onto the county payroll, she invited a "noted Illinois politician" to her home and explained the importance of the bill. He called the House and Senate leaders, gave them the number of the bill and told them to see that it passed. She reflected with some horror that the same method would work for a bad bill. And such success came only when the bill did not conflict with important economic or political interests. Eventually having to work this way became humiliating. Louise deKoven Bowen, as her community work expanded, became an activist for suffrage.[150]

The tax crusade, of course, had opened the eyes of Margaret Haley to the need for suffrage and she moved the Teachers' Federation toward this goal. At the same time, she found it necessary to affiliate with male unions to gain the use of their political power. Jane Addams had tried to organize opposition to Alderman Powers by relying on male voters; she too found that this was insufficient and became an activist for suffrage. One could write endless examples of women in town and city, after being frustrated in their pursuit of a good cause for lack of political power, moving from opposing suffrage to passive or active support.

Temperance and education were the two issues most likely to convert women to this cause. The WCTU early became a powerful and active organization for women's vote since gentle persuasion clearly would be ineffective in their campaign. In 1879 they placed a mammoth petition with 180,000 signatures, before the state legislature; the legislators' scorn created more converts. Ten small Illinois cities then allowed women a straw vote on the license question for saloons. But since men elected the aldermen who carried out city laws, the men controlled the results.

Suffragists continued their organizing and conversion work. The Equal Suffrage Association, among whose leaders were Mary E. Holmes, Zerelda Wallace and Catherine McCulloch, held conventions all over Illinois between 1888 and 1891. Those in favor of women voting used many methods of pressing the issue. In 1891 Ellen Martin, a Chicago lawyer, finding that the town charter of Lombard had omitted the word "male" in its voting ordinance, demanded the right to vote. When the stunned judges let her, she rounded up 14 more women who also voted. The Supreme Court declared the faulty ordinance unconstitutional, but the effort may have helped pass the 1891 bill allowing women to vote in school board elections. Frances Willard and Helen Hood of the WCTU had "mothered" this bill. Eighteen other states had already granted women the right to vote for school board members; in 1891 Illinois women rushed to register and use it.[151]

All through the 1890s these women were active in having bills introduced in the legislature. In 1893 when the legislature met, there were more petitions for women's suffrage than for all other subjects. Emma Ford Altgeld, the governor's wife, came onto the floor of the Senate and personally thanked all the Senators who had voted for the bill. In 1898 suffragists persuaded Senator George H. Munroe of

Will County to introduce a bill exempting women's property from taxation until they could vote. It failed, but it made a telling point.

Women made effective use of petitions. In 1899 the teachers convinced 25,000 union men in Chicago to sign suffrage petitions. For one hearing in Springfield, Iva G. Wooden pasted them on muslin, and draped 75 yards from the galleries down through the house aisles. In 1901 a Joint Guardianship Bill, for which the persistent Reverend Kate Hughes had worked, passed; the bill at least showed progress in giving women some equal rights to their children.[152]

The women kept everlastingly at it. When Grace Wilbur Trout became president of the Chicago Political Equality League in 1910, one of her first projects was a gigantic float in the Fourth of July parade which drew cheers from the crowd. Next an automobile tour was sent from Lake Forest through 16 towns, ending in Wheaton. Its success stimulated similar tours throughout the state.[153]

The National Progressive Party advanced the cause by including suffrage in its platform in 1912. Jane Addams seconded the nomination of Theodore Roosevelt for president; she and other settlement workers travelled and spoke for him. Their actions emphasized the demand that if parties could use women's efforts in this way, the least they could do was to give them the vote. They were so effective that the Democrats sought the support of other prominent women settlement house workers.[154] After Wilson was elected, suffragists held a pre-inaugural parade in Washington, D.C. in which 83 women from Illinois marched. With no police protection, the women were jeered, spat upon and manhandled so roughly by men along the line of march that many people were converted to their cause in the hope that the vote would prevent such disgraceful treatment.

The Illinois movement went forward at the same time. Education campaigns were carried on in the most remote parts of the state. A suffrage bill was introduced into the state legislature in 1913 as a non-partisan measure though it had much party support. The bill was unique, as it gave women the vote in presidential and municipal elections. It exempted the state elections—the elections of the group who would be deciding the issue, as well as other state officials. Called the "Illinois Law," it became a model for other states. After its introduction, legislators and lobbyists worked to see that it went to the right committees and that those who had promised votes thinking it would not pass did not back out when it became evident that it had enough votes. When the Speaker was pressured by those against it, a campaign was organized so that he had telephone calls every 15 minutes in Chicago on weekends and was inundated with letters and telegrams in Springfield.

When the vote came up, Grace Trout, knowing that the doorkeeper was opposed to the bill, stationed herself at the door to make sure no friendly legislator left nor unfriendly vote or lobbyist illegally entered after the session started. The vote was successful and a milestone; Illinois became the first state east of the Mississippi to grant women suffrage in a presidential election. The conservatism of the Midwest toward women voting was broken. The Illinois law is even given credit for making possible the success of the New York suffrage bill in 1917 which in turn made national success possible.[155]

The effort did not end there. After the banquet for the men who had voted for the bill, much hard work was still to be done. Legal arguments to prove the constitutionality of the bill had to be prepared for the inevitable court challenge. Legislative resolutions to repeal or broaden the law had to be fought since they could jeopardize the fight to prove it constitutional. Money raising continued, parades were organized; over 15,000 marched in Chicago in May of 1914 to prove that public sentiment backed women voting. Over 200,000 women registered to vote in Chicago and thousands more registered downstate.[156]

The effects of women attaining the right to vote were greater than had been anticipated. The effect on the nation was astounding; some felt suffrage sentiment doubled over night.[157] Women were immediately appointed to many offices and boards, not because they had been elected, but because the powerful feared women would use the vote as a reform weapon. The appointments were to placate them. In Chicago, almost at once, a commission, with two women and Mary McDowell as chairman, was appointed to provide for the installation of the long sought municipal garbage reduction plant. The city also appointed 40 policewomen and created a court for boys too old for the juvenile court. Women could now be found at all levels of city government, although still in token numbers.

The newly enfranchised women forced the Board of Education to restore Ella Flagg Young to her position as Superintendent. Dr. Clara Seippel became assistant county physician; Mary Bartelme, assistant judge of the juvenile court; Leonora Meder, a lawyer, chief of the Social Service Bureau. By 1915 the *Women's Civic Magazine* claimed that 7,000 women were on the city payroll, most of whom of course were teachers.[158]

Chicago civic reformers' ability to take advantage of suffrage was in part due to the Women's City Club which had been organized in 1910 at the behest of Medill McCormick to help clean up the city. Women such as Jane Addams, Mary Wilmarth, Hannah Solomon, Grace and Anna Nicholes, Mary Bartelme, Harriet van der Vaart, Rachelle Yarros and Mary McDowell—in essence the activists of the Woman's Club and the settlement workers—decided to make use of this Club "to coordinate and render more effective the scattered social and civic activities in which they are engaged; to extend a knowledge of public affairs, . . . and to assist in arousing an increased sense of social responsibility for the safeguarding of the home, the maintenance of good government, and the nobling of that larger home of all—the city."

With branches in all the wards and committees focused on city waste, clean air, municipal citizenship, animal protection and public schools, the club collected complaints and sought to educate women to put pressure on aldermen and government to improve services. Special committees were formed for specific issues. Membership climbed to over 5,000 by 1922 and then slowly declined, probably due to the emergence after 1920 of competing groups, such as the League of Women Voters, and the regular party organizations.[159]

The great political issue of the war years was liquor. Before 1918, 158 towns, cities and villages had voted dry; in that year 62 more did, including Springfield. The success of prohibition has been attributed to women voting. Even in Chicago, which voted wet in a referendum in 1919, women of all social classes and backgrounds voted differently from men on an issue traditionally viewed as dangerous to the home. In high rental districts women voted four times as heavily as men in favor of prohibition. In the low rental ethnic districts, men opposed prohibition by a vote of four to one but women opposed it by less than two to one, indicating that in these areas, on an issue pertaining to the home, many women voted differently from their husbands or fathers.[160]

The granting of partial suffrage to women in 1914 inspired women to run for office. In Cook County, a Suffrage Alliance was formed to help women run for office; petitions were filed in the aldermanic races in eight Chicago wards. The candidates ranged in social background from Harriet Vittum, president of the Woman's Club and head resident of the Northwestern University Settlement, to Bernice Papieralski, a seamstress with six children. The Socialist Party ran four women candidates.

The campaign which attracted the greatest attention, however, was that of Marion Drake, a lawyer, reporter, suffragist and president of the Cook County Suffrage Alliance. She ran in the first ward, the notorious vice district, against its long time alderman, Bathhouse John Coughlin. Hundreds of women flooded into the district, canvassing from door to door. The campaign had the quality of both a revival and a fairy tale, for in one blow they hoped to slay the monster vice and to demonstrate the political strength of domestic ideals.

While Marion Drake did better than expected, she could not seriously compete in an area where too many voters, legally and illegally, depended upon the protection and services provided by the machine. Although 95,000 women came out to vote, the results were disappointing.[161] Having seen the futility of poll watching when the police ignored their protests, many women thereafter did not vote in local elections, where the issues and candidates were hard to distinguish; they could not compete with the corruption. But in 1916, 289,444 women in Chicago came out to vote in their first presidential election.[162]

The suffragists continued their efforts for complete suffrage on both the state level and through a national amendment to the constitution. In 1916 when the Republican Convention met in Chicago, 5,000 women marched through pouring rain to demonstrate on behalf of a full suffrage plank in the party platform. When the nineteenth amendment was finally passed, the Illinois legislature was prepared to accept change. It became the first state to ratify the amendment on June 10, 1919. There were just three negative diehards in the House and Senate passage was unanimous.[163]

Women's wartime activities had also made it difficult to deny them the vote. They had joined the armed forces, gone overseas with the YWCA and the Red Cross and had taken thousands of men's jobs at home, from running street cars to making steel. In Illinois 326,323 women had formed 2,136 local groups with 18 departments, directed by 7,700 chairwomen under the banner, "Win the War." They had registered 692,229 women for war work.[164] The energies of many social feminists were deflected from local social problems to the cause.

Many had opposed the war before the United States entered. Only a few, like Jane Addams, remained pacifists. For this posture her image as a "practical saint and the most useful" American shifted to that of "villain" and "the most dangerous American." But in 1931, during the depression, she shared the Nobel Prize for Peace, and once again became an "American heroine."[165]

In looking back over the period from the end of the Civil War to the end of World War I, it is clear that women had traveled far on a long, hard road. They had learned the art of organizing effectively behind a common goal. They no longer fainted at the thought of speaking in public, nor did they think themselves less capable than men in pursuing intellectual goals and careers. They were eager to enter the arena of political affairs. Women had gained not simply the right to vote, but the right, even if they were married, to have legal careers, to make binding contracts, to have equal rights to their children after divorce and to control their own property and income. Moreover, never again could local governments disregard their views on subjects that affected the home, child rearing, and schools; nor could they automatically place economic interests above the human needs of the community.

Yet at the close of the period women still had a long way to go. More women would go to college, but only a small percentage would actually undertake the careers for which they were qualified. Most of their jobs would be, on the whole, defined by their womanhood. And the distance between the homemaker and the worker would grow; they would move more and more in separate worlds. It would be many years and another profound social movement before more progress would be made.

CHAPTER 5

From Flapper to Libber

"I have faith to believe that what we have done is but the earnest of what we shall do."

Ellen M. Henrotin

By 1920 women had the vote and the country was "dry"; the two amendments to the Constitution were the culmination of years of exhausting efforts on the part of women. And in one generation, they had changed from Gibson to John Held, Jr., girl; from wearing long skirts and long hair, presiding over the separate and restricted sphere of the home and children, to short skirts and bobbed hair, dashing around in the world outside that sphere. The flapper of the 1920s was in youthful revolt against restrictions, which symbolized a sense of equality and personal freedom. Cigarettes, cosmetics, speakeasies, tennis and her own flask were expressions of her emancipation.[1]

But after the flapper married, she would settle down to a traditional family life. She was less apt to have a maid than her mother, but she had more household gadgets. Gas stoves, washing machines, vacuum cleaners and a larger variety of canned goods both made her housework easier and raised the standards of housekeeping. And it meant more work if the family were not to suffer the embarrassment of a "gray wash" on the line.

Although domesticity no longer was so backbreaking, it took just as much time, if not more. Advertisements linked love with housekeeping; a wife must have her makeup on straight and be sure she smelled good when her husband came home from work. Those who did the "double job"—working both inside and outside the home—also had these higher standards which made them feel guilty. A new mother took a more clinical interest in child development and read psychology books for guidance.

But the intense reforming spirit of the late nineteenth and early century had collapsed. This may be linked in part to the fact that the worst evils of urban life were not as apparent. By the end of the decade, housing for most of the working class included appliances, hot and cold running water and indoor plumbing. Most streets were paved, playgrounds and small parks dotted town and city, many due to the efforts of women. Classroom size had declined, kindergartens were common and high school education had expanded. At least in Chicago, female teachers, though still badly paid, received the same salaries as their male colleagues. But later when school boards wanted to attract more men to the classroom, they devised the method of paying additional sums for each dependent. Immigration restrictions which had been in effect since World War I had facilitated assimilation, while the spread of the automobile speeded up the process of suburbanization, putting a larger geographical gap between the haves and have-nots. Blacks and Mexicans had replaced immigrants from abroad as the poverty group; the racism of the period dampened enthusiasm for charity and settlement work.[2]

Structural changes in the field of social work—professionalism, specialization and bureaucratization—helped to decrease the club woman's concern and activity. The welfare field was fragmented; the reformer and volunteer became isolated from the paid case workers within social agencies. The paid case workers, who at one time worked side by side with volunteers or even under them, sought to establish their professional identity. In doing so, they downgraded the value of the volunteer. Professional associations further separated them from charity workers. One practitioner, in the journal *Family,* asserted that "The really valuable citizen" realized that "specialists" alone could perform certain jobs and that the public needed protection from "amateur social workers."[3] Bureaucratization, with its stress on efficient service rather than the development of personal contact and understanding between social classes, further restricted the spontaneous desire of the volunteer to serve.

The new focus on individual psychology among social workers also shifted attention away from dealing with the problems of a poor community environment. During the Progressive Era case workers had attempted to understand the individual in terms of his or her social situation and environment; they therefore considered the coordination of community services and the creation of new welfare resources indispensable to giving assistance. To them social work was a great crusade for human betterment; personal contact with the poor would not only raise individual families to a higher level, but would furnish the information to make the upper classes conscious of the need for reforms in the basic environment in order to minimize poverty, disease and crime and to change individual behavior. But in the 1920s social workers stressed human relations skills based upon an understanding of the individual growth process which involved adjusting the individual to the environment. This was a change in emphasis that had far-reaching effects in the future.

Ironically, the clubs themselves had promoted the idea of professional service as a means of improving the work of welfare agencies. Club women and settlement leaders, among them Lucy Flower, Louise deKoven Bowen and Julia Lathrop, who had worked for the Juvenile Court and established the Juvenile Protective Association, were instrumental in creating the Juvenile Psychopathic Institute in 1915. The Institute researched juvenile delinquency as a means of improving the work of probation officers. Becoming a clinic of the court, it also helped to redirect the concerns of social work away from the environment to individual psychology. They also created the job of probation officers, providing the funds themselves until they could persuade the government to take over. But these women, unlike the social agencies of the 1920s which they had helped create, never saw therapy as an alternative to either reform or welfare, but as supplemental to it.

The Chicago School of Civics and Philanthropy, under the influence of Edith Abbott and Sophonisba Breckinridge, differed in the 1920s from most social work schools in the East. The Chicago School showed a distinctive interest in social research and public welfare administration. Since Abbott and Breckinridge were experts both in child welfare and labor legislation, they never lost the progressive vision which was a product of their close association with settlements, the Immigrant Protective League and the Women's Trade Union League. Both wanted to see social work become a profession, but they resisted agency demands for specialized technicians since they believed that social work's future as a profession depended upon the school's ability to produce administrators equipped to handle the broad problems of legislation and community welfare. Their emphasis was exceptional.[4]

Not only did the humanitarian work of volunteer women become a career area in the 1920s, but women's concern with improving the internal environment of the home had become an important profession, opening up career opportunities in academics, business and government. Marion Talbot and Alice P. Norton, at the University of Chicago, were active in making home economics an academic specialty. They turned the older preoccupation with household management into a discipline with social research significance. Home economics now stimulated studies by the government and by social agencies on American buying habits, on wages, on family budgets and on the time housewives spent on domestic chores. The gospel of home economics, household sanitation, diet and efficiency propagated by public schools, charitable societies and magazines helped direct business enterprise to the potential market for labor saving home devices and prepared foods.

The home as a physical and social arrangement became a model for transforming institutional life. As dean of women at the University of Chicago, Marion Talbot arranged college dormitories as residential clubs to simulate the "simple, quiet attractions of a home," with housemothers, self-government and a hospitality program. Philanthropists introduced the "cottage system" into reformatories and orphanages in an effort to make these dreary and depressing institutions more resemble a home. Cottages, rather than a single large building, were to be the units of social organization. The Park Ridge School for Girls, a favorite philanthropy of the Illinois Federation of Women's Clubs, served as a model.[5]

Thus in the course of time the very efforts of club women and reformers to create a system of improved and enlarged social services to the community and to gain public recognition for the social importance of domesticity had produced a culture that downgraded benevolence, made the professional-client relationship the model for welfare work and the home a laboratory to test professional theories. The trend towards relegating the non-professional women to the home and narrowing the limits of volunteer activities was most pronounced in metropolitan cities such as Chicago. Even parent-teacher associations came to be dominated by the professional teacher. In town and suburb, however, the non-career women had more diverse opportunities for volunteer work and retained a larger measure of influence over school policies and the activities of social agencies.

When viewed in this way, it is not surprising that women's clubs tended increasingly to become centers for socializing and less centers for mobilizing social services. They did remain vital institutions. While they continued or extended old projects, they redirected more of their energies to expanding cultural life. The Chicago Woman's Club, for example, continued the progressive tradition of extending the services of the public schools to home and neighborhood. They funded a model nursery and an adult education class. They continued the experiment of an Infant Welfare Station, which they saw both as providing clinic care and as stimulating democratic participation, while linking neighborhood groups and professionals into a new social unit. Such projects, however, gained less attention than efforts to make music and drama more widely available. The Chicago Woman's Club took the lead in the formation of the Civic Music Association which made available in neighborhoods and parks free or inexpensive concerts. Children were trained in choral and instrumental work and many adults began in this way to become professional musicians.[6]

The scale of social welfare services and cultural institutions had by then become so large that they demanded coordination through joint councils and through government participation. The type of activity best suited to the volunteer clubs became the organizing of single events and money raising. Through white elephant sales, entertainments and the eliciting of pledges, women's groups could promote projects of special interest to them. In these ways the Illinois Federation of Women's Clubs raised $73,000 in different communities for the Park Ridge School for Girls.[7] Wealthy individual club women also carried on this philanthropic tradition. Edith Rockefeller McCormick belonged to 28 organizations, founded the Chicago Zoological Gardens in 1923 to further the study of experimental psychology, helped support the Chicago Opera Company and in 1925 was the chief sponsor of an attempt to begin a Chicago Civic Theatre to bring reasonably priced drama to the city[8]

One of the most striking of these fund raising events was the Women's World Fairs in Chicago. The fairs served not only to raise money for wortwhile organizations but also to provide women with a chance to display their talents and to learn about new vocational opportunities. The first one, in 1925, was sponsored by the Women's Roosevelt Republican Club and the Illinois Republican Woman's Club; Helen Bennett, who managed the Collegiate Bureau of Occupations, suggested it and Louise Bowen ran it. In eight days, 200,000 people attended the fair which netted $50,000. This fair was unique in that everything was done by women. The program, with a cover by Helena Stevens, was printed in a plant owned and operated by a woman. A small emergency hospital was staffed by women physicians. Over 200 exhibitors from the United States and some foreign countries displayed women's work and demonstrated the diversity of women's interests and skills. A women's symphony orchestra gave concerts; a pageant, "Women in Industry," was performed; ballets, choruses and wandering musicians amused the crowds. The Famous Women's Luncheon seated 700 and turned away 900, entertaining such notables as Jane Addams and Nellie Taylor Ross, governor of Wyoming.[9] These money raising activities were outgrowths of the Columbian Exposition and the Civil War Sanitary Fairs.

The Women's Trade Union League also continued its activities during the 1920s but on a diminished scale until it was disbanded in the late 1940s. Unions in general failed to sustain the same rate of growth as in the early part of the century. Unionization among women proved still more difficult. Women faced hostility from the American Federation of Labor, which undercut in many subtle ways women's access to jobs. As in the past, the unskilled nature of so many women's jobs and their dispersal in small shops on the craft model, made their situation particularly unsuited to unionization or joint action of any type. Realizing this, the League concentrated its efforts on securing protective legislation.[10]

Even though the Loeb Rule, which prohibited teachers' unions, was overturned in the courts, the Chicago Teachers' Federation experienced setbacks as they continued to work for the improvement of the teachers' economic situation and attempted to increase their influence in the schools. After the founding of the union, teachers' salaries had risen from a maximum of $825 in 1897 to a plateau of $2,200 in 1922. As in the past, the Federation resorted to the tactics of civic and political pressure. They sought to bring more money to the Board of Education through changes in the tax structure—a slow process which in the end backfired as those in power lowered tax assessments. The teachers' struggle to achieve professional status, by giving the classroom teacher a role in shaping educational policies, brought them into bitter conflict with the superintendent. He sought to eliminate their political influence through the abolition of the teachers' councils and to centralize decision-making power in the hands of professional administrators, who of course were all men. In what can be described as a battle of the sexes, since the teachers' councils were predominantly female, the influence of the new ideas of professionalism on the outlook of club women is evident. In all the earlier struggles, the women's clubs and their representatives on the Board of Education had identified with the teachers. In the 1920s they identified with the superintendent; although they did not like his tactics, they refused to aid the teachers, preferring to support what they considered would lead to more efficient services rather than democratic participation in school decision making.[11]

The Depression and the war would obscure the consequences of this split, but in the affluent post-war years, the dominant teachers' union would be the American Federation of Teachers whose goals would be primarily economic issues. Teachers would seek to achieve these when necessary by exerting their power through strikes.

The increased emphasis on professionalism and the environment of moral exhaustion from the earlier efforts proved inhospitable to the continuation of the social feminism of the Progressive Era. Perhaps more important, the success of the suffrage movement brought to the surface differences among leaders as to how to use the vote. After the first election, the number of women voting declined. Further, the number was usually highest in national and state elections and lowest in local ones. Some thought it was even more disturbing to find that women divided their vote in much the same way that men did; they did not act as a separate force. This was partially due to lack of interest and knowledge, but it was also due to disagreement among the women leaders. Those who felt most strongly the need for equal rights and having women elected to office continued the National Women's Party. This group began to work for the Equal Rights Amendment, which was first introduced into Congress in 1923.[12]

Many members of the National American Women's Suffrage Association, after it disbanded in 1920s, agreed with Ruth Hanna McCormick of Chicago that women should work through the regular political parties. She felt so strongly about this that she tried to prevent the formation of the League of Women Voters. The League had been started by those who felt that the first step was to educate women politically and that this could best be done through a policy of non-partisanship. Their main goal was to provide women with citizenship training and an opportunity to study issues.

In Illinois, with Flora Sylvester Cheney as president, the League began a program to help women become politically knowledgeable. A two week leadership course taught by professors, public officials and other authorities led to the one day Citizenship Schools. During the next few years hundreds of women listened to the rudiments of government and methods of political action at these schools. By 1927 women were going to Springfield to see government in action, escorted by the League. A bulletin was published to keep members informed on issues and on legislators' voting records. The *Illinois Voters' Handbook,* first published in 1923, has become a classic. The *Handbook,* now published on the average every two years, is a reference book on the structure of state government.

Later "Know Your Town" studies were encouraged which resulted in booklets with information on taxes, government expenditures, boards, elections, as well as local history. At the same time, members selected areas of interest for study, such as welfare, the status of women, and war and peace; the information gathered helped the League take political action on proposed legislation. The Leagues did not work officially for candidates, though members were encouraged to participate in all aspects of the political process.[13]

The Chicago City Club, which was also nonpartisan, continued to act as a watchdog over municipal government. While it had clubs in local neighborhoods all over the city, there were few in working class, ethnic and black neighborhoods; the best leaders among women in these neighborhoods tended to enter the major parties. After 1925 its membership declined.[14]

When women first gained suffrage, the women's clubs, at the invitation of the League of Women Voters, set up the Joint Congressional Committee in Washington, to coordinate efforts on legislation and to act as a lobbying arm for member organizations. By 1922, national women's groups were members of the committee which lobbied for the Child Labor Amendment and social legislation of benefit to women.[15]

Political party leaders, having at first assumed that woman suffrage would mean an unpredictable block of votes which would have to be wooed, appointed women as heads of committees to work for candidates' elections; an exceptional woman might even be asked to run for office or later even put herself forward as a candidate. Although in the cities, neither party seriously considered running a woman for high public office, at least one woman sought the nomination for mayor." In 1925 Johanna A. Griggs, a member of the school board, tried to get the Republican nomination in Chicago." A municipal housecleaning by a woman mayor," was her slogan; she contended that men "have lacked the stamina and moral courage to repel the ever-encroaching demon of graft," and "cannot be depended upon to exterminate the social vipers who poison the streams of public virtue."[16]

When Big Bill Thompson ran for mayor, his campaign illustrated the divisions among women. In 1915 he was the Republican candidate and presented himself as a reformer. He promised to put a mother on the school board and "to protect the fair womanhood of Chicago." He made Mrs. Page Waller Eaton chairman of women's activities and later superintendent of social surveys; he appointed Louise Osborn Rowe commissioner of public welfare. Marion Drake, who had run against Bathhouse John Coughlin in the first ward, knew the candidate better; she held a "Can't Stand Thompson" meeting. But he proved irresistible, winning with 63 percent of the women's vote.

It was not long before community conscious women's groups discovered that Thompson not only was one of the most corrupt mayors in Chicago's history but also that he was determined to destroy the reform oriented school board, oust Ella Flagg Young as superintendent and destroy the Teachers' Federation through the "Loeb Rule." In March 1916, Louise Bowen, head of the Illinois Republican Women, organized a protest meeting of 3,000 women against his maladministration. Mrs. Eaton resigned her position, saying that Louise Osborn Rowe had demanded from her a $600 kickback for the mayor. In 1923 Thompson was defeated by William E. Dever, a judge with an impeccable record for honesty, who, nonethleless, won only 23 percent of the women's vote.[17] This vote seems to indicate that women were not voting in terms of the social feminism of the pre-suffrage era.

Under Dever, women's special interests were given political recognition. He appointed Mary McDowell as commissioner of public welfare, probably considered a woman's post because of the social feminism of the Progressive Era. Mary Margaret Bartelme became the first woman judge in Illinois that same year and presided over the Juvenile Court for ten years. Bartelme was noted for her concern with the problems of young women, helped establish three homes for girls, known as the Mary Bartelme Clubs, and raised funds to help those who needed foster homes.[18]

A few women sought election successfully. Ruth Hanna McCormick, a Republican Party loyalist after a brief foray into the Progressive Party in 1912, sought election to Congress in 1928. She won a stunning victory, topping Hoover's vote that year. She successfully ran for the Senate nomination in the 1930 primary but her campaign expenditures of over $300,000 helped to alienate voters and defeat her in the election.[19]

The first woman from Illinois to serve in Congress was Winifred Mason Huck, who was elected to finish the unexpired term of her father in 1922. Many congresswomen gain their positions through descent usually through husbands. Huck was defeated in the primary for a full term; she then joined the National Woman's Party Political Council, organized to help elect women to office. She pioneered as a journalist, having herself committed to prison and released to write a story. She then traveled East, taking whatever jobs she could with such a record. Her subsequent newspaper articles on her experiences both as a prisoner and as an ex-convict stressed the humanity she had found among other prisoners and among her employers[20] some of which may have been in response to her own charm and assurance.

A few women ran for state office, but fewer were elected. Lottie Holman O'Neill of Downers Grove was the first to serve in the General Assembly. Elected in 1922, she served 13 terms, first in the House and then in the Senate, interrupted only once when she made an unsuccessful try for the U.S. Senate. In 1924 Katherine Hancock Goode, a Republican from Cook County, joined O'Neill. The number of women doubled with the election of two Democrats, Sarah Bond Hanley of Warren County and Mary Cowan McAdams of Adams County, in 1926. In the next elction Florence Fifer Bohrer of Bloomington became the first woman senator, and Flora S. Cheney and Anna Wilmarth Ickes won seats in the House, for a total of seven women by 1928.[21] In 1971 the total was four: Representatives Eugenia Chapman, Lillian Karmazyn and Giddy Dyer and Senator Esther Saperstein. A breakthough came in 1972 when the total was eleven, eight in the House and three in the Senate—still under 5 percent.

A few women could be found in county government. In 1971 there were 22 women treasurers, 17 county clerks and 2 superintendents of schools. In the court system, just over 1 percent of the circuit court judges and 18 percent of the clerks were women. Curiously, most of the counties electing women to major offices were under 25,000 in population. Putnam County with a population of 5,077 even elected a woman sheriff.[22] Apparently the only important positions voters trusted women to hold had to do with money, education or records.

Inspite of brief initial success, reform measures supported by women's organizations often failed to gain headway. A general distrust of government support for welfare programs came as an aftermath of the "Red Scare" of the post-war period when such action seemed like socialism or even communism. On the national level women supported the Sheppard-Towner Act, which provided funding for education in health care and for facilities for mothers and infants. Congress soon failed to appropriate the money necessary to put it into action. Women supported the Child Labor Amendment to the Constitution which failed to pass in most states, including Illinois, where so much had been done to expose the evils of child labor and where state laws had been passed against it. The Women Patriots and the Daughters of the American Revolution, among other groups, charged that Jane Addams, Mary Anderson of the Women's Bureau, Grace Abbott of the Children's Bureau and Florence Kelley of the National Consumers' League were helping the communists; a chart called the "Spider Web" claimed to show that women and their organizations were working for legislation that would subtly enhance communism. This aroused enough fears so that even legislators who wanted to vote for such legislation found it politically difficult to do so.[23]

In the state legislature, the difficulties faced by Lottie Holman O'Neill were similar to those of later years. In 1923, after sponsoring 13 bills, only three of which passed, she wrote,

Perhaps never before have women's organizations of the state considered legislation so carefully, discussed it so fully, and agreed so fully in their endorsement of several measures introduced so that their failure to achieve success is all the more conspicuous. The three measures which passed . . . were "to save the wild flowers, to help the crippled children, and to assure some added rights to the inheritance of wives."[24]

Divisons within and between women's groups made it difficult to advance women's rights. The clearest example of this was the Equal Rights Amendment. Settlement house groups and women's clubs had labored long for special laws to protect women in their daily working hours, to gain minimum wages and safety in work places and to limit the demands made on women. The courts had ruled against much of what they had gained, but they had kept on

(Manuscript Collection, UICC Library)

Immigrants being received at Hull House.

rewording laws until they did have shorter hours and other protections not extended to men. Women trade union leaders and the club women who worked with them felt that such laws were essential. Thus when the Woman's Party began its push for an Equal (BPW) began in 1937 to work to change the law, but it was 1967 before a bill was passed in Illinois which exempted executives, administrators and their assistants and professional women from that provision.

Only the Business and Professional Woman's Club stayed neutral.[25] Started by the YWCA in 1918, and a member of the Women's Joint Congressional Committee, the BPWC had helped support progressive legislation. But on the question of protective laws they could see that such legislation could handicap them in competing with men for jobs. The eight hour law in particular came under attack because it limited what women could do in comparison with men on the same job and could, therefore, stop their advancement. In 1935 Amelia Earhart, who had become a famous flyer after graduating from Chicago's Hyde Park High School, told the Business and Professional Women's Club of Decatur that she was more "concerned with the eight-hour-law than she was with women in the air." If it applied to men also, she went on, it would be fair, but it kept women out of the better jobs which would demand more time. In Illinois the Business and Professional Woman's Club (BPW) began in 1937 to work to change the law, but it was 1967 before a bill was passed in Illinois which exempted executives, administrators and their assistants and professional women from that provision.

Martha Connole of East St. Louis chaired the national committee of the BPW which made a survey on discrimination against women; as they studied the issue further from their point of view, they swung gradually to agreement on the need for the Equal Rights Amendment. When the National Organization of Business and Professional Women decided to support it, the Illinois branch followed, becoming in 1937 the first of the major women's clubs to do so.[26]

The issue of birth control information was controversial in the 1920s, and is still so today. In 1916, the initiator of the birth control movement in the United States, Margaret Sanger, gave a speech to a crowd near the stockyards of Chicago which led to the organization of the Parents' Committee. This group asked the Illinois attorney general about the legality of giving out birth control information; in 1917 he ruled that no law in Illinois prevented a licensed physician from giving birth control instructions. And because of the efforts of the committee, attempts during the next few years to pass laws to prevent dispensing such knowledge failed. In 1923 the Parents' Committee tried to set up a clinic to provide poor women with birth control information but Chicago's Health Department refused to issue a license. They then changed the name from clinic to center;

since licensed physicians could give such advice legally in their offices, Dr. Rachelle Yarros began to use her office under the auspices of the committee.

The next year the committee organized the state chartered Illinois Birth Control League. On its board initially were six women and sixteen men, most of whom were doctors. James A. Field, a professor of economics at the University of Chicago, was the first president, soon followed by Helen Fairbank Carpenter, long an advocate of birth control. By 1927 there were six centers functioning in Chicago.

Denied entry to the Chicago Council of Social Agencies because of the opposition of Catholic members, the Birth Control League was finally admitted to the Illinois State Welfare Association in 1936. Its membership in the state association provided it with contacts in downstate communities which desired their help. The number of clinics in small towns and rural areas were few, due to local pressures and transportation problems. When there were residents who were social workers or who had connections with the Chicago group and did not have to worry about local pressures the clinics could be operated. But the development was slow and the number served small.

The expansion in the number of clinics began after the League's first exhibit at the 1936 Illinois Welfare Conference in Bloomington. Danville's clinic was opened rather easily in 1937; but a woman doctor had to travel from Chicago every two weeks to the newly opened Springfield Maternal Health Center because the only hospital refused to allow the center to use its facilities. The hospital's policy changed during the war. In Peoria Dr. Ethel Cooper started a service on a small scale in the 1920s; when the county medical society expelled Dr. Cooper, a group organized to defend her.

Evanston's center was the most successful because it received cooperation from the director of social services for the Outpatient Department of the Evanston Hospital and was admitted to the Evanston Council of Social Services. The growth of Planned Parenthood Centers on the whole was slow until 1965 when the State Birth Control Commission appointed by the governor made a favorable report.[27] Their growth since then is due both to the dedicated services of many women and men, and to the demonstrated need for their services.

While the new freedom of the 1920s did not open new opportunities for most women, there were some who achieved business and professional success. Numerous women became insurance and real estate agents. Lorna Taboern Cardevaant owned and managed the Cardevaant Laboratories, which made microscope slides. Fannie C. Baldwin of Peoria inherited the *Evening Star;* she initiated a management committee, a system which some called "socialistic" and other "impractical," but which proved to be very successful. Minna Schmidt made a fortune designing costumes. Dr. Annabel Anderson became owner and president of the Chicago Law

School, the second woman in the United States to attain this distinction. Pearl Hart, who graduated from John Marshall Law School in 1924, was public defender in the Morals Court and helped curb the practice of arresting young girls and lodging them in jail overnight. Sarah Bacon Tunnicliff became interested in trying to eliminate smoke from Chicago air; in 1922 she was a member of the Chicago Health Commission Advisory Staff and the Citizens' Advisory Smoke Abatement Commission. She was director of education and of domestic heating in the Conservation Department of the United States Fuel Administration for Illinois.[28]

Another woman in a government position was collector of internal revenue for Illinois. However, in 1931 she was forced to resign when she played faro with some politicians. Nothing was wrong with her conduct of the office;[29] the double standard had been applied. Such application of double standards was typical. Women stayed in their sphere or encroached on men's terms—taking jobs the men deemed suitable for them and accepting less pay. If in a man's job, they were expected to work as well as a man, yet not lose what men considered their femininity.

The depression of the 1930s weighed heavily on the middle and working classes. Women resorted to all types of work to supplement the family income. They read the "Prudence Penny" column in the *Herald Examiner* by Leona Alford Malek, who tried to help women stretch their few dollars.[30] They made money however they could, from taking in boarders and laundry to selling baked goods. As today, unemployment was higher among women than among men, who were often given preference when jobs were available as "heads of families." Working women who married often tried to keep the marriage secret in order to keep their jobs. Lower wages were paid to women, which led to some men being laid off because women could be hired for less.

When the state passed a minimum wage law in 1933 it examined five industries in which women worked. Laundries paid 23 cents an hour in southern Illinois to 28 cents an hour in Chicago. Beauty parlor operators in Chicago made $16.60 for a 45 to 48 hour week, working full time, but they could be called in to work part time and paid as little as a dollar a day. Women's average earnings in the survey ranged from $10.12 to $16.50 a week. A survey by the Division of the Chicago Relief Administration and the United Charities showed that necessary expenses of a woman living alone were from $17.94 to $19.08 weekly.[31]

The settlement houses had difficulty, as did most charity organizations, in raising sufficient money to carry on their services. Increasingly, responsibility for programs was transferred to government. Staffed by professional workers and volunteers, they provided curtailed service. The changing character of neighborhoods also increased their difficulties. With black migrants increasing, integration was a problem. Some houses avoided it;

others closed or moved to a new location. The Abraham Lincoln Center, however, made integration work.

Settlement leaders like Lea Taylor, head of Chicago Commons, Charlotte Carr of Hull House and Harriet Vittum of the Northwestern settlement acted as spokeswomen for the poor in the legislature. With the Chicago Workers Committee on Unemployment, they took part in demonstrations against relief cuts or curtailment of President Roosevelt's W.P.A.[32] While these allies continued to be helpful, as in the past, workers themselves became more active on their own behalf.

Ethnic and black women carried out numerous sit-down strikes to protest wages, layoffs and unsafe machinery. One of the most notable—because it led to a clash between the women and the police—was the sit-down strike at Great Western Laundries led by a young black woman from New Orleans, Sylvia Woods. She lost her job but went on to organize workers during World War II at Bendix Aviation. In 1931 Christine Ellis, a 20 year old Jugoslavian immigrant, organized workers to protest layoffs at the Kendall Corporation. She too was fired, but went on to organize one of the most effective councils to stop evictions for the unemployed in Chicago. In the Back-of-the-Yards a young woman from Michigan, Stella Nowicki, started a sit-down strike over unsafe machinery. After she too was fired, she went on to organize the bacon-wrappers for the Packinghouse Workers Union.[33]

In the southern part of the state, Agnes Burns Wieck, a former school teacher, carried on in the tradition of Mother Jones. She wrote articles for *The Illinois Miner* and helped form a Ladies Auxiliary of Progressive Miners of America, earning herself the nickname, "the Illinois Hellraiser." Catherine De Rorre, also working with the Ladies Auxiliary, was called "the Good Samaritan of the Coal Fields" for the soup kitchens she set up.[34] These women helped the miners—the support system in operation again—partly because it meant more for their families.

Radicalism and unionism were in the air. Clerical workers responded to the CIO's organizing efforts in their workplaces, as did women working for newspapers and public employees. Elizabeth Dilling, and many other women and men, saw these as communist conspiracies. In her book, *The Red Network*, she criticized settlement leaders for their support of the Workers Alliance.[35]

Some women did well financially during the Depression. Two who had begun in the 1920s were Neysa McMein of Quincy and Helen Hokinson of Mendota, trained in Chicago art schools. Beginning with fashion sketches, they went on to make over $40,000 a year during the Depression. McMein did covers for well-known magazines, from *McCalls* to the *Saturday Evening Post*. Helen Hokinson's cartoons of matronly clubwomen acting foolish, or stupid, were even better known;[36] no one calculated how much harm they did to the efforts of women's clubs.

Sally Rand was another financial success. As the chief performer and attraction in the Streets of Paris at the Century of Progress Fair in Chicago in 1933 and 1934, she is credited both with making the fair a financial success in the Depression years and with raising a "tease" dance to an art form. It was simply merchandising, she said, which used fans and the music of Debussy to make the difference between a performer and a star.[37]

Some women were fortunate enough to have special training they could use. Mary Long Whitmore, born to wealth, had studied landscape architecture in college, "for want of anything better to do." When forced to support her mother and son, she designed gardens, parks and even cemetery vaults. In 1938 when the Gallatin Housing Authority decided to move Shawneetown away from the river after the devastating flood of 1937, she won the contest they held for the best design of the new town.[38]

The Depression directed attention once again to the problem of housing for the poor. Public housing, long advocated by some forward-looking women but resisted by those in government, finally was introduced by the federal government, supported by labor unions, contractors and social workers. The public housing built in Chicago before the 1960s incorporated in its design and social policy the concepts of good domestic environment held by women reformers. Low rise developments, with green spaces for light and air and playground facilities, rather than institution-like high rises, were built. They were meant to be family homes. Until the 1960s regulations prevented unmarried mothers from living in public housing. Income policies discouraged eligible mothers from working; a dual income would place a family too easily above the income group permitted and force them into less desirable and more expensive private housing. In this way public housing policy helped perpetuate the ideal that a mother should be married and that her place was in the home.

Public housing did open up new career opportunities for women with social work qualifications at various levels. In 1948 Elizabeth Wood became chairman of the Chicago Housing Authority after a varied career in housing and social work. Coming to Chicago in 1922 from Vassar College, she began working in the Home Modernizing Bureau of the Building Industries. Then she moved to the United Charities of Chicago and from there to the Metropolitan Housing Council and the Illinois State Housing Board. As chairman of the Chicago Housing Authority she struggled, over the objections of politicians, to maintain a policy of selecting sites where housing was needed, without regard to race or the racial balance within projects. She opposed the building of high rises, which she felt promoted anonymity and set public housing apart from the rest of the neighborhood. The projects opened during her short tenure remain both the most humane of the post-war period and the most visually

(Chicago Historical Society)

Demonstrating for change. 1915 Suffrage parade

(Photographer Mike Tropea

1976 demonstration for ERA in Springfield

attractive. According to Carl Condit, the architectural historian, "The period of civic enlightenment of the CHA culminated in the three years of 1948-51 under the chairmanship of Elizabeth Wood." Public housing of the 1960s reversed these principles and became a social disaster.[39]

With the coming of World War II, women were once again welcomed into the job market—often in industries where they could not have obtained a job during peacetime. The armed forces developed special women's corps to use their talents. Each of the forces had nursing corps; women also went overseas with the Red Cross and the Salvation Army. On the home front, as "Rosie the Riveter," they took over formerly male jobs as fast as the men left for the services. Since it was assumed that the men would return after the war to take back their jobs, some women were paid the same wages as men; had women been reclassified at a lower rate, the transition would have been more difficult. Some wartime industries did try to conform to the equal pay scales urged by the government; half of the 80 contracts surveyed in the midwestern states abided by that provision. The CIO wrote such provisions into their contracts and tried to correct inequities.[40]

Despite these efforts, discrimination continued and women were still concentrated in the lower level jobs. When a Women's Advisory Council was finally appointed to advise on women in the war effort, their advice was not asked, and when given, was usually ignored. Elizabeth Christman, a Chicago member of the Women's Advisory Council, commented that "the only place you can make yourself felt is if you are where a thing happens, [and] they apparently don't happen [here]." The members were not allowed to participate in other advisory bodies. They were separate and unequal.[41]

Both the good and the bad treatment was possible because few people expected women to continue working after the war. A close look at war films, usually made by men, shows women yearning to return to the home as soon as their men returned. Some did, but many did not want to leave the work force. They had left laundries, domestic service and other low paying jobs to find the best pay and conditions they had ever known. This was particularly true of black women. Sylvia Woods, for example, who had helped organize a local for the United Auto Workers at Bendix Aviation, moved into the factory from laundry work.

When the soldiers returned, women were released despite their protests. Many women had to seek other less desirable work. Protective legislation continued to make it difficult for them to get certain jobs; yet within two years of the war women had regained their immediate losses in numbers working. By 1950, 32 percent of women were employed, a greater growth in the ten year period since 1940 than in the previous 30 years. Married women were now a majority of those working and the average age of working women had jumped.[42]

But if reality showed such numbers of women with jobs, a host of books, articles and movies appeared to convince women that if they didn't prefer the home and motherhood, something was wrong with them; that the "double job" both inside and outside the home led to being an inadequate wife and mother. Many of those who did work had a guilty conscience; and society did not make it easy for them. What little child care had come about through the Lanham Bill during the war was gone by 1946, but more and more women managed to find child care or to develop cooperatives.

Yet the literature was designed to make such mothers completely out of step with the accepted ideas of the time. Philip Wylie had attacked "Mom" in *Generation of Vipers* in 1942, setting the stage at least for criticism of the way in which mothers were carrying out their role. Later books told mothers how to do their job to avoid being like Wylie's negative model. This entailed, of course, staying home and devoting full time to child and home care.

Marynia Farnham and Ferdinand Lundberg in *Modern Women: The Lost Sex* implied that any woman who did not prefer such a life should consider herself neurotic. They deplored what they considered the decline of the home—and held feminists responsible. A true woman achieved fulfillment by assuming her proper role—being dependent and giving of herself fully to the family.[43]

Dr. Benjamin Spock reinforced this view in *Baby and Child Care*, the most popular book since the Bible in terms of sales. It reached new mothers with the message that their presence in the home during the early child rearing years was essential to the future of the children. His humane and warm approach was attractive to women brought up by more rigid standards which had less meaning in a more affluent, sanitary and open setting. He joined old ideals of education—that every individual had a potential that would grow if properly nurtured—to new methods of child rearing growing out of Freudian psychology. Spock placed so much importance on full time mothering in the early years that he recommended government allowances for mothers otherwise compelled to work. He implied, though never said, that only a full time mother could avoid bringing up a child who would later be a social problem. He observed that "a few mothers, particularly those with professional training" might be so unhappy not working outside the home that it would affect their children. In this situation an alternative "ideal arrangement" was needed. But he induced guilt in the woman professional by suggesting that "if a mother realizes clearly how vital this kind of care is to a small child, it may make it easier for her to decide that the extra money she might earn, or the satisfaction she might receive from an outside job, is not so important after all." He not only perpetuated the idea that women worked just for extra money, but also that only the mother could give the child what he or she needed.

Spock's influence was not completely negative. He transformed child rearing into a creative art, needing on the part of the mother some of the skills of a clinical psychologist. The mother who concentrated on her own children gained new social significance. Spock was able, in this way, to divert some of the criticism of Wylie's attack.[44]

Many mothers accepted the Spockian challenge to rear a child who would become creative, intelligent, kind, generous, brave, spontaneous, good and happy, each in his or her own special way The Spockian vision made sense to many because it fit their deeply rooted expectations imposed by society and at the same time challenged their creative impulses. It made particular sense in a society which provided no ideal alternative and few opportunities in the occupational structure for a woman to achieve professional success, and further offered little encouragement to try. Spock was an expert, a professional; the words of such people are not taken lightly.

Other experts talked of "maternal deprivation" as if it were a "deficiency disease."[45] All this fit into psychiatric theories, the belief that an early childhood trauma or upsetting experience could be the root cause of later troubles. Most literature strongly implied that there was no such thing as a good substitute for a mother, and the magazines and newspapers and films all carried the same message.

At the same time, manufacturing swung once again to consumer items which, after wartime shortages, were in great demand. The increased production created a need for more workers who could be paid low wages. Women were working in ever-growing numbers,even though all the old inequities persisted. By 1950, 31.8 percent of women and 22.8 percent of married women worked.[46] They received less for the same work, were denied admission to training programs for fetter jobs, and discriminated against in education. It was as though all the forces of society suddenly united to re-Victorianize women. The automobile, easy mortgages and a growth in the size of the middle class made the realization of the ideals of the 1890s—the isolated single family house in a garden— possible for a large number of people. Most blacks, because of lower income and zoning policies, were of course excluded; the ethnic groups whose memories of tenement life were not yet clouded by nostalgia could and did take advantage of the new opportunities.

The situation included within itself the seeds for change; the 1960s provided the catalyst. The civil rights and the anti-war movements generated a broad critical perspective on the American social and economic system. Concern with the status of women was naturally included; the movement which resulted is both a revival of older ideologies and solutions and a new developmental stage.

The sixties offered both a propitious climate and new leaders ready to sound the alarm. But another factor may have been that the generation of the sixties was the first in large numbers to be the beneficiaries of the Spock-type individualized child care; they found conformity to institutional regulations stifling and rebelled against the life styles of their parents. College women fought the double standard on campuses, demanding more personal freedom; they disregarded the programs of "gracious living" provided by dormitories. In some ways this duplicated the earlier rebellions against Victorianism and ethnicity.

Although representing only a small percentage, this group was vocal in their critiques. "Mom"was once more subjected to ridicule, accused of being boring and narrow-minded because immersed in child care and housework. Betty Friedan, originally from Peoria, was an insider with experience in the "Mom" field. When she wrote *The Feminine Mystique* in 1963, many women who had conscientiously filled the Spock-type role recognized their situation as she described it—stripped of illusions fostered by experts and romance. Those in their middle age, married and unmarried, were particularly interested in equal rights in the economic arena. Many had never completely abandoned hopes for a career and had had vague ideas of continuing their education or taking up interrupted careers after children were in school. The number of those with children ranging from 6 to 17 in the work force has been rising steadily; the national figure is now 55 percent.[47] This change in work patterns represents the experience of white women; black women have always worked in large numbers.

Yet women returning to the labor force after child rearing faced both the disability of their sex and their age. John F. Kennedy, an astute politician attuned to the civil rights mood, gave recognition to the growing militancy of women's groups by establishing a National Commission on the Status of Women in 1961. Even before this group brought out their report in 1963, state women's groups were pressuring for similar bodies at that level.

In May of 1963 Esther Saperstein, Frances Dawson and Lillian Piotrowski introduced a bill in the Illinois legislature to create a Commission on the Status of Women. The commission was to have 18 members to study and recommend action in seven areas, with an appropriation of $10,000. Both houses passed it in June and Governor Kerner signed it in August. By 1964 the members were appointed and holding meetings. In spite of the use of this commission for patronage appointments, and the hindrance of small appropriations, enough dedicated people have served to make the commission an important force in shedding light on women's situation in employment, in law, in education, in credit, as volunteers and on methods of discrimination in many areas.[48]

The first report of the National Commission, in 1963, documented many inequities. An Equal Pay Act was passed in 1963, and Title VII of the Civil Rights Act of 1964 prohibited sex discrimination in employment. These provided women with the necessary legal means to try to correct at least some of the worst abuses. But the difficulty in ensuring enforcement has led to the formation of new women's organizations. Such frustration was behind the formation of the

National Organization for Women (NOW) in Washington, D.C., in the fall of 1966, with Betty Friedan as president.

Early in 1967 members from four states met in Chicago to organize locally; the Illinois chapter with its local units was born. That same year they protested against actions of the Equal Employment Opportunity Commission (EEOC); women who had never before undertaken such an activity found themselves marching with placards proclaiming "Women Are People." They protested newspapers' help wanted ads divided by sex. Major efforts were mounted to get the Equal Rights Amendment through Congress and then to press for the right to abortion. With each of these campaigns, some members who disagreed were lost, while others joined. Illinois had developed an active NOW with many local units.[49]

Other national groups, such as the Women's Equity Action League (WEAL) and the National Women's Political Caucus (NWPC) also have chapters in Illinois. WEAL helps women who are discriminated against bring complaints to the right places; NWPC works to convince more women to run for political office and to get more support for those who do.

At the beginning of his first term President Richard Nixon did not seem to be taking action to continue the national effort. In 1969 four women representatives, among them Charlotte Reid of Rockford, met with him on this subject; he then appointed new members to the Citizens' Advisory Council on the Status on Women and a Task Force on Women's Rights and Responsibilities. The task force included in its 13 members Sister Ann Ida Gannon, then president of Mundelein College, and Pat Hutar, president of Public Affairs Service Associates, Inc. and a Republican active in Nixon's election campaign. A report of this task force, "A Matter of Simple Justice," was finally published and some of its recommendations implemented.[50]

The Illinois Constitutional Convention successfully submitted a new constitution to the voters in 1971; many women and women's organizations were active in bringing about both the convention and its results. Fifteen women delegates, 13 percent of the delegates, served in the convention and many went on to political careers. The document itself represents a step toward equality for women under the law. Article I declares that "All persons shall have the right to be free from discrimination on the basis of race, color, creed, national ancestry, and sex in the hiring and promotion practices of any employer or in the sale or rental of property." The next article provides that "the equal protection of the laws shall not be denied or abridged on account of sex by the State or its units of local government and school districts."[51] These provisions are now being incorporated into law by the rewording of old statutes to conform with the constitution and the introduction of new laws. Many women have worked to make this a reality.

The existence of such an article in our state constitution makes doubly ironic the opposition to the Equal Rights Amendment to the U.S. Constitution. Over 75 organizations, with both men and

(Chicago Historical Society)

Float in "Sane 4th" Parade, 1910

women members, have given their approval to the ERA and many have worked for passage in the legislature. Yet in the spring of 1976, these efforts were still blocked by political maneuvering—the kind that made Illinois the only state to require a three-fifths majority—and by an active "Stop ERA" group. "Stop ERA" is led by Phyllis Schlafly of Alton, past president of the Illinois Federation of Republican Women, a mother and recently a law student. This organization has flooded the state with leaflets; they claim, for expample, that ERA will "wipe out women's present freedom of choice to take a paying job *or* to be a fulltime wife and mother supported by her husband." They also claim that ERA would eliminate preferential treatment for women by insurance companies and the social security administration.[52] Proponents respond that women are not now legally assured of support by husbands and that present insurance and social security laws and rates actually discriminate against women; the issues are obviously politically controversial.[53]

ERA's aim is to equalize and thus increase women's choices. With a similar article in the state constitution for six years which has produced none of the consequences predicted by the "Stop ERA" group, it is obvious that such amendments do not create changes by themselves. They can facilitate change in legal, economic and even social practices, but only so far as the public is willing to accept it.

Women working in what later would be called the more traditional organizations, such as WEAL, NOW and the Illinois Women's Political Caucus, have long realized how deeply embedded sexism has been in our culture. These organizations are feminist; that is, they are interested in providing more opportunities and alternatives for women. Members, many from an older generation, are women concerned mainly with expanding opportunities within the established social and economic system. They concentrate on surveying different facets of sexism in advertising, in the teaching of history, literature, psychology and sociology, in medical services and in employment and credit practices. These women have been trying to bring about change by using established institutions such as the courts and the legislature.

(Manuscript Collection, UICC Library)

Cartoonists' expectation of what women would do in community - Reform efforts, women at the washtub.

(Newberry Library)

Woman as an independent voter.

Another branch of the movement was begun by many of the young radical women who fought for civil rights in the 1950s and 1960s. They became conscious of the realities of sexism in the late 1960s While helping organize for radical change, they discovered that they were expected to play conventional subordinate roles in the movement—to do the typing, make the coffee and keep quiet in the decision making meetings. This led them to re-examine their own situation. In 1965 Heather Booth and Naomi Weinstein started theoretical discussion sessions at the University of Chicago, believed to be the first campus group talking about women's liberation. By 1966 a seminar on women's issues was part of the offerings of the Center for Radical Research, a free university program at the University.

When the New Politics Conference met in Chicago in the fall of 1967, members of the Chicago group formed an ad hoc radical women's caucus and tried to get recognition for resolutions on women's rights. When the chair refused them, Jo Freeman and Shulamith Firestone went up to protest. The chairman reportedly patted Firestone on the head and told her to be a "good girl."[54] The indignation this denial stimulated caused the formation of several groups which eventually emerged as parts of the women's movement.

The first Chicago group expanded; one section, the Women's Radical Action Project, took part in the 1969 sit-in at the University of Chicago in support of Marlene Dixon, a controversial sociology teacher whose contract had not been renewed. Another section, the Westside Group, began in March of 1968 to publish the first newsletter of the movement, *The Voice of the Woman's Liberation Movement.* Growing to more than 20 pages and a circulation of over 2,000, it ceased publication a year later because it had become too large for volunteers to publish.[55]

In 1968 a national women's conference held in Chicago attracted over 200 women from 37 states and Canada. It also brought to the fore the diversity of viewpoints within the movement.[56] The basic difference between the original feminists and the new radicals is essentially over whether women should gain rights within the present system or become liberated through radical alteration of that system. These "politicos" as Jo Freeman has called the latter, link women's issues to a democratic-socialist framework.[57]

The Chicago Women's Liberation Union is an example of this kind of group. Their literature states, "We will struggle against racism, imperialism, and capitalism, and dedicate ourselves to developing a consciousness of their effect on women." This group is also dedicated to a democratic organization through full and free exchange of ideas and "through unity of theory and practice." Their programs serve an educational and consciousness raising function, while at the same time some are very practical and directed toward dealing with immediate problems faced by women. In addition to operating a Liberation School for Women three times a year, with courses ranging in content from self-defense to poetry, Marxism and feminism, they operate a health referral office, called HERS, with 24 hour service on questions about abortion, birth control, VD tests, and a rape crisis line. The Union also runs a legal clinic and agitates for more women's sports facilities from the Chicago Park District.[58]

Because so many of the programs created by young radical groups dedicated to reforming society involve building alternate institutions for women and family life—day care centers, abortion clinics, liberation schools, and newsletters—as well as consciousness raising, radical feminism in its early phases bears considerable resemblance to the early phases of social feminism. Many local women's groups who do not perceive themselves as politically radical have started similar programs. They too are searching for new institutional, but non-bureaucratic, forms to bridge the social distances beteen women of different social backgrounds. The younger organizations often rose from consciousness raising sessions, referred to as "rap groups." These would go from the state of awareness of problems to special projects, often conducted by "task forces," to solve whatever problems seemed most important. Some of the older organizations, leery at first of "rapping" as an infringement on privacy, have used it, especially with their younger members.

The distinctions in ultimate goals remain very important, even though the very diversity of organizations and programs means that there is an overlap of support on specific issues. It is still possible for women to be "for" one aim such as ERA and to be "against" another, such as abortion on demand. The conflict between those who want to reform society as a whole and those who would concentrate on just certain segments is similar in many ways to the splits within the women's movement of the 1890s. Then many felt suffrage was enough; but a few, like Elizabeth Stanton, saw the need to reform the church, an institution basic at the time in shaping women's world view. Eventually there may be an organic unity, but in the meantime the new consciousness among politically conservative and politically radical women has resulted in a proliferation of groups all working on women's problems.[59]

The new consciousness of rape as a serious and neglected social problem is an original contribution of the modern women's movement. Until recently the police have not kept adequate statistics on rape victims, nor has there been much awareness of how rape victims should be treated by police and hospitals. And, of course, there had been no special training for women on how to prevent violent attack.

Rape was not discussed by newspapers, social agencies or the police in the nineteenth and early twentieth century. It seems to have been covered by the vague and broad rubric, "seduction." Women's groups were preoccupied with what they thought were its consequences—"white Slavery." Yankee, ethnic and black women's organizations always viewed the seduced woman as the victim of her environment and training. But other than creating agencies that would isolate women from immoral influences and shore up their moral resolve, women's groups did not treat rape as a distinct and unique problem.

Contemporary women's groups no longer worry about "white slavery" and they clearly distinguish between seduction and rape. This new consciousness of the helplessness of women and the way a rape victim is treated by the established powers has brought about efforts to rid the system of this evidence of sexism. It has been shown that police and even the hospitals have tended to treat the victim as perpetrator of the crime.

In 1972 groups on Chicago's North Side formed Rape Crisis, Inc., to investigate and help rape victims. They have developed a program for training police and hospital personnel in handling cases and have suggested means for improving the security and safety of all women. They have also developed programs to train women in self-defense. Many women are now taking judo and karate classes in community centers and private schools. DuPage Women Against Rape, Champaign-Urbana WAR and the Southwest Rape Crisis Line in the

Chicago area are just a few of the groups which have come forward to help women rape victims.[60]

As a result of their work, new legislation has been passed to deal with the problem. In December 1974 Chicago passed a Rape Treatment Center Act. As a result of this ordinance, rape treatment centers have been established in 30 of Chicago's 66 hospitals. Means have been developed to make it as easy as possible for a woman to report a rape. A booklet is being distributed in schools, drug stores and police stations telling women where to go if raped, what treatment to expect and how to help law enforcement agencies. The booklet also provides advice on how to avoid rape. The police are now for the first time collecting more accurate statistics. Figures compiled for January through March 1976 show that one of every four rape victims being treated in Chicago hospitals was a child, 14 or under, and that three of every four victims was black.[61] In January 1976 the state passed a similar act, and the Illinois Department of Public Health is preparing state rules.

Many women's centers have been established to aid women in need and to create a women's network for information dispersal and social interaction. The process of organizing the centers, raising money, finding a location, furnishing it and developing programs of service have created a new sense of purpose among volunteers and a new elan among those involved. Some centers are part of college and university programs in women's studies and counseling; others have been formed by community groups to meet local needs. Some offer legal and medical advice. Others, like those in Carbondale, Elgin and Springfield, provide temporary shelter on a 24 hour a day basis to women—some running from abusive husbands or boyfriends, others trying to get away from traumatic home situations and some recently released from institutions who need help in finding jobs and housing. All these centers have been overwhelmed by the need their presence has uncovered.[62]

Many organizations deal with the problems of working women. Federally Employed Women, Inc. (FEW), works to end discrimination and to increase job opportunities for women in government service. Women Employed (WE) has similar aims for women not in unions. It has been effective in the Chicago area in gaining the support of lower income women, office workers, secretaries and women in insurance and banking. Its detailed planning and skillful use of the media in winning a case against Kraft Foods at the request of some of its workers has made it a model for other groups.[63]

Unions for women are once again growing in number and membership. In 1974 union women met in Chicago from all over the country to organize a Coalition of Union Women. Addie Wyatt, the first woman president of a packinghouse local, became vice president of the coalition.[64] Leadership positions in existing unions, like those in the corporate structure, have been almost entirely closed to women; they have found, as they did in the 1890s, that their own organization will give them greater scope for action and training.

The large number of organizations seeking to improve employment opportunities for working women in Chicago has led to the formation in 1975 of a Chicago Coalition on Women's Employment which acts as a clearing house. Its members come from govenmental agencies and women's professional organizations. It has started a skills bank for Chicago women.[65] Professional women also have numerous organizations. In 1970 the University and College Women of Illinois was formed to promote the exchange of information and to coordinate efforts to enforce affirmative action programs in colleges and universities.[66] The Professional Organization for Women's Rights, a national group with a branch in Illinois, has helped with litigation. The POWR appealed a lawsuit against six private clubs and the Illinois Liquor Control Commission for discriminating against women.[67] Other women in broadcasting, publishing, law, medicine, banking and education have either formed caucuses within their professional groups or independent organizations to disucss the status of women in their field and to provide counseling to women.

Professional groups are also forming clearing houses and coalitions. Traditionally the YWCA has acted as a mail drop for new women's groups and has provided many of them with a meeting place. Now many groups with similar membership and goals are forming their own umbrella organizations. In higher education, in addition to the University and College Women of Illinois, there is a Council on Women's Programs begun in 1974 which includes all groups in the metropolitan area involved in the education of women. The Chicago Consortium of Women in Education Programs, serving the college and university community, was initiated in 1975 by Jean Gillies of Northeastern Illinois University and a group mainly from Northwestern University and the Circle Campus of the University of Illinois. The Eleanor Club has recently begun the Clearing House International with a newsletter to keep subscribers informed of what women are doing both nationally and locally.

Another new effort is the National Women's Agenda, begun in the fall of 1975, which has 11 items on its national program. In Chicago this group operates out of the Institute on Pluralism and Group Identity, with a newsletter funded by the Playboy Foundation. It functions through a steering committee comprised of representatives from its task forces; it welcomes all women's groups to free membership.[68] Many of these groups overlap in membership as well as purpose, but they do help the left hands know what the right hands are planning; they help to prevent duplication of effort, to coordinate plans and to engender more ideas.

· Women have also been active in forming community groups to protect their neighborhoods when threatened either by urban renewal or by the social changes which have led many to escape to new suburbs. In the Pilsen district of Chicago, now heavily Spanish-speaking, women have formed the Outreach Center and have successfully demanded community involvement in school decisions affecting their neighborhood. In Austin, Gale Cincotta, a housewife and a mother before she was out of high school, became involved in community organization through the PTA. As her neighborhood disintegrated through overcrowding, decaying schools, "redlining," and absentee landlords raising rent and cutting services, she decided that it was time to mobilize. She helped form the Organization for a Better Austin and became its president in 1969. Realizing that local success rested on being able to influence federal policy in relation to housing, she organized the Metropolitan Area Housing Alliance, becoming its president, and then the National People's Action on Housing. She is now the director of the National Housing, Training and Information Center. Cincotta has used statistics, discussion and even confrontation in her efforts to make politicians more responsive to local needs; she is now paid for the type of work she once did as a volunteer.[69]

Cincotta represents two changes which have come to the volunteer scene since the 1890s. The first volunteers came from middle and upper class groups of women with leisure time, able to afford household help, who could give of themselves to good causes in the community. Moreover, as professionals arrived, many of the volunteers found themselves in the position of supervising the trained personnel. Today the number of volunteers available is not great enough to meet the needs; they are in demand still in community improvement projects, in hospitals, in institutions and even in education. More of these volunteers are now coming from the lower middle class, like Gale Cincotta, as these women rise up to combat the ills of their neighborhoods and of the times, from crime to poor education. Many volunteers today, working under the trained professionals, are using this as a means to step into a paid job. With additional training they are becoming paraprofessionals and earning money after their initial apprenticeship as a volunteer. Many women have found that their volunteer experience has been counted as an asset in the job market, and further, has been useful to them after they are hired.

The women's movement seeks to be inclusive, but it has in practice been dominated by articulate middle class women whose style, language and concerns have often alienated working class and ethnic minority women. They see the movement as an attack upon their own traditional values and life styles. Yet such women are becoming restive, no longer willing to remain undemanding, hardworking and without clout. Their activism in neighborhood groups is one sign of change. Minority women entering the women's movement have preferred not to join already existing feminist groups such as NOW and WEAL, but to establish their own local and national organizations. Examples of this trend include the National Black Feminist Alliance, the Coalition of Labor Union Women, the

National Conference of Puerto Rican Women and the National Congress of Neighborhood Women. The importance of life styles, language, race and ethnicity in separating women comes out clearly when one considers that black women as a whole consistently outpoll white women in their support of what are called feminist issues but have refused to identify themselves as feminists.[70] For working class women, the union provides the social benefits of a woman's group; but it is also the best vehicle for the improvment of wages and working conditions, as well as encouraging job advancement. Women's groups are often only interested in the latter, ignoring what is of immediate importance to working women.

Women from the working class and the lower middle class, both ethnic and native, are also beginning to return to school when their children are grown. They do so either to acquire job skills or simply to expand their horizons. Many prefer the community colleges where attempts are made to help such women develop self-confidence in a strange environment. Counseling services, programs in assertion training and programs such as one designed by Rose Levinson of Northeastern University called "Life-Span Planning for Women" are designed to appeal to these women. Minority women, who come from highly traditional cultures, such as the Spanish-speaking neighborhoods, need supportive services, because they do not receive much moral support from within their own families.

The Institute on Pluralism and Group Identity in Chicago is particularly interested in finding ways to bridge the gap between working class and minority women and the women's movement and to find ways to encourage leadership from within ethnic groups. It has been holding a series of seminars that bring together people from diverse backgrounds.[71]

A series of nine Saturday workshops called "Women and Work" were held at Chicago State University during the winter and spring of 1976, in an attempt to break down "barriers in communication between the academic world and the working world by focusing on issues that involve all women who work."[72]

The women's movement has not transformed many traditional organizations, but it has definitely altered their programs. Sexism in education is often a top priority. The AAUW of Wheaton-Glen Ellyn began in 1972 with a study of "herstory," and continued with a report to the school boards of both suburbs on sexism in elementary school readers. In 1976 they prepared curriculum materials for fourth, fifth and sixth grades on the history of women in DuPage County. The National Council of Catholic Women has been running articles on feminism in their magazine, *Catholic Women.* One issue in 1975 begins with a piece called "Feminist Liturgies" and makes a case for referring to God as "She." The author also points out that all the saints in the Christian Era were chosen by celibate men, and that today women "want to reevaluate these figures."[73] In addition to its anti-abortion stand, the Council of Catholic Women opposes the

ERA on the grounds that the amendment would jeopardize family support laws; but there are Illinois organizations of Catholic women who are working for ERA.[73] The Institute of Women Today, which provides courses and sets up workshops on women's history and women's problems, is sponsored by Catholic, Protestant and Jewish women's organizations searching for the religious roots of women's liberation.[74] Both old and new groups are being affected by the ideas of the women's movement.

The women's groups least affected are probably those which are auxiliaries to men's groups, particularly such groups as the American Legion Auxiliary. Other groups have always stood for the equality of all; they have not changed. The Women's International League for Peace and Freedom, begun in 1915 by Jane Addams, sees women's rights as part of the larger problem of justice for all and continues to work for both equality and peace. Another group set apart from the movement is Women for Peace, formed in the 1960s, which publishes a newsletter and holds protest meetings against government actions they consider inimical to peace. Such issue-oriented groups have, in a sense, a broader outlook than many other women's groups who focus on issues only in relation to women.

A recent single issue group is the Right-to-Life group which is forming chapters in Illinois to disseminate information against any interference with a fetus after conception   which it calls "pre-natal child abuse." They provide counseling for women and referrals. They are also working to change the Supreme Court decision which permits abortion on demand.[75]

Because of the proliferation of single issue groups and the continuation of older groups, no one single organization represents the entire women's movement. Neither is there any group today which brings together women of different backgrounds as did the settlement houses. She has lived at the Center on Maxwell Street, in scale, the YWCA comes closest to mixing disparate groups. On a small scale, Dr. Beatrice Tucker and the Chicago Maternity Center might be called a one-woman, one-service descendant of the settlement houses. She has lived at the Center on Maxwell street, in the midst of one of Chicago's worst slums, for over 40 years and estimates that she and her crew have presided over 100,000 home deliveries. Dr. Tucker was the first woman obstetrics resident in Chicago Lying-In Hospital in 1929; she took over the Maternity Center in 1932. Yet she is a rare example; sadly, at 79, she had to see the Center close for lack of funding.[76]

Bridging of the class structure by women is now being attempted by many in the movement, but thus far the mixing seems to involve only the leaders of the established bureaucracies within the women's organizations. After an initial consciousness raising stage, they have become structured in order to provide consistent service to meet the needs of their members. Many new groups which wanted to operate without a governing structure or bureaucracy, on either a volunteer or consensus system, have found it too difficult to get things done and much harder to participate in the wider movement. They have set up councils or boards and task forces, and have almost as many reports as the Federation of Women's Clubs had departments. Some groups that have resisted this process have lost members who have split off to accomplish a specific purpose.

Financing problems still plague women's groups; the solutions show both continuity and change. Traditionally the source of funds was either through the husband's pocketbook or through money raising fairs and sales. Big business and big events like fashion shows are still a source, but today grants from both government and private foundations are being sought. The Donors Forum has been organized in Chicago to help women learn how to write grant proposals and to learn where to apply for funding of particular kinds of projects.[77] This may mean twisting a project to conform to the specifications of the donors and sometimes delaying its start until notification. Applications, too, may or may not be successful, since some sources only fund 5 percent of the requests they receive. Many such grants are for "seed money" to get a worthwhile project started; then there is the problem of how to carry on when the grant runs out. Such sources are a mixed blessing, though they have provided many women's organizations with funds to make new programs possible.

While many women have been involved in both volunteer and paid labor, in the factory, office and school, others have been excelling in the arts. Illinois has had many outstanding women writers. Twenty percent of a list of major authors in Illinois for 1966 were women, a higher participation level than in most fields. Some have won Pulitzer prizes; Margaret Ayer Barnes received the prize in 1930 for her novel, *Years of Grace*. Prize winner Gwendolyn Brooks of Chicago became poet laureate of Illinois in 1968 and has taught poetry in several colleges. Many women writers are authors of children's books: Grace Humphrey of Springfield, Lillian Budd of Lombard and Rosamond Neal DuJardin of Glen Ellyn.[78]

In music Mahalia Jackson raised the singing of gospel hymns to a high art. Eight of her recordings have sold more than a million copies. In dance, Katherine Dunham, with a degree in anthropology, brought ethnic folk culture into her art; she was also a financial success.[79]

These were fields in which women have traditionally found opportunities to be successful. The women's movement has also given a boost to women in publishing. *Spokeswoman*, one of the major new vehicles of movement information, was started in Chicago by Susan Davis. The *Chicago Woman's Directory* was published in two languages by the Inforwomen Collective in 1974. Selling for $2.00, the directory contains 225 pages of solid data about women's organizations, compiled and published by seven women.[80]

In fields once dominated by women, men have been competing

successfully. In education the percentage of women in administration is still very small and less in some areas than it was 40 years age. With the exception of Virginia Keehan of Southwest College, Chicago, and Rosetta Wheadon, acting president of State Community College of East St. Louis, women are presidents only of Catholic colleges. Sister Susan Rink is president of Mundelein College, Sister Candida Lund is president at Rosary College, and Sister Irenaeus Chekouris presides at St. Xavier. Rockford College and the National College of Education, once run by outstanding women presidents, have now become coeducational and are headed by men. The percentage of women who are superintendents and principals is less than in 1930. While more women are elected to school boards, a woman elected is usually a single, token woman. In 1974, women were less than 10 percent of the total number.[81]

In domestic labor, where women were once the only workers, and in the scrubbing of public buildings, men have established janitorial service companies and have made a successful business out of cleaning houses and institutions. A few women have begun to organize companies which compete, but the field is still controlled by men.

Nonetheless, women are competing with more success in what are still male dominated fields. The percentage of women in engineering has doubled since 1960—up to 1.2 percent.[82] More women are entering construction work, are climbing telephone poles and driving trucks; many more are making headway in banking. Women police officers are doing the same work as men.

Yet in 1969 the median income of Illinois families with a female head (10.7 percent) was $5,791, while that of a male headed family was $11,652.71.[83] As more women have taken jobs outside the home, many of them without previsous experience, the gap between the pay of men and women has widened. Women are receiving equal pay in some areas, but on the whole they are still in sex-determined jobs. Also most women with families who work—and the majority of working women are married—still contend with the "double job" syndrome, have additional expenses and laws that penalize them for the double income. And those who stay home also work, but with no money to show for it, either in cash or in social security credit.

Women on aid to dependent children and welfare have difficulty getting sufficient training to obtain an adequate job for family support, and even greater difficulty finding a solution to the need for child care. There are also many more "displaced homemakers," as the increased numbers of divorced and widowed women are called. This group has members who may not receive alimony nor be eligible for social security; they are often not qualified for most jobs without retraining.

The need for day care centers for working women has long been recognized, but until recently little had been done to provide enough centers with quality care. Settlements had early recognized its importance and provided this service, and during the wars the federal government gave it some attention. But as long as society accepted the notion that the infant needed the mother's full attention—or else it was a deprived child—it was impossible to make day care, like education, a basic social right. The increase of married women in the work force has made this an issue of national debate, because the absence of sufficient numbers of day care centers means that many children are deprived of quality care. While many still follow the Spock line, new studies have shown the benefits of a well run day care center. It has been found that children become more self-reliant and that the quality of the time the parent spends with the child can more than makes up for less quantity.[84]

In addition to the numerous social service agencies which provide day care facilities, some employers and unions have established centers. For its employees, Illinois Bell Telephone Company in 1972 began setting up small centers near their homes. In the same year, the Amalgamated Clothing Workers Union started the first union sponsored day care center in Chicago for 65 children. But just as philanthropists in the progressive era realized that voluntary efforts were not sufficient to deal with family welfare needs, so women's groups and family relations agencies realize the need for government funding. To advocate and publicize these needs, the Chicago's Day Care Crisis Council, an affiliate of the Day Care Child Development Council of America, has become the leading group working in the field in Illinois, under the leadership of Silvia Cotton.

In our increasingly complex world, more families are moving around; the national and nulti-national corporations' policies of shifting employees creates problems for wives, especially those in dual career families. Stories about couples moving to the wife's new job make headlines, but they are the exception. Meanwhile the homemaker, who is not giving up a job, still has to re-establish roots for the entire family in new surroundings. If involved, she must start all over again in volunteer activities. Again it is a support system for others she is creating and operating; the move which brings exciting new challenges to her husband in his world of work brings to her the same old burdens and problems of resettling in a new place.

Obviously women are still working on many of the same problems—as well as new ones which have been created by our complicated modern society Today women are putting more emphasis on solving women's problems, as well as those of the community. This change in emphasis is evidence that the support system women operate is once again in transition. When women emerged from the home and "went public" in the nineteenth century, much of the effort was concentrated on the community as a whole through such institutions as settlement houses. Proponents of protective legislations, the Women's Trade Union League and other organizations concentrated on assisting women. But their major emphasis had been on women needing special treatment to help them function in both the working world and the family. As they had been set apart in a woman's dometic sphere, so did their special requirements demand their being set apart in the world outside the home.

In today's effort to help women the major emphasis has shifted; it is now on putting women on an equal legal and economic footing with men in every aspect of their activity—from the world of jobs to the world of sports. The support system is focusing on helping each individual woman maximize her talents and compete on an equal basis in that outside world, while not ignoring the same problems within the family. The legislation which is now being supported, the crisis lines and the women's centers are designed to realize the equal rights and opportunities, the ways and means, necessary for women to succeed. Women are to have more choices; and the support system is now lined up to see that they get them, assured that this will also benefit the entire community. Thus women are still playing a part in the success and failure of others; we are exploring new ways of supporting others and ourselves in meeting these new challenges as well as the old. The long range effect of these efforts will be for future historians to evaluate.

This attempt to acknowledge women's efforts in Illinois is incomplete, not only because of lack of space, but also because historians have not felt women's experience worthy of special attention. This is slowly being remedied. Special collections of documents and records about women are being established at the University of Illinois' Circle Campus and Northwestern University Libraries. Many colleges and universities are offering special courses about women in history; their library resources are also increasing. One new organization along this line is the Chicago Area Women's History Conference which meets monthly at the Newberry Library. It brings together women and men interested in exchanging information on our history. More monographs are being written and more research is being done. In the future, more compilations such as this one will be possible.

Surely as we understand more fully what women have done and how all have benefited from their efforts, we shall keep better records of what women are doing today. Future generations can then both appreciate and continue that progress.

THE CARBONDALE WOMEN'S CENTER
Rita Lovell Moss

"What Carbondale needs is a women's center!" These words, lightly spoken more than four years ago, were the beginning of our adventure. At the initial meeting of what was to become the local branch of the Women's Political Caucus, we decided that the establishment of a women's center should be one of the goals of the organization. A small committee was formed which met often and diligently explored ways in which this goal could be realized. We envisioned a house providing temporary shelter for women with no other place to go, a meeting place for diverse women's groups, a library of books and materials concerning women's activities around the country and an information exchange for women's affairs in Carbondale.

Carbondale—roughly 90 miles southeast of St. Louis, 300 south of Chicago and 60 north of Cairo—is a city whose existence often seems to be a matter of doubt and incredulity to citizens of other parts of the country. It takes its name from the fact that it has been a railhead for the coal mining regions to the north and east; it is rural in character and slightly southern in flavor. Its downtown shopping district stretches for eight heartbreakingly ugly blocks along the Illinois Central railroad tracks; the outskirts of the city are being filled in with an assortment of chain stores. But there is lovely country all around the city—man-made lakes, rolling hills, the Shawnee National Forest, a National Wildlife Refuge, and state parks with cliffs and caves, streams and dense woods.

Southern Illinois University, at the southern edge of the city, has a beautiful, sprawling campus with a lake and woods. The University is the community's largest employer; since World War II it has experienced the kind of mushrooming growth that has affected universities all over the country. The population of the community is about equally divided between town and gown, with the city having an edge of 2,000 to 3,000 persons. Nowhere in this community was there a facility which offered temporary shelter or care to women, although an active and responsible group of ministers of all faiths cooperated in providing small amounts of money for food and hotel housing for a night or two.

The practical advantages to the community of a women's center seemed quite obvious. Women, and their children if necessary, would be encouraged to stay at the center for a short while until they felt they could return to their homes, or until they were able to make alternate arrangements, perhaps with the aid and cooperation of social service agencies.

In addition to meeting definite and easily recognized community needs, we felt there were many other benefits to be realized. We knew that women tend to be isolated from each other and are not encouraged to seek advice or help in handling their personal or family problems. Each woman learns to cope with her problems by herself on a trial-and-error basis. Many women are geographically far from supportive family groups, from mothers and relatives who might be helpful. The success with which individual women handle the problems of child-rearing, marital adjustment, social accommodation and personal realization differs, of course, from person to person. A fairly universal fact is that handling these problems is frequently occasion for confusion, loneliness, depression and panic. A women's center, we felt, would provide a warm and friendly place where women could talk with other women—sisters, daughters, mothers and neighbors—about their common problems and ways of coping with them. They would share not only their problems and solutions to them, but their joys and satisfactions as well.

The committee started its work by asking women to pledge a small amount of money each month for one year; collection of the pledges was to begin when a suitable house had been located. Every type of organization in the community was approached by the volunteers to explain the need for and purposes of a women's center and to ask for pledges and donations. We talked to public service agencies, church groups, sororities, the Goals for Carbondale Committee, the city council and members of the police force. Some of these people were warm and receptive and wished us luck; others obviously thought we had holes in our heads. The response from one campus social sorority was, "We don't need a women's center—we know where to go for abortions!"

Throughout the spring the group met regularly to hash out problems and dreams, between times spinning out to talk with more organizations and to appear on local radio and TV talk shows. We discovered, painfully sometimes, that we were separate individuals and that our views of trust, responsibility and reality differed. Over oceans of coffee and tea, and occasional celebratory beers in Carbondale's taverns, we laughed and clashed and defined and refined our aims.

We sold daffodils on campus, held a bake sale and participated in a flea market. With profits of $360 we opened a bank account. We also applied to the State of Illinois for a certificate declaring that we were a not-for-profit corporation and named ourselves members of the requisite Board of Directors. We hammered out a required set of bylaws and in the process got hung up for days on questions of what should constitute membership, quorums, frequency of meeting and so on.

During the summer we watched the newspaper for houses for rent and cruised the streets for likely looking houses with For Sale signs on the lawns. We decided that for easy access we wanted a house near the center of town, which is zoned for multi-family dwellings. Landlords owning four to six bedroom houses easily rent them to students and collect tidy sums, while students, often feeling the total rent for the building is exorbitant, leave the landlords at the end of each school year with large repair bills not covered by damage deposits. Families wishing to live in such convenient locations can't compete with groups of students, and neither could we. We dispiritedly tramped through wrecks remodeled to hold as many bodies as possible, obviously on the theory that students would only be sleeping there. The theory must be accurate, since some houses offered no possibilities for anything called living.

While one of our committee members looked for an apartment for herself and her husband, she learned that her new landlady owned a house in a good location for us. It was occupied by the members of a rock band but they were leaving shortly. The house consisted of two bedrooms and a bath upstairs, two bedrooms and bath, living room, dining room, kitchen and sun porch downstairs; a leak in the roof, hills and valleys in all the floors, dubious wiring everywhere, and rotting screens enclosing the front porch. The rent was $225 per month; we took it and got to work in earnest.

We assembled work crews and started scrubbing and painting and repairing. The owner paid to have the roof fixed, the floor in one room jacked up, the wiring redone and the first $65 worth of paint. Husbands, lovers, friends, and sons and daughters pitched in and helped—they volunteered—and carted out what looked like tons of refuse from attic and cellar, mowed the lawn and tore out the screening on the front porch. About 10 hours of scrubbing and scraping went into the kitchen stove; a repairman put it back together and didn't charge us for his labor. A paint dealer gave us 10 to 15 percent discounts on the gallons of paint we needed to paint the entire inside of the house. We contacted all the people who had promised us used furniture and a car rental dealer donated the use of a pickup truck.

Weary and giddy, having exercised skills we'd forgotten or just discovered, we notified everyone who had expressed any interest in the women's center project and scheduled a meeting. We described our progress and declared that, ready or not, we were having an open house on the 29th of October with everyone welcome and invited. About 40 women attended the meeting and almost all of them agreed to serve on committees.

And we went back to work. We collected a marvelous assortment of used chairs, couches, rugs, drapes and beds. We acquired a typewriter, file cabinet, desk and refrigerator. Those of us who drive vans have hauled so much furniture that we ought to qualify as the Midwest branch of the Mother Truckers! One woman handlettered "The Women's Center" in white on a redwood board for the front of the house. A committee made bright posters announcing the opening and distributed them all over town. (There was a suggestion that we sell raffle tickets for the open house with the first prize being a free vasectomy. We didn't.)

On Sunday noon, the 29th, there we all were, looking like strangers in dresses and hose or respectable pantsuits; the windows of the house were shining and the paint gleaming. The house was filled with flowers, cookies and cakes and coffeemakers; touch-up painting on doorways chipped when furniture was brought in had been done, the porch was appropriately decked with Indian corn and pumpkins. We had a few quiet moments just before two o'clock while we marveled at what we'd wrought and wondered whether anybody would show up. An hour later the house was packed with happy people, newspaper reporters and a TV camera. It was a smashing open house! The first guest looking for emergency shelter arrived within the next week.

The Board of Directors agreed on basic operating policies through a system of argument, counterargument and sweet reasonableness, reminding themselves again and again that the democratic process is remarkably slow. Women are invited to walk into the Center; men are asked to knock. We want to provide a "safe" house for women; the problems of many women are connected with men, and we don't want women who are running from men to have to deal with other men in the Center. There are meetings and discussions and open house events to which men are invited. Counselors or emergency persons from local agencies use the Center occasionally to work with guests.

Legally we are not allowed to shelter runaways; the many calls we receive concerning women under 18 years of age have to be referred to other agencies. The use of alcohol and illegal drugs is not allowed on the premises. Overnight guests are asked to sign a form stating that they are over 18, that they will abide by the simple rules of the house and that they will not hold the Center responsible for their persons or property while there. We define "guests" as women who need to stay at the Center for a short period of time.

After two hectic, crowded years in this location, the Center had an opportunity to rent a much larger house and took it. Originally a large family house which had most recently been used as a day care facility for the Jackson County Mental Health Service, the house has three floors. The lower floor is a large and completely separate apartment for the three residents who live at the Center and are responsible for its operation during the night. The main floor has a large living room, kitchen, dining room, bathroom, counseling room, small library, an office and a room in which pregnancy testing is done. The top floor has two bathrooms, three bedrooms and a meeting room which doubles as a sleeping room.

In the almost four years of its existence, the Center has slowly acquired a solid reputation for reliability. Referrals are made to the Center by almost every Carbondale social service agency, by the police departments and by ministers and private citizens. Referrals are also made by agencies in other southern Illinois communities. The Rape Action Committee, members of which will respond immediately to requests for help on a 24 hour basis, is highly responsible and has developed good working relationships with the hospitals, local doctors and the police forces. The Center has been designated as a practicum site by several graduate departments at Southern Illinois University, and graduate students meet clients for general or problem pregnancy counseling there. Pregnancy tests are done for $2.00 and are anonymous—we keep records of numbers of tests given, but no records of names.

During the day the house is staffed by a constantly shifting roster of volunteers who answer the phone, make referrals to local service agencies, provide willing ears and various kinds of aid and comfort as required or requested. The Center provides training to its volunteers in basic listening techniques and in the operation of the house; volunteers range in age from 18 to 65 and include both university and community women.

Activities have included consciousness-raising groups, car repair clinics, weight reduction classes, health seminars, art shows, poetry readings, yoga meetings and a mom and tots group. The house is available to local women's groups as a meeting place and occasionally provides sleeping space for women attending meetings at the University. Women representing the Center serve as speakers or panelists for a diverse group of local and regional organizations and on radio and TV programs. There is a potluck supper on the first Sunday evening of each month and a brown bag lunch one day a week. A monthly newsletter informs area women of the current happenings at the Center.

Funding for the Center is a rather haphazard thing. We are still receiving pledges and donations from local women, some of whom have been supporting the Center with monthly sums since its inception. The United Fund has included the Center in its list of recipients and the 708 Board of the Jackson County Mental Health Service provides an emergency fund for food, medical and travel expenses for indigent guests. The larder is usually well stocked with everything from disposable diapers to packaged foods and toothpaste. Last fiscal year, and we hope, the next, the Center participated in a HUD sponsored Community Development Block Grant which is administered by the city. The grant money is used to pay for part-time work by a custodian, administrative assistant and coordinator and a portion of the operating expenses. But there have been ominous predictions that funding for a third year may not be forthcoming. The yearly rummage sale may bring in as much as $600, but requires an incredible amount of time and effort on the part of Board members and volunteers, and the monthly expenses of the Center run close to $700. Where have all the fairy godmothers gone? Clearly the Center needs a stable, continuing source of funds. It provides a unique and needed resource, which is used by the entire region; it should have public funding of some kind.

The Center's guests come from a variety of circumstances and places; some of them, recently released from either medical or mental institutions, are staying at the Center while working with other agencies to find jobs and housing; some are visiting inmates of area prisons; some are stranded in town on their way to other parts of the country; some are running from abusive husbands or boyfriends; some need only to get away from traumatic home situations for a few days; some are merely looking for cheap housing for a couple of nights. The Center has a nightly charge of $3.00 to women who can afford it; if they have funds, they are expected to supply their own food. Some guests are able to articulate their problems and make positive moves to solve them, but many others are unable to take necessary measures to improve their situations without the active help and supervision of case workers from state and local agencies.

We are learning as we go. The operating procedures have had to be changed several times to deal with unexpected situations and demands. Limits to the kinds of care which the Center can provide have had to be thoroughly discussed with referring agencies; there is an understandable tendency for some agencies to deposit guests at the Center and then forget about them for a while. Some of the potential guests have problems of such severity, or exhibit such erratic or disruptive behavior, that the Center has to ask the referring agency to place the woman somewhere else. We need to remind people and agencies again and again that, while many of the women associated with the Center are professionals of one kind or another, it is an amateur and volunteer organization. On the whole, we have received excellent help and cooperation from service agencies, crisis intervention personnel and the police.

The Women's Center has never been a part of Southern Illinois University, although many of the volunteers and board members have been university personnel. We have felt that it was important to be an independent, community-based organization; at the same time we have cooperated with university women's groups to sponsor events and have been able to make use of university resources from time to time.

Many of our problems are common to other volunteer organizations. During breaks in the university schedule or vacation periods, we have difficulty in filling the necessary volunteer hours; some volunteers work with great enthusiasm for several months and then go on to other interests. Board members must fill too many jobs from admitting guests to dealing with plumbers and policemen, much of it on an emergency basis which is hard on spouses and families. Our residents carry a very unequal share of the day to day business of dealing with troubled guests. They are usually university students and have exhibited immense good will and kindness, but some of them burn out early on the job because of the intense demands on their time. We need the help of people with blocks of time to devote to exploring the possibilities of funding through grants and of completing such projects; we need people to write budgets and to deal with the large load of statistics demanded by our participation in a HUD grant. Many of our volunteers are women who have other interests and commitments which demand their time; there are never enough people to go around.

The Center has weathered several crises involving intense ideological discussions as to the aims, purposes and directions of the Center. Some women feel that the emergency housing aspect of the Center, with its often chaotic circumstances, precludes the possibility of women finding out about themselves and other women in ways that might lead to growth and change. There is still a segment of the community which views the Women's Center, variously, as a group of busybodies, do-gooders, radicals or man-haters—who would be better off staying at home where they belong!

There have been hundreds of guests and dozens of volunteers in and out of the Center. But we know little about whether or not the reality of women helping other women has had any impact on the lives of our guests. We do know that the rest of us, board members and volunteers, have had opportunities to learn a myriad of public relations skills, and to use our imaginations and ingenuity to hold the house together literally and figuratively.

In spite of the never ending deadlines and emergencies, we continue to dream great dreams of improving the quality of life for women, of helping each other to develop our abilities and perhaps to help change attitudes in our community. The network of affection, fun, and willingness to work and improvise which has developed among the women affiliated with the Center is astounding. It is easy to see that we are indeed filling a community need, that we are providing a "home away from home, a haven, a simmer-down-and-cool-off place" (to quote from one of our early flyers); but there is no way to measure the intangibles of this venture—our pride and joy in the accomplishment and our delight in each other.

Rita Lovell Moss is one of the founders of the Women's Center in Carbondale, Illinois. She works as a secretary in the Law Library of Southern Illinois University, Carbondale.

THE INSTITUTE OF WOMEN TODAY

Sister Margaret Ellen Traxler, SSND

The Institute of Women Today was "born" on a cold February day, 1974, in New York City during a conversation I had with Anna Wolf of the American Jewish Committee. Each of us saw a need for church and synagogue-related women to be part of the women's movement. Yet, by and large, this group of American women had not entered the women's equality effort, except perhaps as evaluators from the outside. We felt that Judeo-Christian values could contribute a deeper richness, which were not reflected to any great measure in the women's search and call for freedom.

The Institute of Women Today, located in Chicago, was designed for the Year of Woman; the Institute intends to continue into the United Nations designated Decade of Women, 1976 to 1986. There are now ten sponsoring national women's organizations; joining with the American Jewish Committee on Women as the major sponsors were the National Coalition of American Nuns and Church Women United. Seven others are participating agencies. The Institute has a faculty of well over one hundred professional women from the four disciplines of law, psychology, theology and history.

The main instrument for meeting women and introducing a climate of change has been a flexible method of workshops. Each workshop is sponsored on the local level by local affiliates and other local women's groups. The sponsoring committee meets and works together with these groups to sponsor the "traveling workshop" which brings four or five faculty to their area. A lawyer speaks about women and the law. She discusses how the law affects women's lives; she speaks on such issues as the Equal Rights Amendment, social security, the Equal Employment Act, credit, welfare, child-care and marriage laws. The psychologist addresses values clarification, for what we value does affect our actions, self-esteem and self-image, women as they see themselves in the media, sibling and spouse relationships, tenderness and other socio-cultural responses. The theologian and scripture scholar speaks of the Bible and such concepts as scriptural roles of women, language and worship, famous heroines of the Book, patriachal systems, religious and sexist interpretations, and new ministries for women in church and synagogue. The historian of course calls forth the "Herstory" of the record of human-kind. The role of the foremothers in building this nation, for example, was highlighted over and over again in the

Bicentennial celebrations of the Institute Workshops.

In the Chicago area, Dr. Kay Asche and Dr. Lillian Vittenson of Northeastern Illinois University and Sheribel Rothenberg, counsel to the Equal Employment Opportunities Commission, among countless others, have been active in the workshops.

In the first year, 1975, there were 30 workshops in as many cities over the country. Participants ranged from 60 in number to 600, the ideal being of course fewer in order to bring faculty and participants closer together. The principle of the workshops is that the value derived by the participants will be in direct relation to the degree in which each has had an opportunity to enter into the discussion and the goal-setting. In this pursuit, the presentations by the faculty are kept to 40 minutes. The presentations are followed by questions and answers and small-group discussions based on questions posed by the presenter. Then a general session of free-form discussion is held, based on the small groups, the presentation and the special interest-group input. Stress is placed upon intervention and individual observation as well as upon questions and answers.

An important aspect of these workshops is not only that a local inter-faith group is sponsoring it, but also that a practical strategy session follows, in which groups decide and plan on the action they will take in the future, based on the locale, the neighborhood, church, synagogue, offices and schools. The follow-up practical planning is essential in keeping the local groups of women working together and planning the future instead of allowing the future to decide for them.

While the local workshops are the major concern of the Institute, we have been active in other areas which are of interest to women, and which contribute directly to our efforts in the workshops.

A major thrust of the new consortium is research in the related fields of women's rights and studies. Dr. Roberta Steinbacher of Cleveland, a clinical psychologist and a faculty member, reported that in one of the national conferences of the American Psychological Association, the few women there had to stand and shout for the right to be heard when the question arose whether there was such a thing as "the psychology of women." The men there insisted there was no such thing; they realized of course that if there were, then they could not specialize in something apart from their own male experience. A separate discipline would then be developed in which they could never play a key role. Dr. Steinbacher and Dr. Faith Dean Gilroy of Baltimore are contributing the first part of a series of research studies for the Institute of Women Today. Their study is a three-part report to be published in the fall 1976 issue of the *Journal of Psychological Research*. It addresses the question of whether women or men more effectively change men's minds. These research efforts are part of the work of the Institute because there is a need to add to the discipline of women's studies. There must be an appreciable body of studies on women by women for graduate and undergraduate study. This aspect also relates well to the over-all purpose of the Institute, "the search for the religious and historical roots of women's liberation."

In July of 1976, Title IX of the Education Amendments of 1972 became federal law. The faculty of the Institute began plans to aid implementation of Title IX which bars sex discrimination in federally funded education programs. Our workers, including Dr. Margaret Carroll and Dr. Kaye Rockwood of Northern Illinois University, have studied the implications of this new legislation; we began helping educators, school systems and classroom teachers to understand not only how not to break the law, but to explain the sound reasoning behind it. We tried to show teachers why Title IX was important and how, if properly understood and implemented, it could make a great difference to both sexes in whatever level of school. Title IX is one of the most fiercely fought equality efforts; now that it is law, we are working to help teachers become aware of how it might be used to change the school world in which youngsters from the very beginning of their schooling could receive equal education opportunities.

Legal services to women in prison was at first an unplanned program of the Institute; later it was to become a most important program. The first invitation came from Dr. Jane Kennedy, the antiwar activist nurse from Chicago. Although recently paroled, she was at the time a resident of the Alderson, West Virginia, Federal Prison, convicted on charges of destroying draft records in 1970.

"Our women need role models," said Jane. "We need to see women who have made the grade, who have succeeded." In response, I explained that we did not realize that the Institute had resources that would be of service to women prisoners; but an invitation from Jane Kennedy was as a command.

The first workshop, on Nov. 1, 1974, was then set up with the cooperation of the warden, Virginia McLaughlin, who is no longer at Alderson. If there was a question about the viability of the Institute's resources, those questions were answered by the first weekend which six faculty members spent with the women at Alderson. Dr. Ralla Klepak, a highly successful Chicago attorney, is head of the Legal Services Program. Indefatigable in her efforts on behalf of women's rights, Klepak found her calling in service to women prisoners.

One of the first members of the "prison faculty" was Dorothy Day. Day, born in 1897, has long worked in Chicago and New York as a journalist, publisher and social activist. Only Dorothy Day, with her long history of serving the poor, could respond to the question of an elderly woman at Alderson. "Why are you here?" Dorothy's reply was: "We have come to wash your feet." Figuratively speaking that was the spirit of the workshops which took place every six weeks at Alderson Prison. In 1976, we also began a series of workshops at the women's division of Lexington Prison in Lexington, Kentucky.

The format of these weekends was a series of private interviews with any of the residents who wished to seek help or counsel from an attorney. It was hard at first for us to believe that some of the women had never talked to an attorney. There were about 70 Hispanic women who spoke no English at all; this was a special hardship for them because of the 250 employees at the prison, only one spoke Spanish. One of the Hispanic women told us that it had taken several days for them to express their need for a bar of soap. Some of them had gone thoughout their trial without anyone to translate for them what was actually happening. Sylvia DeJesus, a computer specialist, now assists the prison projects as translator.

In the second weekend it was apparent to Ralla Klepak that although federal law required that each prison have a law library, none of the women were using the one set apart in the administration building of the prison. "As a rule," said Klepak, "men in prison study and become 'jailhouse lawyers' but women seem to lack the necessary assertiveness to undertake these studies." So there began a course in how to use law reference books and an introduction into the basic tools of legal research. Having once been a teacher, Ralla Klepak knew how to teach   and in the first moment of the opening class, the women knew it too.

Dr. Annette Walters, a clinical psychologist who was with the first faculty at Alderson, discovered that some of the women were keeping prison diaries. Dr. Walters pointed out that keeping a journal can be a therapeutic instrument which can heal and help the person. With this inspiration, there was another "first" initiated for the administration, staff and residents at the prison. Dr. Maureen McCormack began her first intensive journal course for a class which was projected to number about 20 students; 86 finished the first weekend. Dr. Ira Progoff and the Progoff Center in New York, who have developed and spread the idea of intensive journal workshops, furnished the books and journals. Dr. McCormack, with the most excellent evaluations given her course by those who took it, began a series of such Progoff journal keeping workshops in women's prisons all over the country.

After one of the weekends our lawyers asked to see the administrators of the prison in a private interview. Klepak queried, "We have found so many whose basic Constitutional rights have been denied them, do you mind if we prepare some writs of habeas corpus?" she asked. The warden replied, "We've been waiting for some such action and wondered when you'd begin." Thus began the preparation of the writs. The workers gave a file to the residents, with copies to some administrators, in which the forms for the writs were explained, together with minute instructions on how they are to be prepared by the prisoners themselves and the necessary procedures involved. This aspect was extremely helpful to the prisoners; there were so many who had never talked to their court appointed attorney, or who could not speak English, and thus did not have an opportunity to understand either the charges or the dynamics of the court action against them.

"We want to learn welding and they make us work in the garment factory," explained a resident. "We want to learn a job that will give us an income for our family," said another woman. "Many states do not even allow ex-felons to have a beautician's license and they teach us that." Since welding was a desired course, the Institute applied for and received a grant to teach a complete course in welding. Spot-welding in itself brings an income of close to $8.00 an hour. The master-welder, a woman who was hired as teacher, assured us that she could rent the equipment from her company and could prepare her class of up to 20 members for the master-welder status, which included heavy welding in all its forms. During the fall and winter of 1975 and 1976, this course progressed with unusual speed. The skills achieved were influential in impressing the parole board with the promise that a woman could have a marketable skill and thus qualify for a parole as soon as the opportunity and dates were available.

On July 3, 1976, the Supreme Court handed down its decison on capital punishment, which meant that the 599 people on death rows were again faced with execution. According to the decision, about one half of those would be in the category affected by the capital punishment verdicts. Ten of these were women. Five were black women, four were white and one was a native American. Ralla Klepak, as head of the Legal Services of the Institute, began contacting lawyers on the faculty in order to set up a visit with each of these women in order to assure that each had had sound legal counsel."As a criminal lawyer for the past ten years, I know how poor legal counsel can oppress someone on trial," said Ralla Klepak, "and I want to see that each of the women facing death has had proper advice and also I want to know what, if anything, we can do to provide services of any kind to each woman." She also expressed the desire to see that the remaining 589 men on death rows likewise received the same assistance; but with the limited resources of the Institute, that was impossible. Ten women was a limited goal and was achievable, but not the other 589 persons included in the Court decision. Thus in the fall of 1976 and early winter, a series of visits to women on death rows will begin.

There is a world of communication between prisoners, with one another and with those in other prisons; there is also such a world of communication between wardens and administrators. The news sent out by Assistant Warden Doris Martin and Warden Virginia McLaughlin at Alderson, was good news about the Institute; as a result, many invitations were received to spend weekends in other prisons. Because Lexington Prison was most persistent, their women's division was the next scene of the services. At one time, Donald Finger, a unit manager at Lexington, even set a date for the "traveling workshop." But as director, I had to explain that it was the need for funds which prevented our coming and that appeals were underway. It cost about $1,400 to set up a weekend visit. When

Helen and Leland Schubert of Cleveland heard the need, they gave the gift which made possible not only the continuation of the Alderson visits but also extending the visits to Lexington Prison. Ruth Goldboss of Highland Park (wife of Willard Goldboss) also helped financially but gave even more in motivation and encouragement.

Future needs are clear. The workshops of lawyers and psychologists are needed wherever women are in prison, especially state and county prisons. Class action suits are needed for such abuses as unjust sentencing. For example, a married couple committed the same crime; when sentenced the man got two years and the woman six. Women oftentimes receive more severe sentences because as women they are expected to have better conduct; when convicted, their breaking of "the code" is considered a more serious infraction simply because "women don't do such things."

Also in the future are hopes for bringing women physicians to women in prison. An elderly resident showed the visitors her open breasts, filled with what was obviously skin cancer. Yet she was asked to wait by the prison doctor until there was an opening in a nearby prison health facility. Requests for immediate medical care by the Institute faculty brought her help the very next day.

When entering the prison the first time, faculty were asked to do what all visitors are required to do: write down their name, show identification and then write the purpose of the visit. Dorothy Day, in signing herself into the compound, turned around and asked us, "Shall I say that I am a revolutionary?" We smiled at the venerable woman, realizing that revolutionaries can come on quiet feet and through processes already approved can bring needed change. The purpose of Legal Services to women in prison is devoted to bringing change through orderly process.

As Dr. Judith Schloegel, a regular faculty member of Atlanta, wrote in a journal, "We go to prison to bring the good message of law and basic rights. We come to heal and unite, to free and make ready for the greater freedom." In a brief statement Dr. Schloegel has stated the purpose of Legal Services.

The larger goal of the Institute of Women Today remains the same: to search for the religious and historical roots of women's liberation. Reaching church and synagogue-related women with this message seems more important now than ever before, so that in the decade ahead all women may share with men the same role in the voice, presence and vote wherever decisions are made that affect the human family.

Sister Margaret Ellen Traxler, of the School Sisters of Notre Dame, is the director of the Institute of Women Today. A resident of Chicago, she is also former director of the National Catholic Conference for International Justice.

THE ILLINOIS WOMEN'S AGENDA

Rebecca Anne Sive-Tomashefsky

We women of the United States of America, join together to challenge our Nation to complete the unfinished work of achieving a free and democratic society, begun long ago by our Founding Mothers and Fathers. In creating the first National Women's Agenda, we are making explicit demands on our Government, and on the private sector as well. Firm policies and programs must be developed and implemented at all levels in order to eliminate those inequities that still stand as barriers to the full participation by women of every race and group. For too long, the nation has been deprived of women's insights and abilities. It is imperative that women be integrated into national life now.

We are women with interests and roots in every sector and at every level of society. Although our programs and goals may vary, still we have agreed upon issues which must be addressed as national priorities so that women will play a full and equal role in this country.

The above words from the preamble to the U.S. National Women's Agenda are the product of the spirit of a new movement among women today, a coalition building effort which reaches across barriers of class, ethnicity, lifestyle and political philosophy. Its credo is that women, drawing strength from their diversity, have a common agenda. Its style is action—action on those fronts important to us all. Here in Illinois, this new spirit is seen in a number of cities and within many different types of organizations. In Peoria, women of the YWCA are organizing with tenants in a local housing project on the issue of battered wives. They formed an influential coalition for the Equal Rights Rally in Springfield in the spring of 1976. In Carbondale, a new women's center has brought women's services and programs to a new audience. In both Rockford and Springfield efforts began in the summer of 1976 to form local coalitions. And on National Women's Agenda Day, December 2, 1975, a state wide coalition, the Illinois Women's Agenda, was launched in Chicago.

Our purpose was to announce and celebrate the National Women's Agenda—a women's bill of rights developed by the

Women's Action Alliance from the contributions of representatives of 92 national organizations. The Agenda enumerates 11 issues of concern:

quality child care for all children;
respect for the individual;
fair representation and participation in the political process;
physical safety;
meaningful work and adequate compensation;
adequate housing;
just and humane treatment in the criminal justice system;
equal access to economic power;
fair treatment by and equal access to media and the arts;
quality health care and services; and
equal education and training.

The purpose of the Agenda is to comprehensively outline the interests and demands of women and then to provide a platform from which to organize. Launching the Agenda gave those of us in Illinois a chance to formalize the new spirit and to join together in a concerted effort to maintain past gains and win new victories.

Many women had been discussing the real need for us to come together, to use our united strength to work for issues of concern to women. This grew in part perhaps from the widespread concern over our failure thus far to see the Equal Rights Amendment (ERA) passed in Illinois—due in some degree to our own inability to mobilize our powers. Therefore passage of the ERA and a call for full employment became the two issues around which representatives of 35 organizations met on November 20, 1975 to plan the first meeting. They agreed that on December 2 we should hear from women representing the different constituencies who would join together to launch a new coalition.

On that day, Marie Fese, vice president of the Chicago Chapter of the Coalition of Labor Union Women, Hilda Frontany, organizer of the Lakeview Latin American Women's Program, Susan Davis, publisher of the feminist newsletter *Spokeswoman,* Connie Seals, executive director of the Illinois Commission on Human Relations, and Heather Booth, long-time movement organizer, verified that white working class women, Latinos, blacks and feminists will work together on mutual concerns. After their participation in this historic meeting, 150 women, representing 100 women's organizations, returned to their members to announce our new unity and to encourage participation in the new coalition.

But why are women in 1976 interested in working together in new ways? Why, after 100 years of significant civic efforts by Illinois women, after eight years of activity by the new women's movement, have spirits and philosophies reached a new stage? Both too little and too much success may cause organizations to not work with others—because of jealousy, fear or pride. It is also true that ethnic organizations, service organizations, advocacy groups and academic groups all have differing approaches to their issues and to their organization's members; they have different degrees of need or interest in communicating with other groups.In addition, difficulties in winning campaigns dampen our spirits and slow the momentum of our efforts. For these reasons, and because we lacked a common platform which stated our beliefs and demands, women of Illinois previously had few ways of getting together and often no incentive to do so, except for single issue, short-term efforts.

The last few years have been difficult for women's organizations. But as the contemporary women's movement has been accepted by greater numbers of people and institutions, as its image has become more positive in the media, and as influential national leaders have adopted some of its demands, its base has broadened. Increasingly, women of diverse backgrounds have been able to appropriate some of the movement's concerns and call them their own. By 1976, previous differences had lessened so that a platform stating our unity was perhaps all that was needed to provide the impetus to coalition-building.

But once the need and willingness to form coalitions is recognized, what is the next step? Organizers of other coalitions in civil rights, the environmental and the consumer movements told us that single issue coalitions formed to win short term goals are different from those which are long term, working on several issues simultaneously. Organizational structure, the development of plans of action and outreach must be approached differently. Also, we know that a coalition can end up as no more than a loose federation, whose only activity is mutual communication, if there is not constant suggestion of new ideas and programs—and some significant victories. These complexities were recognized by both the steering committee of the Illinois Women's Agenda and the organizers from the Women's Action Alliance who were working to create a national women's coalition.

Together, and with the advice of other organizers and theorists, we developed a structure and form of governance which we hoped would encompass the complexities of coalitions and yet keep enthusiasm high. On December 18, 1975 representatives of 75 Illinois organizations met to formally create the Illinois Women's Agenda. It is a coalition organized by task forces; its steering committee is composed of the co-chairs of the task forces and the staff. The Agenda is supported by the Institute on Pluralism and Group Identity of the American Jewish Committee. Formal bylaws were not adopted nor officers elected in December so that we could test out and modify this structure. Plans of action developed by the task forces are outlined to the steering committee; the co-chairs can ask for resources, technical assistance or other task force and organizational support from the committee. Individual member organizations can also announce activities and request support from the steering committee. The May 1976 National Rally for Equal

Rights in Springfield, initiated by the National Organization for Women (NOW) and sponsored by many groups, drew attendants and organizational support from the Agenda.

It is a long and time consuming process both for organizations to learn in depth about each other's efforts and for individuals to develop the level of trust and support necessary to pursue joint activities. After seven months of task force and steering committee meetings, membership events and constant outreach, several of the Illinois Women's Agenda task forces are now planning actions and programs whose participants will include hundreds of organizational members.

The Political Participation Task Force, composed of representatives from the Illinois Women's Political Caucus, Leadership Conference of Women Religious, National Organization for Women, Women's Share in Public Service, League of Women Voters, National Council of Puerto Rican Women and others wrote a questionnaire specifically on issues of concern to women which it sent to the gubernatorial candidates. The candidates' responses to the questionnaire will be analyzed and published; a meeting will be held with them.

Task force projects include both action and service activities. The Education Task Force is preparing an information packet on filing complaints under Title IX of the Education Act of 1972 which prohibits discrimination by sex in education. The packet will be distributed to schools, libraries, community groups and women's organizations. Task force members who have worked on the packet are from the National Council of Negro Women, American Friends' Service Committee, Evanston Women's Liberation Union and the National Black Feminist Organization.

The Economic Power Task Force concluded after a number of meetings and discussions with others that its focus would be on the credit issue. It is planning a rally for October 28, 1976—the anniversary of the passage of the Equal Credit Opportunity Act—at which women will publicize the law and demand coordinated government enforcement. The rally will be held in the plaza of the Chicago Civic Center to dramatize to the public and to the media the urgency of rectifying credit discrimination against women. This event represents the first time that the Women's Rights Committee of the Chicago Council of Lawyers, the Women's Bar Association, the Chicagoland Women's Federal Credit Union, the Consumer Credit Project and others have planned an action together. It also epitomizes the kind of work a coalition can do—drawing on the resources and the expertise of its members and representing the concerns of the thousands of women who are members of its constituent organizations.

While pursuing these joint activities, members of the American Association of University Women, National Organization for Women, National Council of Jewish Women, Illinois Commission on the Status of Women and others have learned much about each other. The result is a steady growth of mutual trust, as well as strength from which to draw. There is no way that this lengthy process can be short circuited, but also no other process that can potentially bring more women together.

As part of community building, of course, formal outreach efforts must be carried on by the coalition. In our original planning for the Illinois Women's Agenda, we identified eight groups of women who could be brought into a coalition: traditional women's organizations, feminist groups, labor, ethnic and community organizations, direct action organizations, academic and professional groups, social service agencies and government associations. Because of differing priorities as well as differences in lifestyle and occupation, direct action groups and ethnic women's organizations are those with whom we have had the fewest discussions. However, the May 6, 1976 program, "Fundraising Techniques for Women's Organizations," which we sponsored with the Donor's Forum, brought in some of these women as participants. Featured speaker Mary Gonzales, president of the Pilsen Neighbors, a Chicago neighborhood group, stressed the common interests of feminists and neighborhood women working on local problems. She affirmed that their individual sense of self may be similar and that they have a common interest in social change.

What can we say we've accomplished in the last year? We co-sponsored an all day fund raising seminar for women's organizations. We have announced and fostered acceptance of a new women's bill of rights and published a newsletter sent to 1,000 organizational representatives. We designed and conducted a three day training program on coalition-building for steering committee members and developed a model women's summer 1976 internship program for volunteers working on the Agenda. The agenda co-sponsored, with local groups, coalitions in Rockford and Springfield. We have become the model nation-wide for the development of state coalitions of women's organizations.

Agenda members continue to be enthusiastic and many activities are planned for the coming months. It is our hope that the Agenda will be able to spin off from the Institute on Pluralism and Group Identity to become an independent service and umbrella coalition for women's organizations. In the meantime, organizers from all over the country will meet on October 2, 1976 in Washington, D.C., to formally create a National Women's Coalition working with state based groups. We are working hard for the day when we can say that our Agenda is "finished."

Rebecca Anne Sive-Tomashefsky is Midwest Director of Special Projects for the Institute on Pluralism and Group Identity of the American Jewish Committee. As part of her work with the Institute she is the co-convenor of the Illinois Women's Agenda. She created and co-edited the recently published Chicago Women's Directory.

WOMEN'S HEALTH CARE

Abby Pariser

I moved to Illinois in the summer of 1968 from the highly political
and activist world of Columbia University in New York. There I had
participated in the Independent Committee Against the War in
Vietnam since the November 1965 conference and march in
Washington, D.C. I also had been one of the founders of the
Columbia chapter of the Students for a Democratic Society. My
involvement with women's issues—even consciousness of
them—had been limited to the problems of planning a career and
finding some means of birth control, via a friend who had a contact in
the East Village. Later I discovered Planned Parenthood, where they
called us all "Mrs."

As a teaching assistant in American history under Jesse Lemisch at
Roosevelt University, I became interested in plans to form the
Chicago Women's Liberation Union (CWLU). I went to its founding
conference in November 1969. Over that weekend I was enormously
excited by what I learned about feminist issues—day care,
employment discrimination, divorce, health care. I also ran into a
repetition of the political factionalism which I had seen in the anti-
war movement. Women from the Progressive Labor Party, Socialist
Workers' Party, International Socialists and Youth Against War and
Fascism were at the conference, trying to mold it to their vision of
radical politics. I think that CWLU was successful in keeping the
organization independent of existing political groups.

One of the priorities established for CWLU was women's health
care. A work group was formed and met occasionally to discuss

possible actions. One of the programs suggested was a women's health center and clinic to be staffed by paramedics trained from our group. The project was to be named after Alice B. Hamilton, one of Chicago's early women doctors.

The Alice B. Hamilton Women's Medical Center did not open; the committee had even found a suitable building to rent at 55th Street and Western Avenue, but could find no reliable source of funding for equipment, supplies and medicines. Instead, a pregnancy testing service, staffed by trained volunteers, was started at the CWLU office.

While I was involved with CWLU, I kept hearing about another work group, the Abortion Counseling Service, also known as "Jane." When I spent one day a week at CWLU's office answering the phone, I had been referring women with problem pregnancy questions to Jane or to the Clergy Consultation Service on Problem Pregnancy. In the summer of 1970, I called Jane to volunteer as a counselor.

At the time, abortion was illegal in Illinois but, on July 1, 1970, it had become legal in New York. Several other states, California, Colorado and Hawaii among them, had liberalized abortion laws, but many restricted legal abortions to state residents. I assumed that ACS-Jane referred all candidates to New York. It didn't occur to me that many pregnant women could neither afford the plane, train or bus fare to New York nor afford to pay the $200 cost of the operation. Soon I learned that alternate methods of getting safe abortions, legal or not, might have to be arranged locally.

I attended two orientation meetings for new counselors, learning about the actual operation, complications and care of the pregnant woman. New counselors were taught about the political realities of abortion—its illegality. Jane was actually a telephone tape machine; we called the woman back to find out her needs, to refer her to New York or to assign her to a counselor. Before the abortion the woman was counseled in person about abortion, health and birth control after the operation. Then she received an appointment.

Abortions in Chicago were done by trained abortionists; some Jane counselors learned by apprenticeship the techniques involved. At first the cost was $450 but decreased to less than $100 by 1972. Since our patients were so poor, we didn't push for the entire amount for fear that they might instead try self-abortion or go to their "neighborhood catheter lady"—both with disastrous results. Jane was handling 50 to 75 women per week and referring many others to New York.

Jane continued to function with ever increasing popularity until Wednesday, May 3, 1972, when seven of us were arrested by the Chicago police and charged with abortion and conspiracy to commit abortion. Although we were indicted, we did not go to trial; on

January 22, 1973, the U.S. Supreme Court overturned restrictive abortion laws in Georgia and Texas. Subsequently, on February 16, the Illinois law was found unconstitutional and our case was dropped. During the year that we were in the court system, Jane continued to function, with slightly more attention to security for the remaining workers. After abortion became legal in Illinois and clinics for abortion opened, the service closed. Some of the former counselors have set up the Emma Goldman Clinic and some work in HERS, the health referral service of the CWLU.

During the time I was working in Jane, I belonged to the DuPage County chapter of Zero Population Growth (ZPG) and did a considerable amount of speaking on women's health, women's liberation and environmental and population issues. I spoke mostly in high school and college classes, but occasionally to a few community groups. I have continued to speak in high schools, primarily on birth control and abortion. I think it is very important to give both girls and boys a sound factual base of sexual information, especially their responsibility for contraception, at the time when they begin to be sexually active. Although the sense of the community usually is that sex education should be done by the parents, the church or the school, judging by the numbers of unplanned teenage pregnancies, not enough has been said about the actual mechanics of birth control, its availability, cost, side effects or effectiveness.

One frustrating aspect of my talks on birth control was that there were very few physicians in DuPage during 1970 and 1971 who would prescribe birth control even for married women, much less for the single woman under 18. I believe this was due to many doctors' attempts to impose their concepts of morality on their patients.

ZPG, attempting to create some alternatives, co-sponsored a planning meeting with the small Planned Parenthood Auxiliary. A hearing at the DuPage County Board of Health was set up to establish the need for a public family planning clinic. Fifty women came; they were from Planned Parenthood, ZPG, NOW and the League of Women Voters. All came as private citizens.

Women spoke of their personal, unsuccessful efforts to obtain contraception in DuPage; they spoke of the high cost of private medical care. We suggested that the Health Department set up a family planning clinic as part of its regular services for the indigent women of the county. The Health Department refused; they maintained that there were no needs that were not already being met by the private sector.

From our own survey of the county, we already knew that the needs were there. The Planned Parenthood group decided to open a birth control clinic in DuPage as soon as funding could be found and a staff trained. Chicago Planned Parenthood had made a tentative commitment to support a DuPage clinic; when the Health Department refused us, they agreed to go ahead.

About 15 women were interested in becoming the volunteer staff for the clinic. A training team from Chicago's Planned Parenthood came out to Wheaton for about eight days of actual class sessions. They gave lectures on the anatomy and physiology of reproduction, methods of birth control and the philosophy and policies of Planned Parenthood. We learned to fill out reams of paper for the never-ending bureaucracy of agency existence; we learned role playing and counseling techniques. Since I had paramedical experience, I was qualified to fill the job of laboratory technician, who does urinalysis, pregnancy testing and syphilis screening.

The Wheaton Planned Parenthood Clinic began May 8, 1973; it was open the second and fourth Tuesdays of the month, with a capacity of 23 patients. Although we had sent a survey to local physicians, not many of them were interested in working for us. We relied on downtown Planned Parenthood for our clinicians. We found that the doctors from the teaching hospitals in the city had better training and were not as hostile to the concept of a clinic with a sliding fee scale as were DuPage doctors.

It took a few months for the clinic to run at full capacity. We had promoted the clinic by mailing announcements of our opening to high school and college guidance counselors, school nurses, social workers, other service agencies and women's organizations in the county, plus the Health Department and the newspapers. We actually expected some signs of distress from the conservative right to life groups, but no overt opposition materialized.

The Wheaton clinic functions in much the same manner as most other Planned Parenthoods. We offer complete gynecological care to any woman 13 or older; we give a methods talk, covering anatomy, reproduction and all methods of birth control. We describe the advantages, disadvantages and effectiveness of each method. We test for syphilis, sickle cell and other hemoglobin anemias, red blood cell anemia, pregnancy, blood pressure and weight; we do a complete individual and family health history in a private counseling interview. The doctor does breast and pelvic exams, including Pap and gonorrhea smears, prescribes birth control pills, inserts IUDs and fits diaphragms. And in cases when we are too late, the doctor estimates length of pregnancy; we counsel the patient.

Of the clinic staff, all except the doctor and the charge nurse are volunteers. The issue of volunteerism has become sensitive under the scrutiny of many feminists who view volunteering as a continuation of the unpaid housewifely labor. But perhaps I can make a case for the positive effect of volunteering in an agency of social change—not just busy work or envelope stuffing, but having an effect on people's lives. An advantage of our volunteer workers is their commitment to the cause—furnishing quality birth control and other related medical services to women in a non-judgmental setting. The Wheaton Planned Parenthood staff work because they believe in the necessity of the service, not because they individually enjoy filing, bookkeeping, washing instruments or filling out bureaucratic forms or need an income. There are disadvantages with a voluntary work staff; family vacations interfere with scheduling, as do children's sicknesses. There are relatively few coercive actions available to the coordinator when a staff person fails to show up for her shift or chooses not to work frequently enough to keep her skills highly polished. There are very few ways to reward good or punish bad behavior; we can't give staff raises nor dock their pay.

As we were planning the clinic, I asked to be hired as the clinic supervisor. I thought that my work with Jane and the Alice B. Hamilton Center had given me a considerable amount of experience with women's health care facilities; besides, I had been a patient at the New York and Chicago Planned Parenthood clinics for eight years. I was not encouraged to pursue the job, however. I had no formal degree or certificate proving my competence nor did I have a long association with the Wheaton group. A licensed practical nurse was hired as the charge nurse and supervisor. Unfortunately, she had little previous experience with gynecology or with non-judgmental, feminist, medical consumer or related social service agency principles.

The problems of our charge nurse/clinic supervisor were only an indication of how special an area family planning is. The handling of women's health care specifically related to reproduction requires a synthesis of many areas and skills—special attention to birth control methods and new research, the skills and tact of social work, a medical orientation, the ability to constantly absorb masses of new information and especially a sensitivity to the personal area of sexuality and the relationships between people. Although birth control and birth control clinics have existed in this country since Margaret Sanger's original women's clinic in 1916, there are very few places to get training in family planning. On the job training, however, is almost the best there is. Our second charge nurse, who had been a volunteer in the clinic for 18 months before she took the job, was much better prepared because she had been working in the field with us.

Technically, the Wheaton clinic was supposed to send all abortion referrals to the Problem Pregnancy Counselling and Referral Service of the Planned Parenthood Association of the Chicago Area. We did make all appointments through the downtown clinic until Planned Parenthood worked out a system which evaluated the abortion clinics in Chicago. We were able then to start referring those women who chose abortion directly to the approved clinics.

Some pregnant women who come to our clinic choose to have their babies; we help them find good pre-natal care and help them find ways to adjust to their new life situation, including the problems of housing, job or other financial support and parenthood. Many of the women we see are teenagers. There is a large amount of planning they must do to work out the choice of having a baby, married or not. Our most important job, especially with teenagers, is referring them to other social service agencies. We do extensive referrals to the Health Department, well child clinics, mental health department, prenatal classes, Catholic charities, many adoption agencies, public aid, the Family Service Association and the Illinois Department of Children and Family Services.

Although we are just as careful in counseling our pregnant women who plan to carry to term—in fact we are very concerned with nutrition, possible side effects of medication to the fetus, proper care for the mother—our reputation in the county among anti-choice or "right to life" groups does not acknowledge this. We are pro-choice—the choice of the pregnant woman to abort or to give birth. We do not make up any woman's mind for her; she decides, after all the altenatives are explored: keeping the child, getting married, adoption, abortion and all combinations. Of course, many of the pregnant women are already married, and they are given the same treatment. Fortunately they don't have the added burden of dealing with parental disapproval and high school problems.

By the summer of 1974, we were so crowded at the clinic, turning 10 and 20 women away at each session, that we asked to increase the clinic to weekly sessions; arrangements with the downtown Planned Parenthood were not completed until January 1975. Because of the post-holiday rush, we were filled again almost immediately. It was constantly amazing to us that the County Health Board had not seen any need for this kind of service when we were full and referring women to other places.

We bought a recording machine for our telephone at the clinic, which gave a message about our hours and one of our phone numbers for further information. At home, we fielded calls day and night, seven days a week, until we learned to limit the times we were available. The volume of calls pointed out once more the inadequacies of available medical help for the sexually active teenager or adult in this county. We averaged 85 calls a month between January and June of 1976. Many were simply requesting information about the clinic; the bulk concerned pregnancy tests, abortions and birth control information.

Calls come, of course, from our own patients and from people trying to find out about the clinic. But people ask where they can get VD tests, which the DuPage County Health Department *does* do without charge; they ask, in great numbers, where to get pregnancy tests when they do not wish to go to their own doctor or to the obstetrician who had delivered the last child; they ask how soon after intercourse they can get pregnancy test, and they ask where to get abortions and female and male sterilizations. Women and many men ask us about the "morning after pill." We also get calls quite frequently from women whose gynecologists have told them to stop taking the pill—often for unspecified reasons—but did not give or offer them another method of contraception. Our phone has become a sort of medical hotline in the county; women now call us for all sorts of non-reproductive medical information: bladder infections, kidney stones, sexual dysfunction and physician referral.

Some few of us shared the telephone duty responsibility. And although at times it could be a strain on our lives to be constantly on the phone with strange people's problems, it was obvious that we were needed, that there was no other source for non-judgmental social and medical information, that men and women were reluctant to chance discussing many topics with their own source of medicine, or that they had gotten some bad or wrong answers to their questions and problems. We also found that some women would call us to complain about shabby treatment they had received from local doctors. We would like to follow up some of these complaints; we are distressed that the county medical society does not make an attempt to police the profession.

In November 1975, the Illinois legislature passed the Kelly Bill, over the veto of the governor. It severely restricted access to abortion for minors by requiring parental consent and also restricted the access of married women by requiring the husband's consent. It completely prohibited second trimester abortions. Fortunately the Illinois Division of the American Civil Liberties Union obtained an injunction against the law, claiming it violated the Supreme Court decision of 1973. The Supreme Court ruled, in July of 1976, that similar laws in twelve states were unconstitutional, maintaining the right of women to decide their own reproductive lives.

The newest expansion of the Wheaton Planned Parenthood is the addition of a second weekly session, a Teen Scene Clinic. This has a basic staff of paid workers, many of them already volunteers at the original clinic. The Teen Scene enables us to focus more directly on teenagers' needs in the area of birth control and sexuality than we were able to do in a mixed age clinic.

The issue of women's health care goes beyond the medical and social services provided by a clinic. I have tried to carry out my interest in women's health in two other women's organizations in DuPage County—NOW and the YWCA. In NOW, I have been active in the Reproduction and Health Committee and in the Pro-Choice Committee. NOW is not restricted in its political activities and lobbying efforts. In fact a great deal of NOW's efforts are expended in trying to change society through its laws and courts. In the fight to keep the option of abortion legal and safe, NOW, along with the National Abortion Rights Action League and its Illinois affiliate, Abortion Rights Association of Illinois, act as watchdogs on congressional legislation and make our stand known to our various representatives in Washington and Springfield.

The Pro-Choice Committee produced a slide show, *Abortion: A Woman's Right to Choose,* to publicize the importance of maintaining legal abortion, rather than prohibiting it. We know that if abortion becomes illegal again, women will return to self-induced and criminal abortions, with the risks of complications and deaths. We have used the slide show most effectively with high school people; they have become sexually active in an era of free choice and do not have much idea of the horrors of illegal abortion.

In the Reproduction and Health Committee of NOW, I have helped construct a physician questionnaire aimed at the consumers rather than the doctors themselves. In this way, we tried to find out how the patients were treated, whether they were considered with dignity, consulted on their own diagnoses and treatment, as well as to discover which doctors are sympathetic in birth control, abortion, sterilization and childbirth matters. The results of the questionnaire are available to NOW and other DuPage women.

Where do we go from here? In talks with members of NOW and in conferences sponsored by such groups as the YWCA, one of the needs identified by many women has been to have a central source for health information and referral, a sort of clearing house of health resources. So far, no one has implemented the suggestion.

We in DuPage who have worked with women's health issues have dreamed of setting up a Feminist Women's Health Center, with a nurse practitioner, childbirth instructors, counselor, therapists, and much learning and teaching. It is too early yet to see if this will happen.

Abby Pariser, whose master's thesis for Roosevelt University is titled "History of the Chicago YWCA," is a volunteer at the Wheaton Planned Parenthood and a member of the board of directors of the West Suburban Area YWCA.

THE COALITION OF LABOR
UNION WOMEN

Interview with Barbara Merrill, President,
Chicago Coalition of Labor Union Women (CLUW).
By Adade Wheeler, July 22, 1976.

WHEELER: First, would you tell me something about yourself? Do you have children and a home to take care of too?

MERRILL: I have two daughters, both married, and two grandchildren, one three and one less than a year old. My husband was killed in the Korean War, and the two girls were kind of raised here in this union hall, and before this one, in other union halls. I'm proud to say that the older one and her husband are both active in the union where they work, and my other daughter and her husband are continuing their education this fall. My three year old granddaughter has been in this union hall at a couple of meetings and she knows how to say "AFSCME" and "solidarity." I suppose someday she'll go to work and will belong to a union.

W: How did you get started? Where did your interest in the unions come from?

M: Well, I guess I was always interested. When I was a young girl, about nine or ten, my grandfather took me to some meetings. He was working with the teachers' union, and I remember going to a place the young people never heard of today—Bughouse Square. He took me with him to open-air meetings, and I heard a lot of labor people. When I was still quite young, I had thought about going into the religious life, but after I'd tried it for a few months I came home. But I still always wanted to do something that would help people. So after I began to get into the work force all that was a natural preparation for coming into unions.

W: What kind of job did you have at the beginning?

M: First I was with the federal government, when the federal employees were beginning to organize. I was involved with the credit union because I had worked with the credit union in my parish. Then I went to the Cook County Department of Public Aid, as it was called then. There was a union, kind of a conglomeration, Local 73 of the old Service Employees' Union, which represented all the employees—everyone in one union, elevator operators, janitors, everyone. With all those we felt they weren't as responsive to us as they should have been, so after a few short discussions, we decided to form our own independent union in the Public Aid Department [later to become the American Federation of State, County and Municipal Employees (AFSCME)].

W: When was that?

M: Oh, it began late in 1964, didn't really get started until 1965. We went to a Local 73 meeting and when we could not get the floor or the mike we just left and went over to a cafeteria. We had some labor friends, and a couple of us knew something about unions; we thought you just got the idea and you up and started your own. That's more or less what happened.

W: Now may I ask you about the women in the union, if you don't mind my hitting this from the women's viewpoint. Just what are the particular advantages for women?

M: I suppose the first advantage for women in a union is that it gives an outlet for what I think is women's tremendous, just natural inborn energy. It provides a platform and place for them to utilize their organizational skills. Women have always been organizers. We organize our homes, we organize our block clubs, our churches and PTAs. And so naturally if a woman works, I think that she brings certain skills and certain characteristics to her job and to the union that are much needed. All that is most important. Secondly, it gives her a greater sense of being, of fellowship. Men often have a camaraderie situation that is not always available to women. I think a union gives this to her.

W: Do unions also give women some special training and help educate them to go further in their jobs?

M: Yes. One thing we've seen is more intra-union training programs, making available to members just the basic union documents that they are all entitled to know about—constitutions, grievance procedures and such. And then women are asking for training in parliamentary procedure and in the handling of grievances. The unions within their own framework are beginning to give women this kind of training.

W: Is the Coalition of Labor Union Women [CLUW] helping with this?

M: Oh, yes. We have had some national meetings. Here in Chicago last year we ran some educationals and we are running a series this year.

W: When do you have time for these?

M: The ones we had last year were on Saturday mornings, from 10 to around 12:30 or so, and we've had a couple in the evening. Then we had that very successful school for women workers—a Midwest School—in South Bend, Indiana, in May of this year [1976]. We brought in women from the Chicago CLUW, the University of Ohio, University of Kentucky, Cornell, University of Indiana; we had 115 women from a six state area for four days. We had intensive training sessions, strictly for women trade unionists. We expected 40 or 50 and got 115, so we are going to do it again next year, perhaps in a different place.

W: Are the colleges—community and university—here receptive to helping with these?

M: There's been a national organization made up of instructors out of various labor education programs of the land grant universities. Many of the members of the University and College Labor Education Association (Barbara Wortheimer of Cornell did much to help set this up) have seen the need for emphasizing labor women's education, so that's what we are doing

W: Would it be harder to do something like that through a single union?

M: Oh yes, this opens it up and makes it wider. We get women from all kinds of unions. I don't think without CLUW that the unions would have embraced such an idea, yet most of the women went at union expense.

W: What other kinds of education have unions been involved in?

M: We've had training classes for women on an ongoing basis, especially for clerical employees—which most of us are—and we would help them study for civil service exams so they could get better placements.

W: What about promoting better health care? What has the union done to help women get better insurance and safety?

M: Health insurance is integral to the union—men and women. We fight for *all* union members. We've just begun to get into the whole area of occupational health and safety. With our particular union, the state dropped its occupational health and safety program. It was turned over to the federal government which doesn't cover state and municipal employees under the OHS Act [Occupational Health and Health and Safety Act.] For the short time that Illinois handled the OHSA program, we did file a number of grievances, and we had begun to really do some education on it for our members, especially for the women. Once again, it was done by those in the clerical classification who worked with copying machines and materials—who, you know, had to sit for hours at desks and typewriters. But now that we have no program, we have to get it back first. We tried at a state convention a year ago to introduce a resolution attempting to get it reinstated, but that failed. So what we've done is to join with some other locals and unions facing the same problem, trying to get this coverage for state, county and municipal employees.

W: What are the major problems that you are dealing with now for union women?

M: I would imagine in unions like ours it would be OHSA. It's probably also the question of insurance and rates. In some contracts, and even in some industries and plants where there are no contracts, you'll find that the insurance rate is generally higher for women than it is for men, or vice versa. I think that what women are saying now is that not only with insurance rates, but with pension payments and deductions, we want the same. In our union we were successful a couple of years ago in getting a standard pension deduction. They had deducted more out of male checks than they did from the women's. It took a long time for the women to understand that while they were giving one-half a percent less from each check, when it came time for retirement, they would also receive less pension. Cook County Public Aid's position was that men are heads of families and when they retire they will need more money in order to support themselves and their families. We had to point out that in this particular department we have one-third more women who were heads of families than we had men. So we had to get them the standard rate.

W: And by the time they reach retirement age, the number would be greater?

M: That has become a big issue with a lot of unions. I think something else that is very important is this whole question of maternity as a disability benefit. A couple of unions have gone into various federal courts and we're hoping that very soon after the national elections, [in November 1976] the Supreme Court will settle the question once and for all, nationally, so that we won't have to continue to negotiate it contract by contract, or court by court. Certainly it is our position as female unionists that it should be treated as any other disability.

W: What about the Equal Rights Amendment? What is the union doing on that?

M: Well, I suppose we've done just about everything. We've lobbied, we have sent telegrams, we have been to just about every rally here in Chicago and in Springfield.

W: Did your own legislator vote for it?

M: Yes, oh yes.

W: Good for you. I can't say that about all mine.

M: Well, we've had our differences, but we felt until the last week of this session that it had a chance.

W: What do you think happened to it?

M: I've had so many different theories each time it's failed to come up for a vote, or failed to get it, that I've almost run out of theories. I just don't know, I just don't know. I suppose that given the way politicians think, if it is going to pass, it will probably pass in the next session, right around election time. They have a tendency to enact legislation oft times when it is to their benefit, and I would imagine the closer we get to November, we may see it. If we don't get it then, we probably might as well forget it.

W: What about the union women? Do you feel they are all behind it?

M: No, they're split. You must remember they worked hard for protective legislation. And then again most of the union hierarchy are males. They for the most part have been against it. Then a lot of the problem has been lack of education and lack of knowledge about it. I have found that in travelling across this state and in the cities. I think union women are still split about half and half on ERA. But then you must remember that it wasn't until about two years ago that the state and the national AFL-CIO endorsed ERA. Before that there were just some local individuals like myself who were for it from the beginning.

W: Tell me more about CLUW, since it's new. What is its main purpose and how did you get involved?

M: I have some information here—I usually have about 50 million pieces of CLUW information. It was, I suppose, a natural outgrowth from what a lot of us who have been in the labor movement for years—ten to fifteen, and longer—have been talking about. It really began about four years ago. We were sitting around talking about what we could do to educate and interest women in the passage of the ERA. We began to say, look, there's one of us in this union, and one or two of us in that union, but for the most part most of our own sister members don't know anything about ERA. So let's get some together (this was before the AFL-CIO came out for it) and we had a series of meetings at the Packinghouse with women from all kinds of unions. We talked about ERA and then about a lot of other things that women didn't know about their own unions and the labor movement. We began to discuss how we have a hard time sometimes functioning within our unions—like trying to go up the ladder of executive offices.

The next year there was a conference of the Midwest women from six states. Women came from all over the Midwest, for one day only, and we were so enthused over it that somebody said, "We shouldn't stop here; we should do something more, maybe form a larger organization." About three months later there was a meeting in New York, a conference, and they were enthused too. And lo and behold, the next year CLUW was born.

For the most part here we worked out of the Packinghouse Labor and Community Center, and we planned for a convention. We expected between 2,000 and 2,500 women and, as everyone knows, over 5,000 showed up. We were caught with not enough rooms, not enough materials—really overwhelmed by the vastness of it, by the kinds of women who came and the distances they came. It was wonderful. We had put together a working document—the Blue Book. We had set up a structure, elected interim officers and a state structure. It fell to me to be the convenor for Illinois—and the puller-together for the Chicago chapter—which has had elections twice since then. Each time it's been my "misfortune" to be elected president. The 18 months before the convention I found myself going into other parts of the state, helping chapters and talking to women about CLUW. That was one of the most interesting times of my life—that opportunity to go into strange towns, and talk to strange union women that I never would have met. And of course I found some beautiful sisters and made some very good friends.

I learned a lot; I think that's what means so much. I'd always been a public employee. And even though you can read about the differences in various kinds of work and job situations, that's not the same as meeting women at work in shops and plants where they are on piecework, or time schedules, and on assembly lines where a minute or a fraction might mean two or three dollars less a day in pay. Well, you can really be at the mercy of a foreman, or a co-worker, and it pits co-worker against co-worker. Some of those situations were really foreign to me. The opportunity to work with those women and to hear their problems as opposed to what I had run into before, that has been an experience I wouldn't take anything for. Of course, driving around off the main highways on some of those little country roads, I would wonder sometimes "Why am I doing this?" but I really enjoyed it. It's been tremendous for me.

W: Does it mean more women may get into the leadership of the unions because of this?

M: Oh yes. At first many of the men took it as a joke—but it is no longer a joke. Some are still apprehensive about it; some resent it. I think that for the most part down deep they are overjoyed and welcome it. A friend of mine in the Textile Workers Union at first wouldn't let any of his women even talk about it; he said, "No, no, no." But by a devious method I got a couple to one of our meetings and one ran for steward. He told me just a couple of months ago that she had made one of the best stewards they had. But he still said, "Pretty soon she'll be wanting to run for my job." And I said, "Well, if she's qualified, let her run!"

W: Are there more women members in many of these unions?

M: Oh yes. That's the ironic thing. The majority of the membership are women. You'll find women holding jobs like secretary or grievance committee chairman. But when you talk about the president, vice president, treasurer and even secretary treasurer, no women.

W: Would the men after all these years be ready to yield that leadership?

M: No, they're not. And I respect that and I can understand it. Power is not supposed to concede anything, and I guess that is what the trade union movement is all about. It's the taking away of some of the power from the employer and giving it to the employees. So I look at it like that and I don't have any problem with it; the only thing is I think there is enough to go around and they could share a bit of it.

W: What if the women started voting for themselves?

M: That's the thing. It's just ironic. We were talking about that in this meeting hall just night before last. We were getting nostalgic and going back over a lot of situations, and one of the sisters said to me, "Well, that's one of the reasons I didn't vote for you when you were running for president, because I don't think that a woman should be president. That's a man's job." There were five of us sitting here in this very room, and we talked about how they still had certain attitudes and feelings about woman's place, how it's okay for them to be stewards, or representatives of the credit union—all the volunteers and officers of the credit union are women—but when it goes beyond that, they still have a thing about women's place.

W: What do you think accounts for that?

M: I think that perhaps for the most part some of the women are—I hate to use the word jealous—perhaps you could say a little leery and suspicious of a woman leader. I don't know why I think that, it's not only in unions, but in politics and government, which are 90 percent populated by male leaders. I'm not saying that there would not have been problems had women been the leaders, but to say that men are leaders and women are followers, I can't subscribe to that.

W: Do you think sometimes some of that is from women who are used to getting their way through manipulation, and you can't do that with another woman?

M: Yes, I think you're right there. On the other hand, I like to say that we have an inherent honesty. I do believe that we're a little shade, a mite more honest than men.

W: To go to another aspect of all this, how do the women divide in the large CLUW meetings between white and black? Does there seem to be tension?

M: There are more white there than black. As to tension, let me put it this way. Various needs bring various people together. And I guess people in unions don't have as much trouble because we have another need that transcends our differences. We all work together, and we all want equal pay, better conditions and standard rates. Now we can get out on the street and fight about some other things, but not in the unions. There are differences, but for the most part the people in unions are liberal in their thinking; the whole trade union movement began with forward-thinking people.

W: But are they sexist?

M: Very. Believe it or not, they are much less racist than they are sexist. Much less. If you're black and you're a woman, you've got a pretty, pretty hard way to go—it can get really rough. For men, there isn't as much problem with racism. I think politics also is much less racist than sexist. I've some experience with this. A number of years ago where I worked, a man took over as lobbyist in Springfield, and then there was a young girl, white, right out of college. Then the next year I was sent down to Springfield, and announced "I am the lobbyist." So I was going to various legislative hearings and committee meetings, and I tell you, for about nine or ten months I had to spend two to three days a week in Springfield. That was the most horrendous experience I have ever had in my life. It was terrible.

W: Didn't they listen to you?

M: Well, yes—and no. Sometimes they listened and they weren't hearing what I was saying. Sometimes they listened and even heard, with a smirk, and even when they did hear they didn't seem convinced. And there were other things. I remember one of our legislators who I asked for a special meeting in his office on a particular bill. I was real proud because I had helped write that bill and we were very, very interested in it. When I had sat down, he peeked over his desk at me, and he said, "Well, now, why don't we talk this over at dinner where there is no . . . " And I said, "Well, I'm here now, why can't we talk now?" That is just one instance, but it happened over and over again. And of course when I'd leave in the evenings, the only place I could go was to my hotel room; I just couldn't venture out socially. It was really a bad situation and I was happy to get out of it. There was resentment when I would go down on the floor, with my attache case, thinking I was wheeling and dealing, but you could cut that resentment with a knife. Anyhow that experience in Springfield is something I wouldn't want to repeat.

W: Now that you have CLUW, have you noticed more participation by women?

M: Yes. women are speaking up more. Women who never said anything are even speaking up for ERA. Another woman who had never opened her mouth was on her feet the other night urging her fellow members not only to support the farm workers' union, but to give them money. Yes, I do think that women are not just learning what their union rights are, but they are becoming willing to use them, even to say what they think.

W: Even to the point of voting for more women?

M: I hope so, I hope so. That has to come in the future.

Barbara Merrill, a mother and grandmother, formed, with others, the Local 2000 of the American Federation of State, County and Municipal Employees (AFSCME), and has served as vice president and president. She is presently president of Chicago's Coalition of Labor Union Women, and has been chosen as an outstanding national female trade unionist in 1973 by the Coalition of Black Trade Unionists, Chicago Chapter, and in 1975 by Operation PUSH.

THE ERA IN ILLINOIS

Charlotte Hunter Waters

My secret fantasy is to tell stories to my grandchildren and great-grandchildren about how the women of my generation fought and *won* for them the uphill struggle for equality. Just as it is hard for us to imagine in 1976 that women have only had the right to vote for 56 years, so too, I imagine, it will be inconceivable to our grandchildren that the women of the seventies were not the legal equals of men. Because it takes a long time for some seeds to germinate, I may be overly optimistic in predicting that our grandchildren will reap the benefits of today's struggle. But I feel very privileged to have been part of this struggle and I can think of no other period of this century in which I would rather have lived.

The struggle for ratification of the Equal Rights Amendment (ERA) has been the catalyst for most of the other pieces of legislation to improve the legal status of women. This essay is a description of the events related to Illinois' struggle to pass the ERA. The purpose is not to suggest that others would trace the legislative and political development of Illinois women in exactly the same way; it is, rather, my interpretation, as a lobbyist for women's rights, of the factors which influenced the legal status of women in this state.

The passage of the ERA in March 1972 by the U.S. Congress coincided with my move to Springfield, the state capital. I had been a member of the National Organization for Women (NOW) for about four months and soon became involved in lobbying for the ERA. I had never lobbied before and knew very little about the legislative process. I learned by watching and talking to others, by trial and error, and by learning everything I could about the political makeup of the General Assembly. At the time the Senate was ruled by Democrats, while Republicans controlled both the House and the executive branch.

The most shocking revelation to me was the gross underrepresentation of women in state government. The Illinois General Assembly was a male fortress, as were the legislatures in the remaining 49 states. Illinois had only four women (1.7 percent) legislators; three in the House and one in the Senate. In retrospect, I consider the great underrepresentation of women as the major factor affecting not only the ERA but other women's rights bills as well.

Female lobbyists were as rare as women legislators. Politics was considered the business of men and all traditional barriers were blocking our way. These barriers included not only the sexual composition of the state legislature, but also the attitudes of the male legislators toward women. Rep. Tom Hanahan (D,33rd district) called the ERA supporters "brainless, braless broads." He is currently under indictment, accused of providing special favors for an auto leasing firm.

In addition, women were only loosely organized, as the second wave of feminism was just beginning to develop momentum. Business and Professional Women (BPW), long active in the fight for an equal rights amendment, had been instrumental in having the amendment passed in the U.S. Congress, but NOW was the most active national organization working on the local level. Other, more traditional groups such as the League of Women Voters (LWV), American Association of University Women (AAUW) and the Young Women's Christian Association (YWCA), while giving ERA workers varying degrees of support, only became active as organizations later. As a result, lobbying for the ERA was conducted mainly by NOW volunteers. We were inexperienced, sterotyped, broke and lacked political power. In short, we were a minority.

Against this backdrop, identical ERA ratification bills (HJRCA13 and SJRCA62) were introduced in the House and Senate in April 1972. The major sponsors were Rep. Eugenia Chapman (D, 3) and Rep. Giddy Dyer (R, 41) in the House and Sen. Esther Saperstein (D, 11) in the Senate. Each bill had a majority of each house listed as co-sponsors. Many of the legislators, however, had not made up their minds as to how they would vote on the issue. For most, it was a low priority. Initially, I was very angry because the majority of them considered insignificant what I saw as a matter of basic human rights. Their attitude seemed to be: "Isn't this cute. Women up in arms again!" Their arguments against ERA ranged from "Women need to be protected, taken care of, loved" to "You already have more rights than men."

On May 3, 1972, the Senate Executive Committee recommended "do pass" for SJRCA62 by a vote of 12 to 1 with 6 answering present. Later that day, the House Executive Committee refused to hear

HJRCA13; the chairman, Rober Juckett (R, 4), was violently opposed to the ERA. He ruled that taking action on the bill was unconstitutional at that time. His rationale for this ruling was based on a provision in the Illinois Constitution of 1970 which stated that the legislature could not act on any proposed amendment to the United States Constitution unless a majority of the members had been elected after the proposed amendment was submitted for ratification. I did not realize that this was only the first of many such tactics which would be used against us.

Approximately 100 women had traveled to Springfield that day, many to testify for the ERA. They were disappointed and angry because the bill was not going to be allowed a hearing in the House Executive Committee. We immediately brought this to the attention of the GOP leadership and other influential Republicans. Later that evening, after Chairman Juckett had received communications personally from Speaker Robert Blair and Governor Richard Ogilvie, he informed the committee that action could be taken if the committee so desired. Thus, our first lobbying effort had succeeded. Juckett angrily turned over the gavel to the vice chairman, Rep. Frank North (R, 34) and stomped out of the hot committee room. The bill (HJRCA13) was then voted out without any testimony being heard, with only two dissenting votes being cast—Henry Hyde (R, 18), now congressman from the 6th Congressional District and George Hudson (R, 41).

With both ERA bills having been voted out of the respective Senate and House committees, the next action was on the House floor. On May 16, 1972, HJRCA13 failed in the House by a vote of 75 to 69, with 34 answering "present." In the vote, 21 legislators who had promised to vote "yes" either voted "no" or did not vote. Since 89 votes were needed to pass the bill, it was clear that had these 21 persons voted "yes" the bill would have passed.

In the Senate, SJRCA62 was passed on May 24, 1972, with a vote of 30 to 21 and 7 not voting. SJRCA62 was then sent to the House; on June 15, 1972, the Senate bill failed by 7 votes on the House floor. What happened to those 7 votes? There were many answers given, some plausible and some very far fetched. The most believable answer—and perhaps the most complex—had to do with the struggle going on at the same time between U.S. Senator Adlai Stevenson and Mayor Richard Daley of Chicago over leadership of the Illinois delegation to the 1972 Democratic Convention in Miami. The mayor, in his typical way, was using every means possible to influence the delegates to vote for him as chairman. Pressures were being brought to bear upon delegates and non-delegates alike in the General Assembly. Rep. Chapman and 10 or 12 other independent type Democrats were actively supporting Sen. Stevenson for the chairmanship.

Even though Daley was to win the leadership of the delegation (which was later unseated by the Singer-Jackson delegation in Miami,those who had the audacity to oppose him would have to be punished. Whether it was Daley's decision or that of loyal followers remains unknown. In any event, Democratic Minority Leader Clyde Choate (D,59), his downstate bloc and several Cook County regulars backed off on their commitments to vote for the ERA.

After the vote, a motion was quickly made by Rep. Giddy Dyer (R, 41) to place the bill on "Postponed Consideration" and her motion passed 93 to 50. We had hoped that 7 votes could be acquired from the lame ducks of the November 1972 election in time for the November 26, 1972 session. However, we were unable to accomplish this goal and for all practical purposes the ERA was a moot issue for 1972. The proponents concentrated all their efforts on the upcoming November elections.

I had learned many tricks of the trade in a very short time. I found out, for example, that timing was key to victory. I quickly found that certain other factors greatly affected passage of a bill. These included sponsorship, opposition and presentation of the facts. But the greatest lesson was one of numbers—we simply needed to elect more women and men who would support women's rights issues.

During the election, some gains were made. Eleven women were elected to the 78th General Assembly; 3 in the Senate and 8 in the House. Illinois, however, still had only 4.9 percent women in the legislature. One of the women elected, Mary Lou Kent (R, 48), was opposed to the ERA, although she was not opposed to all issues pertaining to women's rights.

As a consequence of the November 1972 election the constitutional issue that had been raised earlier as a barrier to passage in 1972 no longer existed. But another constitutional problem had arisen to take its place, the question of the number of votes required to pass the ERA. Three alternatives existed: three-fifths (107) of those elected, a majority (89) of those elected or a majority of those present and voting. New House rules were adopted for the 78th General Assembly; House Rule 42 stated that no resolution proposing an amendment to the state or federal constitutions could pass except upon the affirmative vote of three-fifths of the members. In addition the Democrats had lost control of the Senate; the Senate committees were now in the hands of some very conservative Republicans. These two factors played a major role in what was to happen to the ERA and other women's bills in 1973.

Once again, on February 28, 1973, identical ERA ratification bills (HJRCA14 and SJRCA13) were introduced in the respective houses by Dyer, Chapman and Saperstein. The very next day, March 1, 1973, NOW officially opened the first statewide office for ratification of the ERA in Springfield. (ERA Central, a clearing house, had been established in Chicago.) Carol Dornan was hired as a part-time staff person and I became state legislative coordinator for NOW. My responsibilities, among various administrative tasks, were to lobby, to act as a link between sponsors of the ERA bill and proponents of the proposed amendment both within and without the state and to write press releases. I edited our weekly newsletter, the *Capitol Alert.* I also provided the typewriter!

The first issue of *Capitol Alert* reported that 28 states had ratified the ERA; it also reported that a sudden and somewhat unexpected formation of anti-ERA coalitions had begun to form across the United States. The mounting anti-ERA drive was headed by Happiness of Woman (HOW), the League of Housewives and AWARE (American Women are Highly Endowed). A leader of the anti-ERA forces, Phyllis Schlafly, a right-winger associated with the John Birch Society, argued that the ERA was a Communist-inspired plot. Ironically, the Communist Party platform opposes the ERA. Schlafly's organization, "Stop ERA," is located in Alton, Illinois, but is national in scope. We now knew that we had a fight on our hands and that it was time to take off our "white gloves" and put on "boxing gloves." Time was to reveal, however, that we still had neither the training nor the power behind us to win the first round.

The House Executive Committee voted HJRCA14 out of committee "do pass" on March 22, 1973, by a narrow margin, 13 to 11. The question of the number of votes required by the House to pass the ERA became critical at this point. The sponsors attempted to change the house rule, but failed. The sponsors knew that they had 89 plus votes and hoped that they could muster the 18 more votes needed for passage. They called for a vote on HJRCA14 and it was defeated: 95 "yes," 72 "no," 2 "present" and 8 not voting.

The sponsors decided not to place the bill on "Postponed Consideration" as they had done in 1972. Their rationale for this strategy was that they would seek a mandatory injunction directing House Speaker Blair to sign, authenticate and certify the passage of the ERA. This action could be taken only if the bill had been defeated. A suit was then filed in the U.S. District Court for the Northern District of Illinois. The plaintiff's argument was that Article XIV, Section 14 of the Illinois Constitution, which Juckett had used, and House Rule 42, which required a three-fifths majority for passage, were null and void and of no legal effect by reason of their contravention of the U.S. Constitution.

That same afternoon, April 4, 1973, SJRCA13 was voted "do not pass" in the Senate Executive Committee by a vote of 14 to 7. Determined not to give up, we began a campaign to override the Senate committee action.

The first Illinois ERA coalition was formed, its first meeting on April 14, 1973. The League of Women Voters (LWV), Illinois Nurses

Association (INA), Common Cause (CC) and the Illinois Education Association (IEA) met with NOW to set a grassroots campaign into operation in 17 target districts. Other organizations which pledged support to the strategy were the Business and Professional Women's Club (BPW) and the Illinois Home Economics Association (IHEA).

After an intensive three week lobbying effort, an ERA discharge vote failed by one vote on the floor of the Senate. With the lobbying assistance of the coalition, NOW tallies showed 29 "yes" votes with Senator Donnewald (D, 55) committed to casting the necessary thirtieth vote if it would make a difference in bringing the ERA out of the Senate Executive Committee.

With this assurance, Senator Saperstein had called for a discharge vote on May 3, 1973. All of NOW's vote tallies were extremely accurate, but no one could have predicted the actions of Chicago's Sen. Savickas (D, 27). The good senator was nowhere to be found. After a frantic search for Savickas, it became evident that he did not intend to vote for the ERA. We found out later that he had gone back to Chicago. With 28 votes in, and the one vote hinging on its being the thirtieth, the discharge motion failed.

There is one scene that deserves telling; it is an example of the kind of abuse women legislators often have to endure. Saperstein, in her sixties, was not near her desk when it was discovered that Sen. Savickas was missing. Standing near the president's podium, she quickly raised her hand so that she could be recognized by the presiding officer, Sen. Howard Mohr (R, 5). When he saw her hand waving in the air, he rudely ask, "Senator, do you want to go to the little girl's room or do you want the floor?" Many of the senators thought that Sen. Mohr's comments were quite funny and laughed loudly.

positive results. A total of 37 legislative proposals pertaining to women's rights were considered. Of these, 16 bills were passed by both houses and sent to the governor which he signed on August 26, 1973. This was indeed progress; during the prior 77th General Assembly a total of 28 pieces of legislation pertaining to sex discrimination were introduced and of these only one received the necessary votes for passage in both houses.

The official closing of the NOW-ERA office in Springfield coincided with the beginning of the legislature's summer recess on June 30, 1973. We immediately began fund raising; it was obvious that we needed money if we were to continue our fight. Our opponents were heavily financed and we had a total of only $265.00.

I remained state legislative coordinator for NOW through May 1974, although I had moved to Champaign, Illinois. I was now a full-time student at the University of Illinois and no longer had the time to devote to lobbying. Moreover, I was exhausted both physically and mentally. I felt a great need to be less involved with the women's movement and particularly to be less a part of the rigors of Springfield. Ginny Chanda took over my job in Springfield as NOW's ERA consultant and editor of *Capitol Alert.*

Many factors affecting the status of women in Illinois during this period evolved around the growing number of women who had become actively involved in lobbying at both the state and federal levels. More and more women's organizations began to join in the fight. Coupled with the gains in the state legislature, this increased commitment prompted male legislators to take women's bills a little more seriously.

Dyer and Chapman introduced HJRCA32 (ERA) on April 24, 1974. Their intention was to get the resolution on the House calendar, pending a decision in the court suit filed in the spring of 1973. At the end of May, the long awaited ruling was handed down. The federal three judge panel ruled "that the issue which is now presented is not justiciable because it is not ripe for review," primarily because no Senate vote had been recorded in 1973.

The main roadblock to passage of the ERA was then still in the Senate with the Republican leadership and Executive Committee. Sen. Harris (R, 38), president of the Senate, now candidate for secretary of state, indicated that he would not even let the ERA get to the Senate floor. On June 18, 1974, after a battle to get the resolution discharged from committee which failed to get the necessary 30 votes, Saperstein recalled the ERA resolution from its status of "Postponed Consideration" for a vote on passage. The vote was: 30 "yes," 24 "no," 1 abstention and 4 absent.

The ERA resolution once again received a majority vote as it had in 1972. It had passed so we thought. However, Harris, in contravention of Senate Rule No. 6, ruled that a three-fifths majority was required for adoption of SJRCA68. Due to this ruling, the ERA resolution was ruled "not adopted." We had come so close only to fail again through a leadership ruling.

In light of the Senate vote and its impact on a possible court decision, the House sponsors decided not to call HJRCA32 for a vote. At this point, two ERA resolutions had received majority votes in both houses. With history repeating itself, ERA proponents once again began making plans for the November elections. In the election fifteen women were elected to serve in the 79th General Assembly. And, for the first time in many years, the Democrats had control of both houses and the executive branch. All signs pointed to a successful year for ERA and for women's rights legislation.

The ERA was again victorious in the House, receiving a vote of 113 to 62; but it failed to get out of the Senate Executive Committee. For the first time, however, sponsorship of the ERA changed hands. Sen. Esther Saperstein gave up her seat in the Senate to become an alderwoman in Chicago; Senate President Cecil A. Partee (D, 26) became the new sponsor. Ratification of the ERA seemed imminent—but once again politics intervened.

Ratification of the ERA had been stalled in the Senate for more than a year when 10,000 ERA supporters from 30 states staged the biggest and best organized rally in Springfield on May 15, 1976. It was the first national rally supporting the ERA and the largest rally in the history of the women's movement. As I stood in front of the Capitol, watching my two young daughters march with thousands of other supporters, tears of joy came to my eyes. I remembered when there had been only a handful of us converging on these steps. It was one of the highlights of my life. The rally effort brought new experiences, new skills, new people and new hope into the struggle for equality. The rally brought together labor unions, church groups, civil rights groups, professional associations and campus organizations. It received attention from the national electronic media and coast to coast newspaper coverage.

But despite the success of the rally, Senate sponsor Partee was forced by lack of votes to make the following statement on June 25, 1976:

This issue will pass one day. Today is not the day. But it will pass because it's right, it's proper, and it lessens and destroys one of the eating cancers of America—discrimination.

Later, on June 30, he responded to the telegrams, mailgrams and other missives from people around the state. In a letter about his posture on the ERA he said,

But let me tell you realistically what our real problem was. There are many, many people in this nation, and particularly in this state, who are diametrically opposed to passage of the ERA. I can understand some of it because it is based on a lack of knowledge of what the amendment really does. There have been many distortions as to what this amendment would provide. There are many very active groups who are indeed opposed to ERA.

I was always told that there is no sense in becoming a loser when you know in advance that you are going to lose. This decision to not call the resolution ...was jointly made by all the great and strong proponents in the House whose resolution it was, and by the great and strong proponents of the resolution in the Senate.

While it is true that there are "many active groups" who are opposed to ERA, there are many "behind the scenes" reasons for the losing situation which cannot—by necessity—be told in total today. Some obvious reasons are as follows:

Until 1974, when Rep. Celeste Stiehl (R, 57) was appointed assistant minority leader of the House Republicans, no woman had ever held a leadership position in either house.

Few women have ever chaired legislative committees.

Women make up only 5.5 percent of the membership in the legislature.

Mayor Daley has not lent the full weight of his support to the issue.

Lies and distortion have been spread by Phyllis Schlafly's "Stop ERA" group.

Opposition by some groups within the Catholic Church has been intense.

Labor has not supported the issue as it should; for example, Rep. Hanahan has been labor's spokesman in Springfield. An early rumor also claimed that George Meany opposed ERA, although the AFL-CIO later came out in support.

The "great and strong proponents" in both houses must endure verbal harassment and broken promises of support.

In view of these obstacles, it is almost miraculous that the sponsors have been able to increase the vote in the House from 75 "yes" votes in 1972 to 113 votes in favor of the ERA in 1975. The women of this state owe a large debt of gratitude to the dedicated sponsors who have fought so courageously against formidable odds. Only they can adequately describe the frustration, loneliness and political disadvantages that have been forced upon them by this still unwon battle.

To date, 34 states have ratified the Equal Rights Amendment. Four more states are needed before 1979. When will Illinois' day come? I do not know. Neither do I have any clear cut prescriptions for victory. Women have made some gains—but not nearly enough to achieve legal equality. The 1976 report of the Illinois Commission on the Status of Women gives details of the blatant discrimination which still exists against women in many areas. In fact, it appears that Illinois women are losing ground in some phases of our fight for equal rights. We can only hope that the women of the seventies have laid a strong foundation upon which future generations can build the power needed to improve the situation of all women.

I cannot help but wonder how many generations it will take before the "end" of this story can be written.

Charlotte Hunter Waters is Director of Research and Affirmative Action Officer at Triton Community College, River Grove, Illinois. In 1975, Sen. Cecil A. Partee appointed Charlotte Waters to the Illinois Commission on the Status of Women. She was recently elected a member of the Board of Directors of the National Commissions on the Status of Women.

CHAPTER NOTES

Introduction
1. Mary Burtschi, *Vandalia: Wilderness Capital of Lincoln's Land* (Vandalia: Little Brick House, 1963). pp. 141-144.

Chapter 1
1. Julia Cooley Altrocchi, *Wolves Against the Moon* (New York: Macmillan, 1940), p. 37. The word "squaw" is an anglicized form of an Algonkian Indian word meaning "woman." The word has been widely used to describe an Indian woman, but in general usage has come to have derogatory implication no longer in good repute, such as "squaw-man," as an effeminate person.
2. Mitford Matthews, *A Dictionary of Americanisms on Historical Principles,* 2 vols. (Chicago: University of Chicago Press, 1951), 2:1627.
3. De Gannes, "Memorial Concerning the Illinois Country," published at Montreal, Oct. 20, 1721, p. 24 (also attributed to Desliette).
4. Eve Zaremba, *Privilege of Sex* (Toronto: House of Anansi Press Ltd., 1974), p. 11ff.
5. W. Vernon Kinietz, *The Indians of the Western Great Lakes, 1615-1750* (Ann Arbor, Mich.: University of Michigan Press, 1940), p. 166.
6. Kinietz, pp. 33, 203; James Axtell, "The White Indians of Colonial America," *William and Mary Quarterly* Jan. 1975, pp. 85, 68; De Gannes, p. 18. Axtell writes of colonial America; what he says would be somewhat less true of the frontier where animosity between Indian and white had been heightened.
7. Otis T. Mason *Woman's Share in Primitive Culture* (New York: D. Appleton Co., 1910), pp. 117-119. Indian babies when carried on the mother's back faced away from the mother and were swaddled. Today's back carriers for infants and small children give them some freedom of movement and they can face forward or backward.
8. Juliette A. Kinzie, *Wau-Bun "The Early Days" in the Northwest* (Chicago: The Caxton Club, 1901), p. 274; *Wau-Bun* was actually written in 1856.
9. Kinietz, p. 185.
10. George Smith, *History of Illinois and Her People* (New York: American Historical Society, 1927), vol. 1, p. 54.
11. Milo M. Quaife, ed., *Early Days of Rock Island and Davenport,* (Chicago: Lakeside Press, 1942), pp. 87-88; see the narratives of J.W. Spencer and J.M.D. Burrows.
12. Florence Gratiot Bale, *Galena's Century Milestone* (Galena, Ill.: Bale's Drug Store, 1927), p. 5; "Galena and Its Lead Mines," *Harper's,* May 1866.
13. Axtell, pp. 56-63, 85ff.
14. Milo M. Quaife, *Checagou from Indian Wigwams to Modern City, 1673-1835* (Chicago: University of Chicago Press, 1933), p. 144.
16. Kinzie, p. 190.
17. Elizabeth Ellet, *Pioneer Women of the West* (New York: Charles Scribner, 1852), pp. 192-214.
18. Lucius M.S. Zeuch, ed., *History of Medical Practice in Illinois* (Chicago: The Book Press, 1927), pp. 132-133; Ellet, p. 49ff; Bale, p. 5. The story does not end happily; Dr. Muir died suddenly and his estate was complicated by litigation. Mrs. Muir returned to her tribe's reservation with her children, where she died.
19. Edward F. Dunne, *Illinois: The Heart of the Nation* (Chicago: Lewis Publishing Co., 1933), 1:50.
20. Natalia Marie Belting, *Kaskaskia Under the French Regime* (New Orleans: Polyanthos, 1975), p. 13.
21. Irvin Piethmann, *Indians of Southern Illinois* (Springfield, Ill.: Charles C. Thomas, 1955), pp. 99-100, 101; Quaifte, *Early Days,* p. 45.

22. Virgil Vogel, "Indian Place Names in Illinois," *Illinois State Historical Society Journal*, 55 (1962), 31, 80.
23. W.H. Carpenter and T.S. Arthur, eds. *History of Illinois from Its Earliest Settlement to the Present Time* (Philadelphia: J.B. Lippincott and Co., 1857), p. 167.
24. W.V. Kinietz and Ermine Voegelin, eds., *Shawnee Traditions* (Ann Arbor, Mich.: University of Michigan Press, 1939), p. 12.
25. Edward T. James, Janet Wilson James and Paul S. Boyer, eds., *Notable American Women*, 3 vols. (Cambridge, Mass.: Harvard University Press, Belknap Press, 1974), 1:xxii.
26. Marion T. Gridley, *American Indian Women* (New York: Hawthorne Books, Inc., 1974), p. 11.

CHAPTER 2

1. Emerson Hough, *Passing of the Frontier: A Chronicle of the Old West* (New Haven, Yale University Press, 1918), p. 134.
2. Jack Eblen, "An Analysis of the 19th Century Frontier Population," *Demography*, 2 (1965), 400; less than 2 is transfrontier, more than 6, post frontier.
3. Natalia Marie Belting, *Kaskaskia under the French Regime* (New Orleans: Polyanthos, 1975), p. 40. Belting gives the best description of life in Illinois during the French period.
4. Arthur Clinton Boggess, *The Settlement of Illinois, 1778-1830* (New York: Books for Libraries Press, 1908), p. 190.
5. Robert E. Riegel and Robert G. Athearn, *America Moves West* (New York: Holt, Rinehart and Winston, 1930), pp. 518-519.
6. William W. Fowler *Woman on the American Frontier* (Hartford: S.S. Scranton and Co., 1878), p. 192.
7. Emely Gear Hobbs, in the *Illinois State Historical Society Journal*, 67:4 (1974), pp. 611-714. Before she died, Hobbs picked the person she wanted to be the mother of her children; her husband returned to the East and married Hobbs' choice.
8. William Forrest Sprague, *Women and the West: A Short Social History* (Boston: Christopher Publishing House, 1940), p. 49.
9. Christiana Holmes Tillson, *A Woman's Story of Pioneer Illinois* (Chicago: Lakeside Press 1919), pp. 140-142. Tillson also gives details of the efforts required for making soap, laundering, candle making and many other onerous tasks that fell to frontier housewives. She also describes the differences between settlers originally from the South and from the Northern immigration routes.
10. Belting, p. 60 The high price of slaves is deemed evidence of their being "comparatively well treated."
11. Martin Litvin, ed., *Voices of the Prairie Land* (Galesburg, Ill.: Mother Bickerdyke Collection, 1972), 1:165.
12. Hermann Muelder, *Fighters for Freedom* (New York: Columbia University Press, 1959 1959), pp. 174, 182-184.
13. Earnest E. Calkins, *They Broke the Prairie* (New York: Charles Scribner's Sons, 1937), p. 225.
14. Litvin, 1:167-168.
15. Mary Burtschi, *Vandalia: Wilderness Capital of Lincoln's Land* (Vandalia, Ill.: The Little Brick House, 1963), p. 75.
16. Sprague, pp. 73-74.
17. C. Hall Nelson, ed., *We, The People of Winnebago County* (Mendota, Ill.: Wayside Press, 1975), p. 15.
18. Ray Allen Billington, *America's Frontier Heritage* (New York: Holt, Rinehart and Winston, 1966), pp. 216, 65.
19. Harriet Martineau, *Society in America* (New York: Doubleday, 1968), p. 292.
20. Milo M. Quaife, *The Development of Chicago, 1674-1914* (Chicago: Caxton Club, 1916); Lucius M.S. Zeuch, ed., *History of Medical Practice in Illinois* (Chicago: The Book Press, 1927), 1:160.
21. Odillon B. Slane, *Reminiscences of Early Peoria, Including Indian Stories*, privately printed, 1933 (available at Newberry Library, Chicago, Illinois).

22. Mary Austin, *Earth Horizon* (Boston: Houghton Mifflin Co., 1932), p. 8.
23. Jane Ridgeway, "A Retrospection," privately printed available at Docker Museum, Shawneetown, Illinois.
24. Zeuch, 1:260-261.
25. Elizabeth Woodson Farnham, *Life in Pririe Land* (New York: Aron Press, 1972), p. 168.
26. Eblen, p. 412.
27. John Woods, *Two Years Residence on the English Prairie of Illinois* (Chicago: R.R. Donnelly and Sons, 1868), p. 167.
28. Sprague, p. 55. A graveyard survey after the Civil War showed 50 percent more women died between 20 and 50 than men (pp. 104-5) and that the mortality rate on the far west frontier was 22.5 percent higher for women in 1859-1860. It appears to have been greater on the prairie.
29. J. Gordon Melton. *Log Cabins to Steeples: The United Methodist Way in Illinois, 1824-1974* (Nashville, Tenn. Parthenon Press, 1974), p. 6: Gallatin *Democrat,* p. 1. available at Docker Museum, Shawneetown. One informant says "more children were conceived than saved at camp meetings."
30. William Oliver, *Eight Months in Illinois with Information to Immigrants* (Newcastle-upon Tyne: W.A. Mitchell, 1843), pp. 32-34; Woods, pp. 68-77.
31. Helen Van Cleave Blankmeyer, *The Sangamon County,* (Springfield, Ill.: Sangamon, County Historical Society, 1935), p. 57.
32. Boggess, p. 43.
33. Lydia Colby, "An Elastic Sod House, "*Illinois State Historical Society Journal,* 18: 3-4 (1925), pp. 103-105.
34. Rebecca Burlend, *A True Picture of Emigration,* ed., Milo Quaife (Chicago: R.R. Donnelly and Sons, 1936), pp. 35-36.
35. Solon J. Buck, *Illinois in 1818* (Urbana, Illinois, University of Illinois Press, 1967), p. 63.
36. John W. Allen, *Legends and Lore of Southern* (Carbondale, Ill.: Southern Illinois University Press, 1963), p. 46.
37. Zeuch, I:236.
38. Zeuch, I:273.
39. Euell Gibbons, *Stalking the Healthful Herbs* (New York: David McKay Co., 1966), p. 105.
40. J.S. Haller and R.M. Haller, *The Physician and Sexuality in Victorian America* (Urbana, Ill: University of Illinois Press, 1974), p.116.
41. Boggess, pp. 210-211.
42. Burlend, p. 66ff.
43. Austin, p. 20.
44. Blankmeyer, p. 38.
45. James Gray, *The Illinois* (New York: Farrar and Rinehart, 1940), p. 175.
46. Henry McCormick, *The Women of Illinois* (Bloomington, Ill.: Pantagraph Printing and Stationery Co., 1913), p. 17.
47. Clara Moore, "Ladies Education Society of Jacksonville, Illinois," *Illinois State Historical Society Journal, 18 (1925), 196-200;* George Osborne, comp., *Brief Biographies of Illinois Women* (Springfield, Ill.: State of Illinois, 1932), pp. 17,53.
48. Catherine Clinton, "Pioneer Women in Chicago, 1833-37, "*Journal of the West,* April 1973, p. 322; Bessie Louise Pierce, *A History of Chicago,* 3 vols, (Chicago: Alfred A. Knopf, 1957), 1:270. Pierce notes that salaries for women teachers in Chicago in the 1840s were $200 a year, raised to $250 in 1847. See also Tillson, pp. 81-82.
49. McCormick, pp. 14-17. There are many stories of women who managed to placate Indians who came to their cabins when the men were away. Yet some were scalped, kidnapped or killed, while others survived and were ransomed back later.

50. William S. Hill, "Early Recollections of Steeleville," *Steeleville Budget*, May 1907. The wielder of the auger was a doctor's wife, about the year 1846. Charles Arthur Cole, *The Era of the Civil War: 1848-1870* (Springield, Ill.: Centennial Commission, 1919), p. 211.

CHAPTER 3

1. Thomas Woody, *History of Women's Education in the United States* (New York: Science Press, 1929), 1:372-373.
2. William Forrest Sprague, *Women and the West: A Short Social History* (Boston: Christopher Publishing House, 1940), p. 83.
3. "Mrs. Frances A. Wood Shimer," *Distinguished Women*, p. 202, privately printed, (available at Galesburg Library, Galesburg, Illinois.)
4. John W. Allen, *Legends and Lore of Southern Illinois* (Carbondale, Ill.: Southern Illinois University Press, 1963), pp. 198-199.
5. Emerson D. Fite, *Social and Industrial Conditions in the North during the Civil War* (New York: Frederick Ungar Publishing Co., 1963), p. 246.
6. C. Hall Nelson, ed., *We the People of Winnebago County* (Mendota, Ill.: Wayside Press, 1975), p. 55.
7. Arthur Charles Cole, *The Era of the Civil War: 1848-1870* (Springfield, Ill.: Centennial Commission, 1919), p. 212.
8. Bessie Louise Pierce, *A History of Chicago*, 3 vols. (Chicago, Alfred A. Knopf, 1957), 2:442; Cole, *Civil War, p. 85.*
9. Jean Moore, *From Tower to Tower: History of Wheaton, Illinois* (Mendota, Ill.: Wayside Press, 1974), p. 236.
10. Arthur Charles Cole, *The Irrespressible Conflict, 1850-1865* (New York: Macmillan 1934), p. 167n; the *Aurora Beacon*, April 8, 1858.
11. Ruth P. Randall *Mary Lincoln: Biography of a Marriage* (Scranton, Pa.: Haddon Craftsmen, Inc., 1953), p. 332.
12. Mary Logan, *Reminiscences of a Soldier's Wife* (New York: Charles Scribner's Sons, 1913) p. 41ff.
13. John Y. Simon, ed., *Personal Memoirs of Julia Dent Grant* (New York: G.P. Putnam, 1975), pp. 89, 125, 133.
14. Mary A. Livermore, *My Story of the War* (Hartford, Conn.: A.D. Worthington and Co., 1889) p. 141.
15. Mary E. Massey, *Bonnet Brigades* (New York: Alfred A. Knopf, 1966), p. 66; Agatha Young, *The Women and the Crisis* (New York: McDowell, Obolensky, 1959). These two books give the best overview of women in the Civil War.
16. George W. Smith and Charles Judah, *Life in the North during the Civil War* (Albuquerque, N.M.: University of New Mexico Press, 1966), p. 46.
17. Livermore, p. 587ff.
18. Fite, p. 8; Smith and Judah, p. 167.
19. Jane Martin Johns, *Personal Recollections of Early Decatur* (Decatur, ed., Ill.: Daughters of the American Revolution, 1912), p. 151.
20. Cole, *Irrepressible Conflict*, p. 357.
21. Pierce, *2:455.*
22. Young, pp. 77-80.
23. Livermore, pp. 409-462, contains the best description.
24. Edward James, Janet Wilson James and Paul S. Boyer, eds,.
Notable American Women, 3 vols. (Cambridge, Mass.: Harvard University, Belknap Press, 1974), 1:223-224.
25. Johns, p. 190; Robert Howard, *Illinois* (Grand Rapids, Mich.: William B. Eerdmans Publishing Co., 1972), p. 319.
26. William Collins, *Adams County Illinois* (Chicago: S.J. Clarke Co., 1905), pp. 291, 293.
27. Linus Pierpont Brockett, *Women's Work in the Civil War* (Philadelphia: McCurdy Co., 1867), p. 57.
28. Massey, p. 47.

29. Massey, p. 48ff; Livermore, pp. 481-482; James, James and Boyer, 1:145; Jane Hoge, *The Boys in Blue* (Chicago: Church, Goodman and Donnelly Printers, 1869), pp. 344-347. Nina Baker Brown, *Cyclone in Calico* (Boston: Little, Brown and Co. 1952) is a biography of Mother Bickerdyke.

30. James, James and Boyer, 3:221.

31. James, James and Boyer, 3:87.

32. Mary A. Newcomb, *Four Years of Personal Reminiscences of the War* (Chicago: H.S. Mills and Co., 1893), p. 13.

33. Stella S. Coatsworth, *The Loyal People of the Northwest* (Chicago: Church, Goodman and Donnelly Printers, 1869), pp. 344-347.

34. Clarissa Emely Gear Hobbs, "I am Going Too!" *Journal of the Illinois State Historical Society*, 17:4, 611-714.

35. Livermore. p. 224.

36. George Barton, *Angels of the Battlefield* (Philadelphia: Catholic Art Publishing Co., 1898), p. 186-197.

37. Livermore, pp. 217-218.

38. Coatsworth, p. 100.

39. Livermore, pp. 314-316.

40. Livermore, p. 120.

41. Massey, p. 81.

42. *Chicago Tribune*, Feb. 7, 1909, p. 10.

43. Livermore, p. 120.

44. Livermore, p. 114.

45. Livermore, p. 116.

46. Young, p. 95

47. Wood Gray, *The Hidden Civil War: The Story of the Copperheads* (New York: Viking Press, 1942), pp. 155, 138.

48. Gray, pp. 203-207.

49. Johns, pp. 184-5.

50. Thomas Eddy, "Women of Illinois," in *The Patriotism of Illinois in The Civil War*, 2 vols. (Chicago: Clarke and Co., 1865), 2.539, it is interesting to note that only 8 pages of a two volume, 1,300 page work are devoted to women.

51. Coatsworth, p. 102.

CHAPTER 4

1. Edward T. James, Janet Wilson James and Paul S. Boyer, eds., *Notable American Women*, 3 vols. (Cambridge, Mass.: Harvard University Press. Belknap Press, 1974), 1:224-225. Elizabeth Packard was also involved in the success of the 1869 acts. Committed to an insane asylum in 1860 by her minister husband for publicly and volubly disagreeing with him on a point of theology, she was released after three years. She crusaded for laws regulating the power to commit a person to an asylum as well as women's rights. See James, James and Boyer, 3:1-2; Mrs. E.P.W. Packard, *Modern Persecution: Insane Asylums Unveiled*, 2 vols. (Hartford: Case, Lockwood, Brainard Co., 1891); Mrs. E.P.W. Packard, *Marital Power Exemplified in Mrs. Packard's Trial* (Hartford: Case, Lockwood and Co., 1866).

2. Herman Kogan, "Myra Bradwell: Crusader at Law," *Chicago History*, Winter 1974-75, pp. 136, 138.

3. Harvey Hurd, comp., *The Revised Statutes of the State of Illinois, 1874*, (Springfield, Ill. Journal Co., 1874), p. 478. According to Ruth Ricketts, "First Female Law Graduate. Ada Kepley Paved the Way for Women's Rights" in the *Decatur Herald*, July 22, 1965, Kepley received a bachelor of law degree from the Union College of Law, later attached to Northwestern University.

4. Kogan, p. 138.

5. D.W. Lusk, *Politics and Politicians: A Succinct History of the Politics of Illinois from 1856 to 1884* (Springfield, Ill.: H.W. Rokker, 1884), pp. 358-359; The first woman elected to public office in Illinois was actually Amelia Hobbs of Elsah in Jersey

County. Elected justice of the peace in 1871 because a Captain Starr, a local favorite who had originally been elected, was disqualified. At the time, under state law she was not allowed to serve in that office. Cynthia A. Bunting, "Elsah's Woman J.P., *Elsah History,* 15 (April 1976), p. 7.

6. Lusk, p. 359.
7. William Forrest Sprague, *Women and the West: A Short Social History* (Boston: Christopher Publishing House, 1940), p. 97.
8. Bessie Louise Pierce, *A History of Chicago,* 3 vols. (Chicago: Alfred A. Knopf, 1957), 3:458.
9. James, James and Boyer, 2:412.
10. Arthur Charles Cole, *The Era of the Civil War: 1848-1870* (Springfield, Ill.: Illinois Centennial Commission, 1919), pp. 427-448; James, James and Boyer, 2:413. The split which formed in the late 1860's among women working for suffrage was both national and statewide. In May of 1869, Stanton and Anthony organized the National Woman Suffrage Association, the more radical of the national groups, with its newspaper, *The Revolution.* In November, the American Woman Suffrage Association with Lucy Stone, Julia Ward Howe and Mary Livermore was formed; the following year Mary Livermore edited the *Woman's Journal.* At the same time, the Chicago Sorosis, organized in 1868, also divided. The group in which Mary Livermore, Myra Bradwell and Mary L. Walker were active formed the Illinois Woman Suffrage Association. Its rival, the Universal Suffrage Association, did not last long. See Pierce, 2:456-457.
11. *Appleton's Annual Encyclopedia and Register of Important Events for 1870* (New York: D. Appleton and Co., 1871), pp. 392-393.
12. Janet Cornelius, *Constitution Making in Illinois, 1818-1870* (Urbana, Ill.: University of Illinois Press, 1972), pp. 70-71.
13. James, James and Boyer, 3:524.
14. Elizabeth Kimbell, "We Could Not Do Without the Chicago Fire," *Chicago History, 1:4 (Fall 1971),* 231.
15. Paul M. Angle, *The Great Chicago Fire, Described in Seven Letters by Men and Women Who Experienced its Horrors* (Chicago: Chicago Historical Society, 1946), p. 24.
16. Margaret Hubbard Ayer and Isabella Taves, *The Three Lives of Harriet Hubbard Ayer* (New York: J.B. Lippincott, 1975), p. 79.
17. James, James and Boyer, 1:72-224; 2:462, 3:614-615; Ishbel Ross, *Silhouette in Diamonds* (New York: Harper and Brothers, 1960), pp. 85-86.
18. James, James and Boyer, 2:286-288; Mary Field Parton, ed., *The Autobiography of Mother Jones* (Chicago: Charles H. Kerr Publishing Co., 1974).
19. J.C. Croly, *The History of the Women's Club Movement* (New York: Henry C. Allen and Co., 1898), p. 1.
20. Louise deKoven Bowen, *Growing Up with a City* (New York: Macmillan, 1926), p. 126; James, James and Boyer, 1:409-441.
21. Croly, pp. 54-59.
22. Belle Short Lambert, "The Women's Club Movement in Illinois," *Transactions of the Illinois State Historical Society,* 9(1904), 314-329.
23. Mabel E. Richmond, *Centennial History of Decatur and Macon County* (Decatur, Ill.: *Decatur Review,* 1930), p. 280.
24. Croly, p. 410.
25. Lambert, pp. 320-321.
26. Lambert, p. 317.
27. Pierce, 3: p. 496; Lambert, p. 322.
28. Pierce, 3:486-487; PEO to Adade Wheeler.
29. Lambert, p. 315; Muriel Beadle, *The Fortnightly of Chicago* (Chicago: Henry Regnery Co., 1973), p. 8.
30. Mary Earhart, *Frances Willard: From Prayers to Politics* (Chicago: Henry Regnery Co., 1973), p. 8.

31. James, James and Boyer, 3:615; for a full discussion of the way the WCTU came to terms with woman's suffrage, see Earhart.

32. Frances Willard, *A Classic Town: The Story of Evanston* (Chicago: The Women's Temperance Publishing Association, 1891), p. 365.

33. Frances Willard, *Glimpses of Fifty Years* (Chicago: H.J. Smith Co., 1889), p. 335.

34. James, James and Boyer, 3:613-618.

35. Ray Ginger, *Altgeld's America; The Lincoln Ideal Versus Changing Realities* (New York: Franklin Watts, Inc., New Viewpoints, 1973), pp. 247-248.

36. Lambert, p. 318; Dorothy E. Powers, "History of the Chicago Woman's Club" (Ph.D. dissertation, University of Chicago, 1939), p. 41.

37. Croly, pp. 62-73.

38. Lambert, pp. 324-325.

39. Lambert, p. 326; Sophonisba Breckinridge, *Women in the Twentieth Century* (New York: McGraw Hill, 1933), pp. 70-75.

40. Croly, p. 324; Pierce, 3:462.

41. Croly, pp. 384-385.

42. Abby Pariser, "History of Chicago YWCA" (Master's Thesis, Roosevelt University, Chicago, 1975).

43. Ross, pp. 85-85.

44. Lambert, pp. 320-321.

45. James, James and Boyer, 3:620. Fannie Williams was the only black member of the Chicago Woman's Club in 1895; the controversy over her membership also made her popular on the lecture circuit.

46. Hannah Solomon, *Fabric of My Life* (New York: Bloch Publishing Co., 1946), p. 82.

47. Croly, p. 429.

48. Jane Logan Brown, "History of the Springfield Family Welfare Association," *Illinois State Historical Society Journal*, 22:2 (July 1929), 299-321.

49. Solomon, pp. 92-257.

50. Allen H. Spear, *Black Chicago: The Making of a Negro Ghetto, 1890-1920* (Chicago: University of Chicago Press, 1967), pp. 23-27, 102-106; Pariser, pp. 51n, 78-81; Allen F. Davis, *Spearheads for Reform: The Social Settlements and the Progressive Movement, 1890-1914* (New York: Oxford University Press, 1967), pp. 16, 26, 70. For a discussion of how the black housing problem differed from that of immigrants, particularly that of middle class blacks, see Fannie Barrier Williams, "Social Bonds in the Black Belt of Chicago," *Charities*, 15 (Oct. 7, 1905): 40-41.

51. Elizabeth Lindsey Davis, *The Story of the Illinois Federation of Colored Women's Clubs* (Chicago [?], [1922]; Alfreda M. Duster, ed., *Crusader for Justice: The Autobiography of Ida B. Wells* (Chicago: University of Chicago Press, 1970); James and Boyer, 3:621; Fannie Barrier Williams, "The Club Movement among Colored Women in America," in *A New Negro for a New Century*, ed. J.E. MacBrady (Chicago: American Publishing House, n.d.); Louise deKoven Bowen, "The Colored People of Chicago: Where Their Opportunity is Choked--Where Open," in *Women's Work in Municipalities*, by Mary R. Beard (New York: D. Appleton and Co., 1916), pp. 184-195.

52. R.M. Brown of the Delphian Society to Adade Wheeler.

53. James, James and Boyer, 1:18; Davis, *Spearheads for Reform;* Jane Addams, *Twenty Years at Hull House* (New York: New American Library, 1960); Allen E. Davis, *American Heroine: The Life and Legend of Jane Addams* (New York: Oxford University Press, 1973).

54. Pierce, 3:495-496; Davis, *Spearheads for Reform*, pp. 70, 107; James, James and Boyer, 3:657-660; Duster, pp. 279-309.

55. John O'Grady, *Catholic Charities in the United States: History and Problems* (Washington, D.C.: National Conference of Catholic Charities, 1930), pp. 326-327.

56. James, James and Boyer, 2:370-372; Jane Addams, *My Friend, Julia Lathrop* (New York, 1935); Davis, *American Heroine*, pp. 75-76; Julia Lathrop, *The Child, the Clinic and the Court 1925);* it should be noted that Alta Hulett studied in the law office of Julia Lathrop's father, William.

196

Louise deKoven Bowen, *Growing Up with a City* (New York: Macmillan, 1926); Bowen, *Safeguards for City Youth at Work and Play* (New York: Macmillan, 1914); Mary E. Humphrey, ed., *Speeches, Addresses, and Letters of Louise deKoven Bowen, Reflecting Social Movements in Chicago* (Ann Arbor, Mich: Edwards Brothers, Inc., 1937); Anthony Platt, *The Child Savers: The Invention of Delinquency* (Chicago: Phoenix Books, 1969).

57. James, James and Boyer, 2:316-319; Dorothy Rose Blumberg, *Florence Kelley: The Making of a Social Pioneer* (New York: Augustus M. Kelley, 1966); Josephine Goldmark, *Impatient Crusader: Florence Kelly's Life Story* (Urbana, Ill.: University of Illinois Press, 1969); Maud Nathan, *The National Consumer's League, The Story of an Epoch Making Movement* (Garden City, N.Y., 1926).

58. James, James and Boyer, 1:233-235, 2:316-319; Henry B. Leonard, "The Immigrants' Protective League of Chicago, 1908-1921," *Illinois State Historical Society Journal,* 66 (1973), 270-284; Grace Abbott, *The Immigrant and the Community* (New York: Century, 1917); Abbot, "The Midwife in Chicago," *"American Journal of Sociology,* 20 (1915), 684-699; "The Chicago Employment Agency and Immigrant Worker," *American Journal of Scoiology,* 14 (1908), 289-305; Abbott, "The Treatment of Aliens in the Criminal Courts," *Journal of the American Institute of Criminal Law and Criminology,* 2 (1911), 554-567.

59. James, James and Boyer, 2:123-125, 3:693-694; Alice Hamilton, *Exploring the Dangerous Trades: The Autobiography of Alice Hamilton* (Boston: Little Brown, 1943); William Hard, "Chicago's Five Maiden Aunts: The Women Who Boss Chicago Very Much to Its Advantage, *"American Illustrated Magazine,* 62 (1906), 479, 487, 489. The maiden aunts were Cornelia DeBey, Jane Addams, Julia Lathrop, Mary McDowell and Margaret Haley.

60. Hard, pp. 481-484; James, James and Boyer, 2:462-464; Caroline Hill, comp., *Mary McDowell and Municipal Housekeeping: A Symposium* [1938], available at Newberry Library, Chicago, Ill.); Howard Wilson, "Mary E. McDowell and Her Work as Head Resident of the University of Chicago Settlement House, 1894-1904," Master's thesis, University of Chicago, 1927).

61. Davis, *Spearheads for Reform,* pp. 121-125.

62. U.S. Bureau of Census, *Eleventh Census,* 1890, vol. I., "Population" Pt. 2, lxxix, pp. 410 ff, 551-552, *Twelfth Census,* 1900, vol. II, "Population," Pt, 2, pp. cxxxi, cxli. *Fourteenth Census,* 19020, vol. IV. "Occupations," pp. 913-915. Comparisons not directly comparable due to changes in census categories, We have included changes wide enough to be meaningful.

63. These percentages have been computed from data in the *Eleventh Census,* pp. 551-552; *Fifteenth Census,* vol. V., p. 322. *Fourteenth Census,* Vol. IV, pp. 47.51.

64. Figures and percentages compiled from Eleventh Census, p. clxx; *Twelfth Census.* p. xxcii, xlii; *Thirteenth Census* 1910, vol. IV "Occupations Statistics," pp. 152 ff; *Fourteenth Census,* 1920, vol. IV, "Occupations," pp. 128, 132ff, 802, 816-817. Theresa Wolfson, *The Woman Worker and the Trade Unions* (New York: International Publishers, 1926), p. 38.

65. Mark Haller, "Urban Vice and Civic Reform: Chicago in the Early Twentieth Century," in *Cities in American History,* ed. Kenneth T. Jackson and Stanley K. Schultz (New York: Alfred A. Knopf, 1972), pp. 290-305. For descriptions of vice districts in Chicago, see Charles Washburn, *Come into My Parlor: A Biography of the Aristocratic Everleigh Sisters of Chicago* (New York: National Library Press, 1936); Lloyd Wendt and Herman Kogan, *Bosses in Lusty Chicago* (Bloomington, Ind.: Indiana University Press, 1971), pp. 282-293.

66. Elliot Brownlee and Mary M. Brownlee, *Women in the American Economy* (New Haven: Yale University Press, 1976), pp. 194-196. See also Jane Addams, *A New Conscience and an Ancient Evil* (New York: Macmillan, 1912); Charlton Edholm, *Traffic in Girls and Florence Crittenton Missions* (Chicago: The Women's Temperance Publishing Association, 1893); William T. Stead, *If Christ Came to Chicago* (Chicago: Laid and Lee Publishers, 1894), p. 252.

67. *Chicago Tribune*, June 11, 1885.
68. Wendt and Kogan, 294-295. For the relationship of blacks to vice activities see, Chicago Commission on Race Relations, *The Negro in Chicago* (Chicago, University of Chicago Press, 1922) pp. 342-348.
69. Alice Kessler-Harris, "Where Are Organized Women Workers?" *Feminist Studies*, 3 (Fall 1975), 102.
70. Harris, p. 97.
71. James, James and Boyer, 3:386-389; Barrows, p. 44.
72. Dorothy Richardson, "Trades-Unions in Petticoats," *Leslie's Monthly*, March 1903, pp. 489-500.
73. Blumberg, pp. 137-138.
74. James, James and Boyer, 2:655-656; Barrows, pp. 47-51.
75. Allen F. Davis and Mary Lynn McCree, *Eighty Years at Hull House* (Chicago: Quadrangle, 1969), pp. 34-35; see also Agnes Nestor, *Woman's Labor Leader* (Rockford, Ill.: Bellevue Books, 1954).
76. Mary E. McDowell, "A Quarter of a Century in the Stockyards District," *Transactions*, 27 (1920), 72-83; Barrows, pp. 114-119.
77. Richardson, p. 489. "Rings" refers to politics. 1900 to 1903 were the peak years for union organizing. Between 25 and 30 unions of women were formed. By 1927, only four all-women unions remained. The Illinois State Board of Arbitration estimated that in 1903 women's unions included 31,400 women in Chicago; by 1908 it was estimated that there were only 7,000 to 8,000 left. This follows the national pattern; there was an important surge in 1910 and again during the war. Barrows, pp. 58, 60-62.
78. Carolyn Ashbaugh, *Lucy Parsons: American Revolutionary* (Chicago: Charles H. Kerr Publishing Co., 1976). See also, Ginger, pp. 210-211.
79. For accounts of the strike and the course of unionization, see "Chicago at the Front," *Life and Labor*, 1 (Jan. 1911), 4-13; Chicago Joint Board, Amalgamated Clothing Workers, *The Clothing Workers of Chicago, 1910-1922* (Chicago: Joint Board, 1922). The focus on unions has obscured the role of socialist women. Documents indicating their importance at the grass roots level can be found in Mary Jo Buhle, "Socialist Women and The 'Girl Strikers,' 1910," *Signs*, 1 (Summer 1976), 1039-1051; "Strike Fund Auditor's Report," *Life and Labor*, 1 (May 1911), 159. For biographical data see Judith O'Sullivan and Rosemary Gallick, *Workers and Allies: Female Participation in the American Trade Union Movement, 1824-1976* (Washington, D.C.: Smithsonian Institute Press, 1975), pp. 38-39, 57-58; Richardson, pp. 493-494; Nestor, pp. 131-132. Because women lacked representation in the ACWA, Sarah Roznar, in 1920, organized a separate woman's local. See Barrows, pp. 82-85.
80. Martin A. Cohen, "Jewish Immigrants and American Trade Unions" (Master's thesis, University of Chicago, 1941), pp. 170-174.
81. Barrows, pp. 149-157; S.M. Franklin "Elizabeth Maloney and the High Calling of the Waitresses," *Life and Labor*, 3 (February 1913), 36-40; Nestor, pp. 157-160, 91-95, 102-104, 137, 169-170, 22-224.
82. For an account of the Women's Trade Union League, see Alice Henry, *Women and the Labor Movement* (New York: George Durand, 1923); Barrows, pp. 47-54; Mildred Moore, "A History of the Women's Trade Union League" (Master's thesis, University of Chicago, 1915).
83. James, James and Boyer, 2:181-182.
84. James, James and Boyer, 2:183-184.
85. Beadle, pp. 80-81.
86. Wilson, pp. 95-121, 130-133.
87. Nestor, p. 117.
88. Ralph Scharnaw, "Elizabeth Morgan: Crusader for Reform," *Labor History*, 14:3 (1973), 340-351.
89. Ginger, pp. 133-135; Mary Anderson with Mary N. Winslous, *Mary Anderson, Woman at Work* (Minneapolis: University of Minnesota Press, 1951), p. 6ff.

90. Ginger, pp. 244-245.
91. Robert Howard, *Illinois* (Grand Rapids, Mich.: William B. Eerdmans Publishing Co., 1972), p. 424.
92. Margaret Haley, "My Story," Papers of the Chicago Teachers' Federation, boxes 32, 33, Chicago Historical Society, Chicago, Illinois. Haley wrote numerous incomplete versions between 1910 and 1922; it is most useful for capturing the feelings and attitudes but not facts. See Hard, pp. 484-485; Mary Herrick, *The Chicago Schools: A Social and Political History* (Beverly Hills: Russel Sage Foundation, 1971), pp. 95-103.
93. Haley, "Autobiography," Jan. 23, 1912, box 32, p. 130; Herrick, pp. 106-111.
94. David B. Tyack, *The One Best System: A History of American Urban Education* (Cambridge, Mass.: Harvard University Press, 1974), pp. 264-267; Herrick, pp. 113-144; John McManis, *Ella Flagg Young and a Half-Century of Chicago Public Schools* (Chicago: A.C. McClurg and Co., 1916), pp. 144-155; George S. Counts, *School and Society in Chicago* (New York: Harcourt, Brace and Co., 1928), pp. 107-130.
95. McManis p. 120.
96. McManis, pp. 193-225.
97. V.I. Litvin, ed., *Voices of the Prairie Land* (Galesburg, Ill. Mother Bickerdyke Historical Collection, 1972), 1: 251-258; Charles Chapman, *History of Knox County, Illinois* (Chicago: Charles Chapman, 1878), pp. 713-715.
98. Kay Kamin, "School Governance by Women: The Steppingstone to Political Participation," unpublished paper, 1974, pp. 5-8, 13.
99. James, James and Boyer, 3:105-106; 2:147-148; 1:263.
100. Dee Garrison, "The Tender Technicians: The Feminization of Public Librarianship, 1876-1905," in *Clio's Consciousness Raised*, ed. Mary Hartman and Lois W. Banner (New York: Harper Torchback, 1974), p. 160.
101. Garrison, pp. 161-163.
102. James, James and Boyer, 272-273, 493-494.
103. James, James and Boyer, 1:233-235, 1:141-142, 3:423-424 see also Edith Abbott, Education for Social Work (Washington, D.C.: Government Printing Office, 1915); Arlien Johnson, "Her Contribution to the Professional Schools of Social Work,"*Social Service Review*, 22 (1948), 442-447; Helen R. Wright, "The Debt of the School of Social Service Administration,"*Social Service Review*, 22 (1948), 448-450.
104. *National Cyclopedia of American Biographies*, 55 vols. (New York: James T. White Co., 1891), 6:40.
105. James, James and Boyer, 2:473-474.
106. Edward F. Dunne, *Illinois, the Heart of the Nation* (Chicago: Lewis Publishing Co.), p. 285.
107. Florence Howe, "The Education of Women, 1970," in *The American Sisterhood*, ed. Wendy Martin (New York: Harper and Row, 1972), p. 274.
108. Lucius M.S. Zeuch, ed., *History of Medical Practice in Illinois* (Chicago: The Book Press, 1927), p. 609.
109. James, James and Boyer, 1:265-266; 3:454-455.
110. Martin Kaufman, *Homeopathy in America: The Rise and Fall of a Medical Heresy* (Baltimore: Johns Hopkins University Press, 1971).
111. James, James and Boyer, 3:454; Zeuch, pp. 441-449, 236n; Pierce, 3:488.
112. Emy Ferris, "Crusader for Children," *Illinois* Oct. 1975. p. 11.
113. Zeuch. pp. 63-66; Beadle, p. 488.
114. James, James and Boyer, 3:454.
115. Thomas N. Bonner, *Medicine in Chicago, 1850-1950* (Madison, Wisc.: American Historical Research Center, 1957, p. 62.
116. Peter Filene, *Him, Her, Self; Sex Roles in Modern American* (New York: Harcourt, Brace, Jovanovich, 1974), p. 31; Roy Lubove, *The Professional Altruist: The Emergence of Social Work as a Career, 1880-1920* (New York: Atheneum, 1969), pp. 29-33.

117. Zeuch, pp. 473-479; James, James and Boyer, 3:171-172. For a description of the Visiting Nurses Association, founded in 1889, see Helen Isabel Clarke, "Uniform Areas for Chicago City-Wide Social Agencies," (Master's thesis, University of Chicago, 1926), pp. 80-180.
118. *Daily Inter Ocean*, Oct. 28. 1892; James, James and Boyer, 3:620-621.
119. James, James and Boyer, 3:171-172.
120. Illinois Women's Press Association, *Prominent Women of Illinois, 1885-1933* (Chicago: The Association, 1932), p. 19.
121. Bonner, p. 104; James, James and Boyer, 1:468-469.
122. *Portrait and Biographical Record of Macon County, Illinois* (Chicago: Lake City Publishing Co., 1893), p. 445.
123. Ernest C. Hildner, ed., *Morgan County, Illinois; Twentieth Century*, (Jacksonville: Morgan County Board of Commissioners, 1968), p. 182.
124. Illinois Women's Exposition Board, *Illinois Woman's Work* (Springfield, Ill.: State Register Printing, 1893), p. 90.
125. James, James and Boyer, 3:311.
126. Arthur Charles Cole, "Illinois Women of the Middle Period," *Transactions*, 27 (1920), p. 213; Katherine Stahl, "Early Women Preachers of Illinois," *Transactions*, 9 (1916),. 483.
127. John O. Foster, *Life and Labors of Mrs. Maggie Newton Van Cott* (Cincinnati: Hitchcock, 1872), pp. 98-99.
128. Pierce, 3:489; James, James and Boyer, 1:320.
129. Gertrude Hill Nystrom, "Mama Married Me," unpublished manuscript, 1946; Nystrom to Adade Wheeler.
130. James, James and Boyer, 1:274-275.
131. "Sisters of Mercy," *Illinois Catholic Historical Review* 3:4 (April 1921), 339ff.
132. Pierce, 3:496.
133. James, James and Boyer, 1:589-591.
134. Robert Cromie, *The Great Chicago Fire* (New York; McGraw Hill, 1958), p. 236.
135. Pierce, 3:497; James, James and Boyer, 2:454-455.
136. Herrick, pp. 72-74; Dorothy E. Powers, "History of the Chicago Woman's Club" (Ph.D. dissertation, University of Chicago, 1939), pp. 138-139, 151, 166-169.
137. Alson Smith, *Chicago's Left Bank* (Chicago: Henry Regnery, 1953), p. 105; James, James and Boyer, 3:705-706, 1:1-2.
138. James, James and Boyer, 3:90-92, 50.
139. James, James and Boyer, 2:579-580; 1;675-676.
140. James, James and Boyer, 2:562-564.
141. Smith, pp. 21-31.
142. Elsah *Democrat*, Jan. 22, 1896.
143. James, James and Boyer, 2:577.
144. J.N. Hook, Gerald J. Rubio and Mary Henley Rubio, "Illinois Authors," *Illinois English Bulletin*, 54 (Nove-Dec.), 9-10, 44.
145. Hook, Rubio and Rubio, p. 21; James, James and Boyer, 3:52 2: 541-543.
146. Hook, Rubio and Rubio, p. 20; James, James and Boyer, 2: 336-337.
147. Hook, Rubio and Rubio, pp. 9, 34. Clara M. and Rudolf Kirk, "Edith Wyatt: The Jane Austen of Chicago?" (Chicago History, Spring, 1961, Vol. I, #3) pp. 172-178.
148. James, James and Boyer, 2: 389-390.
149. Illinois Women's Press Association, p. 20.
150. Bowen, *Growing Up with a City*, pp. 106-107.
151. Catherine Waugh McCulloch, "Chronology of the Woman's Rights Movement in Illinois, 1855-1913" (Illinois Equal Suffrage Association, 1913) leaflet on file State Historical Library. College of DuPage, *Courier*, August 14, 1975, p. 2.
152. Catherine Waugh McCulloch.
153. Grace Wilbur Trout, "Side Lights on Illinois Suffrage History," *Transactions*, 27 (1920), 94.

154. Davis *Spearheads for Reform*, pp. 194-206.
155. Trout, pp. 93-108.
156. Trout, pp. 108-116.
157. Carrie C. Catt and Nettie R. Shuler, *Woman Suffrage and Politics* (New York: Charles Scribner's Sons, 1923) p. 189.
158. *Civic Magazine*, 1915, pp. 14-15.
159. Barbara Spencer Spackman, "The Woman's City Club of Chicago: A Civic Group," (Master's thesis, University of Chicago, 1930), pp. 8-19, 20-110.
160. Harold F. Gosnell, *Machine Politics: Chicago Model* (Chicago: University of Chicago Press, 1968), pp. 148-149.
161. Frances M. Bjorkman and Annie D. Porritt, *Women Suffrage* (New York: National Woman Suffrage Publishing Co., 1917), pp. 66-67.
162. Wendt and Kogan, pp. 306-312.
163. Bjorkman, p. 66-67. Illinois ratified a few hours ahead of Wisconsin, but the bill was wrongly worded and had to be reprinted. Wisconsin, therefore, filed its ratification first with the Secretary of State in Washington, Eleanor Flexner, *Century of Struggle* (Cambridge, Mass: Harvard University Press, 1959), p. 315.
164. Trout, pp. 108-114.
165. Davis, *American Heroine*, pp. 232-295; Mrs. Joseph T. Bowen, "The War Work of the Women of Illinois," *Illinois State Historical Society Journal*, 1919, pp. 317-329.

CHAPTER 5

1. Lois W. Banner, *Women in Modern America: A Brief History* (New York: Harcourt, Brace, Jovanovich, 1974), pp. 146-154.
2. Ruth Schwartz Cowan, "The Industrial Revolution in the Home; Household Technology and Social Change in the 20th Century," *Technology and Culture*, 17 (January 1976), pp. 1-23; Heide Hartman, "Capitalism and Women's Work in the Home, 1900-1930," (Ph.D. dissertation, Yale University, 1974); Leila Houghteling, *The Income and Standard of Living of Unskilled Laborers in Chicago* (Chicago: University of Chicago Press, 1927), pp. 109-111, 116-117; Elizabeth Hughes, *Living Conditions for Small-Wage Earners in Chicago* (Chicago: City of Chicago Department of Public Welfare, 1925); J.C. Kennedy et al., *Wages and Family Budgets in the Chicago Stockyards District* (Chicago: University of Chicago Press, 1914); Galen Cranz, "Models for Park Usage; Ideology and the Development of Chicago's Public Parks" (Ph.D. dissertation, University of Chicago, 1971); David B. Tyack, *The One Best System: A History of American Urban Education* (Cambridge, Mass.: Harvard University Press, 1974), pp. 65, 177-255 Mary J. Herrick, *The Chicago Schools: A Social and Political History* (Beverly Hills: Russell Sage Foundation, 1971), pp. 171-179, 209.
3. Roy Lubove, *The Professional Altruist: The Emergence of Social Work as a Career, 1880-1930* (New York: Atheneum, 1961), p. 123; see also pp. 164, 167, 180.
4. Lubove, pp. 139-149, 173-174; Elizabeth A. Hughes and Francelia Stuenkel, *The Social Service Exchange in Chicago* (Chicago: University of Chicago Press, 1929), pp. 1-67; Helen Isabel Clarke, "Uniform Areas for Chicago City Wide Social Agencies," (Master's thesis, University of Chicago, 1926), pp. 1-11, 40-45, 83-179; Louise deKoven Bowen, *Growing up with a City* (New York: Macmillan, 1926), pp. 78-79.
5. Edward T. James, Janet Wilson James and Paul S. Boyer, eds., *Notable American Women*, 3 vols. (Cambridge, Mass.: Harvard University Press, Belknap Press, 1974), 3:423-424, 2:637-638.
6. Dorothy Powers, "History of the Chicago Woman's Club" (Ph.D. dissertation, University of Chicago), pp. 359-361, 382-383; for a good summary and analysis of the role of women's clubs in the community, in the emancipation of women, in the life of their members and the relations of the club to other associations, see Powers' conclusion, pages 370-396.
7. Mary Jean Houde, *The Clubwoman* (Chicago: Hewitt Brothers, 1970), pp. 123-124.

8. Agnes G. Gilman and Gertrude Marcelle Gilman, *Women: Makers of History* (Chicago: Eclectic Publishers, 1927), p. 150.
9. Program of the Women's World Fair, available at Chicago Historical Society; Bowen, p. 281ff.
10. Agnes Nestor, *Woman's Labor Leader* (Rockford, Ill.: Bellevue Books, 1954), pp. 222-252; Emily Barrows, "Trade Union Organization Among Women in Chicago" (Master's thesis, University of Chicago, 1927), pp. 165-179; Alice Kessler-Harris, "Where are the Organized Women Workers," *Feminist Studies,* 3 (Fall 1975), 102-106; Lois Banner, *Women in Modern America: A Brief History* (New York: Harcourt, Brace, Jovanovich, 1974), pp. 159, 221.
11. George S. Counts, *School and Society in Chicago* (New York: Harcourt, Brace, and Co., 1928), pp. 92, 227-228; Herrick, pp. 151-161, 177-190.
12. Sophonisba Breckinridge, *Women in the Twentieth Century* (New York: McGraw Hill, 1933), p. 325; Lemons, p. 49.
13. Program for Fiftieth Anniversary, League of Women Voters.
14. Barbara S. Spackman, "The Woman's City Club of Chicago: A Civic Pressure Group" (Master's thesis, University of Chicago, 1930), pp. 8, 11, 84-90, 95-110.
15. Breckinridge, pp. 257-274.
16. "Fifty Years Ago," *Chicago History,* Summer 1975, p. 119.
17. Herman Kogan and Lloyd Wendt, *Big Bill of Chicago* (Indianapolis: Bobbs Merrill, 1953), pp. 91, 105, 109, 115, 138-139, 141, 332.
18. Commission on the Status of Women, "Report on the Status of Women," State of Illinois Printing Office, 1976, p. 35.
19. Breckinridge, p. 341.
20. James, James and Boyer, 2:231-232.
21. John Clayton, *Illinois Fact Book and Historical Almanac, 1673-1968* (Carbondale, Ill.: Southern Illinois University Press, 1970) pp. 279-283.
22. Secretary of State, *Illinois Blue Book* (Springfield, Ill.: State of Illinois, 1971-1972), pp. 770-783, 104.
23. Lemons, pp. 209-225.
24. Breckinridge, p. 325.
25. Lemons, pp. 45-46.
26. Zola Grove, former state president, Illinois Business and Professional Woman's Club, to Adade Wheeler.
27. Bernice J. Guthman, *The Planned Parenthood Movement in Illinois* (Chicago: Planned Parenthood Association of Chicago Area, 1975), pp. 3-4, 6-27.
28. Illinois Women's Press Association, *Prominent Women of Illinois, 1885-1932* (Chicago: The Association, 1932), pp. 17, 43, 80; Illinois Biographical Association, *Illinois and Its Builders* (Chicago: James O. Jones Co., 1926), pp. 207, 247; Gilman and Gilman, p. 208.
29. Breckinridge, p. 341.
30. Illinois Woman's Press Association, p. 17.
31. Bernice V. Westerlund, "Illinois Experience with Minimum Wage Legislation" (Ph.D. dissertation, University of Illinois, 1943), abstract.
32. Judith Ann Trolander, *Settlement Houses in the Great Depression* (Detroit: Wayne State University Press, 1975), pp. 92-99.
33. Alice Lynd and Staughton Lynd, eds., *Rank and File* (Boston: Beacon Press, 1973), pp. 9-35, 67-89, 111-131.
34. Judith O'Sullivan and Rosemary Gallick, *Workers and Allies: Female Participation in the American Trade Union Movement, 1824-1976* (Washington, D.C.: Smithsonian Institution, 1975), pp. 49, 88.
35. Allen Davis, *American Heroine* (New York: Oxford University Press, 1973), p. 268n; William H. Chafe, *The American Woman: Her Changing Social, Economic and Political Role, 1920-1970* (New York: Oxford University Press, 1972), pp. 152-154, 155-158.

36. James, James and Boyer, 2: 476-477, 211-212.
37. Charles Van Doren, *Webster's American Biographies* (Springfield, Mass.: B. and C. Merriam Co., 1974), p. 855.
38. Karen Walsh, article in newspaper at Docker House, Shawneetown, Illinois.
39. Deborah Gardner, "Federal Housing Projects and Women's Lives," paper presented at the Third Berkshire Conference on History of Women, Bryn Mawr College, Bryn Mawr, Pa., June 1976; "Elizabeth Wood," *Who's Who in Chicago and Illinois* (Chicago: A.M. Marquis, 1950), p. 634; Carl W. Condit, *Chicago, 1930-1970: Building, Planning and Urban Technology* (Chicago: University of Chicago Press, 1974), pp. 150-157.
40. Chafe, pp. 155-158; Chafe explains the complexities and variations in women's pay.
41. Chafe, p. 154.
42. Chafe, pp. 181-183 for more details.
43. Chafe, p. 202-207.
44. Benjamin Spock, *Baby and Child Care* (New York: Pocket Books, 1968) pp. xvi, 12, 10-23, 563-564.
45. C. Christian Beels, "The Case of the Vanishing Mommy," *New York Times Magazine*, July 4, 1976, pp. 28-46.
46. U.S. Department of Commerce, Bureau of Census, *United States Population Census*, (1) D15 table 156, (1) D15 table 165; (1) C15 table 53; vol. II, pt. 13, table 70.
47. Beels, p. 28.
48. Commission on the Status of Women, "Report on the Status of Women, 1965," State of Illinois, 1965, pp. 4-8; state commissions have met in Washington, D.C. on several occasions, which has led to the establishment of an informal women's network for the exchange of information. A formal network, the National Commission on the Status of Women is now elected by the state bodies.
49. Judith Hole and Ellen Levine, *Rebirth of Feminism* (New York: Quadrangle Books, 1971), pp. 81-95.
50. Hole and Levine, pp. 47-49, 95-98, 440.
51. Secretary of State *Handbook of Illinois Government* (Springfield, Ill.: State of Illinois, 1974), p. 73; *Constitution of the State of Illinois, 1970*, sec. 17 and 18; Sixth Illinois Constitutional Convention.
52. *STOP ERA*, pamphlet.
53. See essays by Charlotte Waters and Barbara Merrill.
54. Hole and Levine, pp. 112-116.
55. Jo Freeman, *The Politics of Women's Liberation* (New York: David McKay Co., 1975), pp. 108-110.
56. Maren Carden, *The New Feminist Movement* (New York: Russel Sage Foundation, 1974), p. 67.
57. Jo Freeman, ed., *Women: A Feminist Perspective* (Palo Alto, Calif.: Mayfield Publishing Co., 1975), p. 448.
58. Brochures of the Chicago Women's Liberation Union.
59. See Hole and Levine for the development of many of these groups.
60. Rape Crisis Inc. to Adade Wheeler; Susan Brownmiller, *Against Our Will* (New York: Simon and Schuster, 1975); Mary Scott Welch, "What Every Woman Should Know About Rape," *Seventeen*, May 1975, pp. 146-147, 190.
61. *Chicago Sun-Times*, July 15, 1976, p. 61.
62. See essay by Rita Lovell Moss.
63. Federally Employed Women and Women Employed, information to Adade Wheeler.
64. See interview with Barbara Merrill.
65. Chicago Coalition on Women Employed, information supplied to Adade Wheeler.
66. Brochures of UCWI.
67. Professional Organization for Women's Rights, information supplied to Adade Wheeler.

68. The groups listed supplied information and brochures to Adade Wheeler.
69. *Chicago Tribune Magazine,* May 23, 1976, p. 6; *Chicago Sun-Times,* July 11, 1976, p. 4.
70. Catherine Samuels, "The Women's Movement Meets the Challenge of Diversity," in *Dialogue on Diversity: A New Agenda for American Women,* ed. Barbara Peters and Victoria Samuels (Chicago: Institute on Pluralism and Group Identity, 1976), pp. 60-61; Marge Albert, "The Trade Union Woman," in *Dialogue on Diversity,* pp. 52-56; Kathleen McCourt, "Grass Roots Politics and Working Class Women," paper presented at the Midwest Political Science Association Meeting, Chicago May 1975.
71. "Working Class Women in the Schools and Community—Where Are They?" Summary of Proceedings, Seminar on Expanding the Human Ties to Ethnic and Working Class Women, Institute on Pluralism and Group Identity, Chicago, May 18, 1976.
72. Babette Inglehart to Adade Wheeler.
73. Peggy Anderson, "Women's Organizations: It's a Whole New Scene," Family *Circle,* April 1976, p. 19; article treats the women's movement on a national scale. Additional information from Wheaton-Glen Ellyn AAUW, and Catholic Women for ERA groups in Elmhurst and Joliet.
74. Institute of Women Today brochure. See essay by Sister Margaret Traxler.
75. Brochures and data from these groups to Adade Wheeler.
76. *Life* Magazine, August 18, 1972, p. 58; Paul de Kruif, *The Fight for Life* (New York: Harcourt, Brace and Co., 1934), pp. 84-114.
77. Donor's Forum to Adade Wheeler.
78. J.N. Hook, Gerald J. Rubio and Mary Henley Ruio, "Illinois Authors," *Illinois English Bulletin,* 54 (Nov.-Dec., 1966), pp. 1-30.
79. Van Doren, p. 297.
80. See copies of these publications.
81. "Report on the Status of Women,"1975, p. 36. Illinois was in a group of four states at the median; the range was from 40 to 2.
82. *U.S. Census,* 1970, "Population Characteristics," 1, Section D 15, Section C 15, 171. In Illinois the percent of engineers who were women in 1950 was 1.1 and it fell to .6 in 1960.
83. *U.S. Census,* 1970, "Pupulation Characteristics," Part 15, Section 2, from table 156, computation table 198. If female head is in labor force, median income is $7,047
84. Beels, pp. 28-46; *Chicago Tribune,* October 15, 1976, IV, p. 6; Monty Hoyt, "Firms Find Day Care Helps Working Mothers," *Christian Science Monitor,* Mar. 16, 1972; for a critique of the 1960s, see Philip Slater, *The Pursuit of Loneliness: American Culture at the Breaking Point* (Boston: Beacon Press, 1971), pp. 53-90.

Bibliography

The following books are suggested as offering information and insights into the activities of Illinois women. No general book of Illinois history is listed unless more than five percent of its contents involves women and it is indexed to women. No book on women's history is included unless more than ten percent involves Illinois.

GENERAL:

Amberg, Mary, *History of Madonna Center*, Chicago, Loyola University Press, 1976.

Belting, Natalia Marie, *Kaskaskia Under the French Regime*, New Orleans, Polyanthos, 1975. Best description of this period of Illinois history, with the most about woman's role.

Barton, George, *Angels of the Battlefield*, Philadelphia, The Catholic Art Publishing Co., 1898.

Brockett, Linus Pierpont, *Women's Work in the Civil War: A Record of Heroism and Patriotism*, Philadelphia, Zeigler, McCurdy & Co., 1867.

Breckinridge, Sophonisba, *Women in the Twentieth Century*, New York, McGraw Hill Co., 1933.

Chafe, William R., *The American Woman: Her Changing Social, Economic and Political Roles, 1920-1970*, New York, Oxford University Press, 1972.

Coatsworth, Stella S., *The Loyal People of the Northwest*, Chicago, Church, Goodman and Donnelly Printers, 1869. About women during the Civil War, autobiographical.

Davis, Allen, *Spearheads for Reform: The Social Settlements and the Progressive Movement 1890-1914*, Oxford University Press, New York, 1967.

Dannett, Sylvia, *Noble Women of the North*, New York, McGraw Hill, 1958. About the Civil War.

Ellet, Elizabeth, *Pioneer Women of the West*, New York, Charles Scribner, 1852.
—*Summer Ramble in the West*, New York, J.C. Riker, 1853.

Frost, John, *Pioneer Mothers of the West*, Boston, Lee and Shepart, 1869.

Gilman Agnes G. and Gilman. Gertrude Marcelle, *Women-Makers of History*, Chicago, Electric Publishers, 1927.

Ginger, Ray, *Altgeld's America, 1890-1905*, New York, Funk and Wagnalls, 1958.

Hoge, Jane, *The Boys in Blue*, Chicago, C.W. Lilley, 1867.

Kogan, Herman and Wendt, Lloyd, *Bosses in and Lusty Chicago,* Bloomington, Ind., Indiana University Press, 1971.

Lemon, J. Stanley, *The Woman Citizen,* Urbana, Ill., University of Illinois Press, 1973. About women in the 1920's.

Lopata, Helena Z., *Occupation: Housewife,* New York, Oxford University Press, 1971.

Mason, Otis T., *Woman's Share in Primitive Culture,* New York, Appleton & Co., 1910.

Massey, Mary Elizabeth, *Bonnet Brigades,* New York, Alfred A. Knopf, 1966.

McCormick, Henry, *Women of Illinois,* Bloomington, Pantagraph Printing and Stationery Co., 1913.

Henry, Alice, *The Trade Union Woman,* Chicago, D. Appleton and Co., 1915.

Newcomb, Mary A., *Four Years of Personal Reminiscences of the War.* Chicago, H.S. Mills and Co., 1893.

Pierce, Bessie Louise, *A History of Chicago.,* 3 Vols., New York, Alfred A. Knopf, 1957.

Sochen, June, *Movers and Shakers: American Women Thinkers and Activists, 1900-1970,* New York, Quadrangle, 1973.

Sprague, William Forrest, *Woman and the West: A Short Social History,* Boston, The Christopher Publishing Co., 1940.

Terrell, John Upton and Donna M. Terrell, *Indian Women of the Western Morning,* New York, Dial Press, 1974.

Trolander, Judith Ann, *Settlement Houses and the Great Depression,* Detroit, Wayne State University Press, 1975.

Young, Agatha, *Women and the Crisis,* New York, McDowell, Obolensky, 1959.

BIOGRAPHY:

James, Edward T., Janet and Paul S. Boyer ed., *Notable American Women, 1607-1950,* 3 vols., Cambridge, Mass., Belknap Press, Harvard University Press, 1974. Indispensable, with over one hundred entries on Illinois women.

Addams, Jane, *Twenty Years at Hull House,* New York, 1910. The most important of all her many published works.

Davis, Allen, *American Heroine, The Life and Legend of Jane Addams,* Oxford University Press, New York, 1973.

Austin, Mary, *Earth Horizon,* Boston and New York, Houghton Mifflin 1932.

Ayer, Margaret Hubbard and Isabella Taves, *The Three Lives of Harriet Hubbard Ayer,* Philadelphia and New York, J.B. Lippincott, 1957.

Baker, Nina B., *Cyclone in Calico,* Boston, Little, Brown & Co., 1952. The biography of Mother Bickerdyke.

Bowen Louise DeKoven, *Growing Up with a City,* New York, Macmillan, 1962.

Burlend, Rebecca, *A True Picture of Emigration,* ed. Milo Quaife,

Chicago, R.R. Donnelly & Sons, 1936.

Farnham, Elizabeth Woodson, *Life in Prairie Land*, New York, Harper and Brothers, 1846.

Simon, John Y., ed., *Personal Memoirs of Julia Dent Grant*, New York, G.P. Putnam's 1975.

Hobbs, Emely Gear, "Vivid in my Mind" and "I am Going Too!" published by the Galena Historical Society.

Johns, Jane Martin, *Personal Recollections of Early Decatur*, Decatur, Decatur Daughters of the American Revolution, 1912.

Jones, Mary Harris, *The Autobiography of Mother Jones*, Chicago, Charles H. Kerr Publishing Co., 1976.

Kinzie, Juliette A., *Wau-Bun: The "Early Days" in the Northwest*, Chicago, The Caxton Club, 1901.

Blumberg, Dorothy Rose, *Florence Kelley: The Making of a Social Reformer*, Augustus M. Kelley, New York, 1966.

Randall, Ruth Painter, *Mary Lincoln: Biography of a Marriage*, Scranton, Pa., The Haddon Craftsman, Inc. 1953. Randall is from Urbana, Illinois.

Livermore, Mary A., *The Story of My Life, or the Sunshine and Shadow of Seventy Years*, Hartford, Conn., A.D. Worthington & Co., 1889.
—*My Story of the War: A Woman's Narrative of Four Years of Personal Experiences*, Hartford, Conn., A.D. Worthington & Co., 1889.

Logan, Mary, *Reminiscences of a Soldier's Wife*, New York, Charles Scribner's Sons, 1913.
—*Reminiscences of the Civil War and the Reconstruction*, Carbondale and Edwardsville, Southern Illinois University Press, 1970.
Edwardsville, Southern Illinois University Press, 1970.

Nestor, Agnes, *Woman's Labor Leader*, Rockford, Bellevue Books Publishing Co., 1954.

Powers, Thomas, *Diana: Making of a Terroist*, Boston, Houghton Mifflin, 1971. Biography of Diana Oughton.

Rittenhouse, Isabella Maud, ed., Richard Lee Strout, *Maud*, New York, Macmillan Co., 1939. The diary of a young girl growing up in Cairo.

Ross, Ishbel, *Silhouette in Diamonds: The Life of Mrs. Potter Palmer*, New York, Harcourt Brace, 1960.

Ashbaugh, Carolyn, *Lucy Parsons*, Chicago, Charles H. Kerr Publishing Co., 1976.

Ets, Marie Hall, *Rosa: The Life of an Italian Immigrant*, Minneapolis, University of Minnesota Press, 1970. Life around the Chicago Commons neighborhood.

Tillson, Christiana Holmes, *A Woman's Story of Pioneer Illinois*, Chicago, Lakeside Press, 1919.

Duster, Alfreda M., *Crusader for Justice: Autobiography of Ida B. Wells*, University of Chicago Press, Chicago, 1970.

Willard, Frances, *Glimpses of Fifty Years: Autobiography of an American Woman*, Chicago, The Woman's Temperance Publication Association, 1889.

WOMEN'S CLUBS:

Beadle, Muriel, *The Fortnightly of Chicago: The City and Its Women, 1873-1973*, Chicago, Henry Regnery Co., 1973. Discussion of both the Fortnightly and its members' activities.

Croly, J.C., *The History of the Women's Club Movement*, New York, Henry G. Allen & Co., 1898. Covers the nation, with a long chapter on Illinois.

Davis, Elizabeth Lindsey, *The Story of the Illinois Federation of Colored Women's Clubs*, Chicago, 1922.

Houde, Mary Jean, *The Clubwoman: A Story of the Illinois Federation of Women's Clubs*, Chicago, Hewitt Brothers, 1970.

Guthman, Bernice J., *The Planned Parenthood Movement in Illinois*, Chicago, Planned Parenthood Association of Chicago Area, 1975.

Inforwomen, *Chicago Women's Directory*, Chicago, Inforwomen, Inc., 1972. Reference of Chicago women's groups, in Spanish and English.

Most clubs have a brochure, describing their purpose and membership policies; many include a summary of major accomplishments.

FICTION:

Altrocchi, Julia Cooley, *Wolves Against the Moon*, New York, Macmillan, 1940. The story of fur traders in the Great Lakes region during the French and English periods.

Aschman, Helen T., *Connie Bell, M.D.*, New York, Dodd, Mead & Co., 1963. The story of a young woman becoming a doctor and attending the first woman's medical college in Chicago.

Barnes, Margaret Ayer, *Years of Grace*, Boston and New York, Houghton Mifflin Co., 1936. A family saga of three generations over the turn of the century, emphasizing social change and generation gaps among the upper class.

Budd, Lillian, *Land of Strangers*, Philadelphia, Lippincott, 1953. Immigrants in Chicago and northern Illinois.

Dreiser, Theodore, *Sister Carrie*, New York, Airmont Publishing Co., Inc., 1976. First published in 1900, the story of a country girl in Chicago and then New York.

Fairbanks, Janet Ayer, *The Bright Land*, New York, Houghton Mifflin 1932. The story of pioneers in the Galena region.

Gibson, Margaret Wilson, *Emma Smith: a Historical Novel of Her Life*, Independence, Mo., Herald House, 1966. The story of the wife of Joseph Smith, Mormon leader.

INDEX

Abbott, Edith, 73, 113
Abbott, Emma, 102
Abbott, Grace, 72, 119
abortion, 31, 135, 165, 171
Abortion Rights Association of Illinois, 171
Abraham Lincoln Center, 124
Addams, Jane, 70-74, 80, 83, 107, 108, 110, 115, 119, 141
AFL-CIO, 176, 188
Agitator, The, 54
Aiken, Aunt Lizzie, 44
Alderson Prison, 155
Alice B. Hamilton Medical Center, 165, 168
Altgeld, John Peter, 72
Altgeld, Emma Ford, 106
Altrua, 60
Amalgamated Association of Miscellaneous Restaurant and Hotel Employees, 77
Amalgamated Clothing Workers of America (ACWA), 81, 144
Amalgamated Meat Cutters and Butcher Workmen of North America, 80
Amanda Smith Home for Children, 68, 83
American Association of University Women (AAUW), 61, 121, 162, 181
American Civil Liberties Union, Illinois Division, 170
American Federationist, 77
American Federation of Labor, 77-78, 84, 115
American Federation of State, County, and Municipal Employees (ASSCME), 173
American Federation of Teachers, 116
American Friends' Service Committee, 162
American Jewish Committee, 153, 161
American Jewish Committee on Women, 153
American Legion Auxiliary, 141
American Library Association, 92
American Medical Association, 95, 96
American Psychological Association, 154
American Social Hygiene Association, 98
American Society of Superintendents of Training Schools for Nurses, 97
Anderson, Margaret, 103
Anderson, Mary, 81, 84, 85, 119
anti-war movement, 129
Arche Club, 60, 102
Armour Institute of Technology, 93
Asche, Kay, 154
Associated Charities, 67
Association for the Advancement of Women, 61
Austin, Mary Hunter, 104
Autumn Leaf Club, 68
AWARE, 184
Ayer, Harriet Hubbard, 57, 102

Back of the Yards Settlement House, 73, 79
Baldwin, Fannie C., 122
Barnes, Margaret Ayer, 142
Barnett, Ferdinand, 68
Bartelme, Mary, 108, 118
Bates, Mary, 96
Beecher, Catherine, 35
Bendix Aviation, 124, 127
Bennett, Helen, 115
Bevier, Isabel, 93
Bickerdyke, Mary Ann ("Mother Bicker-dyke"), 42-43, 50
birth control, 98, 121-122
Birth Control League, 122
Bixby, Anna, 31
Black Codes, 25
blacks, 24, 68, 69, 71, 73, 112, 123, 130, 140, 178
Blackhawk, 20
Blackwell, Elizabeth, 42, 95
Blair, Robert, 182, 184
Bohemian Club, 60
Bohrer, Florence Fifer, 119
Bond, Mrs. Shadrach, 28
Booth, Heather, 134, 160
Bourbonnois, Rancois, 20
Bowen, Louise de Koven, 57, 59, 69, 72, 105, 106, 112, 115
Bradley, Mary Hastings, 104
Bradwell, Bessie, 52, 57
Bradwell, Myra, 41, 52, 54, 102
Breckinridge, Sophonisba, 72, 94, 113

Breese, Sidney, 25
Brooks, Gwendolyn, 142
Brown, Caroline, 63
Brown, Katherine Holland, 104
Brown, Mary E., 97
Buckel, Cloe, 95
Budd, Lillian, 142
Bureau of Employment, 73
Bureau of Social Surveys, 73
Burlend, Rebecca, 29, 32
Burnt Records Act, 57
Business and Professional Woman's Club, 121, 185
Bytord, William, 96

Cabrini, Mother, 101
Camp Douglas, 41, 49
Candee, Isabella, 64
Candy Dippers, 77
Capitol Alert, 184, 186
Cardevaant, Lorna Taboerne, 122
Carpenter, Helen Fairbank, 122
Carr, Charlotte, 124
Carroll, Margaret, 155
Carse, Matilda, 65
Casey, Josephine, 84
Cassatt, Mary, 66
Catherwood, Mary Hartwell, 104
Catholic charities, 169
Catholic Women's League, 71
Center for Radical Research, 134
Century of Progress Fair, 125
Champaign-Urbana Women Against Rape, 136
Chanda, Ginny, 186
Chapin, Augusta, 67, 100
Chapman, Eugenia, 119, 181, 182, 183, 186
Chappel, Eliza, 33
Chautauqua plan, 60
Chekouris, Irenaeus, 143
Cheney, Flora Sylvester, 116, 119
Cherry mining disaster, 86
Chicago Area Women's History Conference, 145
Chicago Board of Education, 64, 89, 90, 91, 115
Chicago City Club, 117
Chicago Coalition on Women's Employment, 138
Chicago Commons, 124
Chicago Consortium of Women in Education Programs, 138
Chicago Council of Lawyers, Women's Rights Committee, 162
Chicago Council of Social Agencies, 122
Chicago Day Care Crisis Council, 144
Chicago Federation of Labor, 77, 87, 89
Chicago Female Guardian Association, 36
Chicago Fire, 56-57, 62, 96, 101, 102
Chicago Health Department, 98
Chicago Health Commission Advisory Staff, 123
Chicago Health Officers Association, 97
Chicago Hospital for Women and Children, 95
Chicago Housing Authority, 125
Chicago Kindergarten College, 92
Chicago Legal News, 52, 57, 102
Chicago Library Board, 67
Chicago Lying-In Hospital, 98, 141
Chicago Manual Training School, 92
Chicago Maternity Center, 141
Chicago Medical College, 101
Chicago Normal School, 90, 91
Chicago Political Equality League, 107
Chicago Relief Administration, 123
Chicago School of Civics and Philanthropy, 94, 113
Chicago State University, 140
Chicago Teachers' Federation, 86-91, 106, 115
Chicago Woman's Club, 63, 67, 79, 85, 86, 91, 99, 114
Chicago Woman's Directory, 142
Chicago Women's Liberation Union, 135, 164-165
Chicago Women's Liberation Union, Abortion Counseling Service ("Jane"), 165, 168

Chicago Workers Committee on Unemployment, 124
Chicago Working Woman's Union, 77
Chicagoland Women's Federal Credit Union, 162
child birth, Indians, 15; frontier, 28
Child Labor Amendment, 119
Child labor law (1903), 85
children, Indians, 15; frontier, 16; guardianship, 54; labor law, 85; child care, 128; child rearing, 128-129
Children's Bureau, 72
Children's Memorial Hospital, 96
Christian Science Association, 64
Christman, Elizabeth, 127
Church of Latter Day Saints (Mormons), 100
Church of the Assumption, 101
Cincotta, Gale, 139
CIO, 124
Citizen's Advisory Committe on Smoke Abatement, 123
Citizen's Advisory Council on the Status of Women, 131
Civic Music Association, 114
Civil Rights Act (1964), Tittle VII, 130
civil rights movement, 129
Clark, Catherine, 23
Clearing House International, 138
Clergy Consultation Service on Problem Pregnancy, 165
clubs, 59, 63 66, 68-69, 85, 105, 112-113, 114
Coalition of Labor Union Women, 137, 139, 160, 172-179
Coatsworth, Stella, 44, 45, 50
Collegiate Bureau of Occupations, 115
Collins, Naomi Pierce, 99
Columbus Hospital, 101
Company of New France, 19
Common Cause, 85
Confederacy, 38, 48, 49
Congdon, Maggie, 79
Connole, Martha, 121
Constitutional Convention (1870), 54
Constitutional Convention (1971), 132
Consumer Credit Project, 126
Cook County Board of Commissioners, 84
Cook County Department of Public Aid, 172
Cook County Hosptial, 96, 97
Cook County Insane Asylum, 64
Cook County Suffrage Alliance, 109
Cooper, Ethel, 122
Coughlin, Bathhouse John, 109
Council on Women's Programs, 138
Crimean War, 42, 49
Croly, Jennie June, 59, 61
Crothers, Rachel, 103
Cryer, Sadie, 100

Daley, Richard, 183, 188
Dames of theh Loyal Legion, 60
Darrow, Clarence, 78, 81
Daughters of the American Revolution (DAR), 60, 119
Davis, David, 32
Davis, Elizabeth Lindsay, 68, 69
Davis, Jefferson, 48
Davis, Mary Brown, 25
Davis, Susan, 142, 160
Dawson, Frances, 130
Day, Dorothy, 155, 158
day care, 143-144
Day Care Child Development Council of America, 144
De Bey, Cornelia, 73, 79
Decatur Woman's Club, 65
De Jesus, Sylvia, 156
Delphian Society, 69
De Rorre, Catherine, 124
Dever, William E., 118
Dewey, Grace, 99
Dewey, John, 90, 91
Dewey, Melvil, 93
De Witt, Lydia, 99
Dick, George, 99
Dick, Gladys, 99
Dilling, Elizabeth, 124
Dix, Dorothea, 42

Dixon, Marlene, 135
Doggett, Kate, 59, 61
Domestic Science Associations, 64
Donnelley, Michael, 79
Donnewald, Sen., 185
Donors Forum, 142, 163
Dornan, Carol, 184
Drake, Marion, 109, 118
dress reform, 36, 67
Du Jardin, Rosamond Neal, 142
Dunham, Katherine, 142
Dunne, Edward, 86, 87
Du Page Women Against Rape, 136
Dyer, Giddy, 119, 181, 183, 186

Earhart, Amelia, 121
Eaton, Mrs. Page Waller, 118
Edgar, Rachel, 33
education, frontier, 33; Civil War era, 35; Chicago Teachers' Federation, 86-91
Education Act of 1972, Title IX, 155, 162
Edwards, Ninian, 32
Edwards, Elizabeth Todd, 37
Eleanor Clubs, 78, 138
election campaigns, political action, 74, 87-88, 106-107, 109-110, 116-120, 180-188
Elevated Railway Employees' Union, 84
Ellis, Christine, 124
Ellis, Frances Brard, 33
Ellis Island, 104
Emma Goldman Clinic, 166
Equal Credit Opportunity Act, 162
Equal Employment Act, 153
Equal Employment Opportunity Commission (EEOC), 131, 154
Equal Pay Act (1963), 130
equal rights (women's rights), 51-54, 116, 120, 154
Equal Rights Amendment (ERA), 116, 120, 131-133, 153, 160, 175, 179, 180-188
Equal Rights Rally, 159
Equal Suffrage Association, 99, 106
ethnic groups, 74, 77, 112, 140
Evanston College for Ladies, 57, 104
Evanston Hospital, 122
Evanston Women's Liberation Union, 162
Everleigh, Ada and Minna, 76, 102

Factory Act of 1893, 85
Family Service Association, 169
farm, 40, 65
Farmer's Institutes, 64
Farnham, Marynia, 128
Federally Employed Women, Inc. (FEW), 137
Federation of Women's Clubs, 142
Feeney, Mary Ignatius, 101
Female Anti-Slavery Society, 25
Female Relief Society (of the Mormon Church), 100
Fese, Marie, 160
Field, James A., 122
Finger, Donald, 157
Firestone, Shulamith, 134
Fitzpatrick, John, 77
Flower, Lucy, 92, 112
Flowers, John, 31
Fort Dearborn Massacre, 18
Fortnightly, 63, 99
Frank, Henriette Greenebaum, 67
Frederick Douglass Center, 70
Freeman, Jo, 134, 135
Friedan, Betty, 130-131
Friends in Council (Quincy), 59
Frontany, Hilda, 160
frontier, definition of, 21-23
Fuller, Loie, 103
Furgeson, Mrs., 29

Gabrie, Mary, 101
Gaines, General, 20
Gallaton, Housing Authority, 125
Ganeer, 20
Gannon, Ann Ida, 131
Garment Strike (1894), 79
Garment Strike (1910), 81-82

General Federation of Women's Clubs, 63, 64, 83, 98, 121
Gillespie, Angela, 45
Gillies, Jean, 138
Gilroy, Faith Dean, 154
Goals for Carbondale Committe, 147
Goggins, Catherine, 86
Goldboss, Ruth, 158
Goldman, Emma, 103
Gompers, Samuel, 78
Gonzales, Mary, 163
Goode, Katherine Hancock, 119
Graham, Hannah, 32
Granges, 64
Grant, Julia Dent, 38, 45, 104
Grant, Ulysses S., 38, 42, 45
Great Western Laundries, 124
Gregory, Cinderella, 35
Griggs, Johanna, 117
Gulliver, Julia, 94

Hahnemann Homeopathic College, 95
Haines, Elijah, 54
Haley, Margaret, 86-90, 106
Hamilton, Alice B., 73, 99, 165
Hanahan, Tom, 181, 188
Hanks, Nancy, 31
Hanley, Sarah Bond, 119
Hapgood, Neith Boyce, 104
Happiness of Women, 184
Harkins, Lily, 77
Harris, William C., 186
Harrison, Elizabeth, 92
Hart, Pearl, 123
Hart, Schaffner and Marx, 81
Hartrath, Lucy, 102
Haskell, Harriet, 94
Hayden, Sophia, 66
Haymarket Riots, 80
health care, 28, 31, 164-171
Helm, Capt. Linai and Mrs., 18
Helm, Emilie Todd, 38
Henrici strike (1914), 82
Henrotin, Ellen Martin, 66, 83, 91
Henry, Alice, 83
Henry, Lily, 100
HERS, 135, 166
Hershey-Eddy, Sara, 103
Hillard, Martha, 94
Hillman, Bessie Abramovitch, 81
Hillman, Sidney, 81
Hobbs, Emely Gear, 44
Hodges, Jennie (Albert Cashier), 49
Hoge, Jane, 41, 44
Hokinson, Helen, 124
Holmes, Lizzie, 80
Holmes, Mary E., 106
home economics, 93
Home for the Friendless, 49
Hood, Helen, 106
Hook, Frances (Frank Miller), 48
Household Econmic Association, 67
Howells, William Dean, 104
Hubbard, Mrs., 100
Huefner-Harken, Mrs. H., 102
Hughes, Kate, 107
Hulett, Alta, 53
Huling, Caroline Alden, 104
Hull House, 66, 70, 71, 72, 78, 79, 80, 83, 84, 94, 98, 99, 124
   Women's Club, 72
Hudson, George, 182
Humphrey, Grace, 142
Hutar, Pat, 132
Hyde, Henry, 182

Ickes, Anna Wilmarth, 119
Ida B. Wells Club, 68
Illinois Bell Telephone Co., 144
Illinois Birth Control Commission, 122
Illinois Birth Control League, 98
Illinois Board of Health, 97, 98
Illinois Commission on Human Relations, 160
Illinois Commission on the Status of Women, 130, 162-163, 188
Illinois Department of Children and Family Services, 169
Illinois Department of Public Health, 137

Illinois Education Association, 184-185
Illinois Federation of Republican Women, 132
Illinois Federation of Women's Clubs, 85, 93, 114
Illinois Home Economics Association, 185
Illinois Industrial Survey Commission, 82
Illinois law (suffrage), 107
Illinois Liquor Conrtol Commission, 138
Illinois Medical Society, 96
Illinois Miner, The, 124
Illinois Nurses Association, 184-185
Illinois Republican Woman's Club, 115
Illinois State Housing Board, 125
Illinois State Welfare Association, 122
Illinois Teachers' Association, 92
Illinois Training School for Nurses, 97
Illinois Woman Suffrage Associaion, 54-55
Illinois Woman's Alliance, 64
Illinois Women's Agenda, 159-163
Illinois Women's Political Caucus, 133, 162
Illinois Women's Press Association, 99
immigrants, 23, 67-68, 70
Immigrants' Protective League, 72, 113
Industrial Workers of the World, 80
Infant Welfare Station, 114
Inforwoman Collective, 142
Institute of Women Today, 141, 153-158
Institute on Pluralism and Group Identity, 138, 140, 161, 163
International Boot and Shoe Workers, 81
International Council of Women, 62-63
International Glove Workers Union, 78
International Harvester Co., 101
International Kindergarten Union, 92
International Socialists, 164
isolation of women, 27, 29, 37, 56, 57-59, 104

Jackson, Mahalia, 142
Jackson, County Mental Health Service, 149, 150
Jacksonville Art Association, 60
Jacksonville Female Academy, 33, 35
Jane Club, 78
John Birch Society, 184
John Marshall Law School, 123
Johns, Jane Martin, 60
Joint Congressional Committee, 117
Joint Guardianship Bill, 107
Jones (Mother Jones), Mary Harris, 57, 80, 124
Jucker, Robert, 181-182
Juvenile Court, 71-72, 105-106, 112-113
Juvenile Court Committe, 72
Juvenile Protective Association, 69, 72, 105-106, 112-113
Juvenile Psychopathic Institute, 72, 112-113

Kansas Women's Aid and Liberty Association, 36
Karmazyn, Lillian, 119
Keehan, Virginia, 143
Kelley, Florence, 72, 78, 85, 86, 104, 119
Kellogg, Alice, 102
Kelly Bill, 171
Kennedy, Jane, 155
Kennedy, John F., 130
Kent, Mary Lou, 183
Kepley, Ada, 53
Kerner, Otto, 130
Kilvert, Margaret Cameron, 103
kindergartens, 92
King, Aurelia, 56
Kinzie, Juliette, 16, 104
Klepak, Ralla, 155, 157
KLIO Association Noonday Rest, 65
Knab, George, 82
Knights of Labor, 57, 62-63, 77, 85
Knox Female Seminary, 91
Kollock, Florence, 100

Labor Day Parade (1903), 79-80
Ladies Education Society, 33, 60
ladies' fairs, 34
Ladies, Federated Labor Union, 85
Ladies Library Associaion (Decatur), 60
Lady Core-Makers Union, 77-78
Lady Quartette, 103

Lake Geneva Fresh Air Fund, 84
Lakeview Latin American Women's
  Program, 160
Lanham Bill, 128
Lathrop, Julia, 70, 72, 112-113
Latham, Veta, 96
Lazarus, Josephine, 67
Leadership Conference of Women's
  Religions, 162
League of Housewives, 184
League of Women Voters, 99, 109, 116, 117,
  121, 166, 181, 184-185
Le Compt, Madame, 33
Lefevre, Marie, 20
legislation, 52-53, 106, 180-182
Lemisch, Jesse, 164
Leslie, Amy, 104
Leslie's Monthly, 77
Levinson, Rose, 140
Lexington Prison, 155-158
Liberation School for Women, 135
libraries, 60, 92-93
Lincoln, Abraham, 38, 41, 45
Lincoln, Mary, 38
Lindstrom, Ellen, 81
Livermore, Mary, 40, 41, 44, 45, 48, 52, 54, 61
Lloyd, Henry Demarest, 78
Loeb Rule, 88-89, 115
Logan, John, 38
Logan, Mary, 38, 104
Logsdon, Margaret, 31, 95
Lombard University, 67
Lund, Candida, 143
Lundberg, Ferdinand, 128

MacLeish, Andrew, 94
Malek, Leona Alford, 123
Maloney, Elizabeth, 82-84
marriage, Indians, 13-14, 19; interracial, 18;
  frontier, 25-26; divorce, 54
Marshall Sara, 28, 104
Martin, Doris, 157
Martin, Ellen, 106
Martineau, Harriet, 26-27
Mary Bartelme Clubs, 118
Maud Gonne Pleasure Club, 79
Maurice Porter Memorial Hospital for
  Children, 96
May Day (1886), 80
Meany, George, 188
Meder, Leonora, 108
Medical Standard, 96-97
Meigs, Cornelia, 104
Mergler, Marie, 96
Mercy Hospital School for Nurses, 101
Meyer, Carl, 81
Metropolitan Area Housing Alliance, 139
Metropolitan Housing Council, 125
Michael Reese Hospital, 98
Miller, Emily Clark Huntington, 104
Milligan, Josephine, 99
minority women, 139-140
Mitchell, Ellen, 61, 92
Mohr, Howard, 185
Monroe, Harriet, 103
Monticello, 94
Morgan, Anna, 103
Morgan, Elizabeth, 85
Morgan, Helen, 103
Morris, Mary B., 49-50
Mothers' Pension Law, 86
Mount Carroll Seminary, 35
Muir, Dr. Samuel and Sophia, 18-19
Mulligan, Marian, 45
Mundelein College, 131, 143
Municipal Art League, 60
Munroe, George H., 106
Music Service League, 103
Music Teachers National Association,
  102-103
McAdams, Mary Cowan, 119
McCormick, Edith Rockefeller, 114-115
McCormick, Medill, 108
McCormick, Mrs. Medill, 82
McCormick, Nettie Fowler, 101
McCormick, Ruth Hanna, 116, 118

McCormick Institute for Infectious
  Diseases, 99
McCulloch, Catherine, 106
McDermott, Mary, 77-78, 108
McDowell, Mary, 79, 83, 84, 105, 108, 118
McLaughlin, Virginia, 157
McMein, Neysa, 124

National Abortion Rights Action League, 171
National American Women's Suffrage
  Association, 116
National Association for the Advancement
  of Colored People (NAACP), 73
National Association of Colored Women's
  Clubs, 68
National Black Feminist Organization, 162
National Black Women's Alliance, 139-140
National Coalition of American Nuns and
  Church Women United, 153
National College of Education, 92, 143
National Commission on the Status of
  Women, 130
National Conference of Puerto Rican
  Women, 139-140
National Congress of Neighborhood
  Women, 139-140
National Consumers' League, 85
National Council of Jewish Women, 67,
  162-163
National Council of Negro Women, 162
National Council of Puerto Rican Women,
  162
National Editorial Association, 104
National Education Association, 90
National Housing, Training and Informa-
  tion Center, 139
National Organization for Women (NOW),
  130-131, 133, 139, 161-163, 166, 171,
  180, 183-185
National People's Action on Housing, 139
National Progressive Party, 107
National Teachers' Federation, 90
National Women's Agenda, 138, 159-160
National Women's Coalition, 163
National Women's Party, 116
National Women's Party Political Council,
  118
National Women's Political Caucus, 131
National Women's Trade Union League,
  82-84
Nealy, Mary, 18
Negro Fellowship League, 71
Nestor, Agnes, 78, 81, 83-84
New Politics Conference, 134
Newcomb, Mary 44
Newberry Library, 145
Nicholes, Grace and Anna, 108
Nightingale, Florence, 42
Niké, 60
Nixon, Richard, 131
North, Frank, 182
Northeastern Illinois University, 138, 140,
  154
Northwestern Female College, 62
Northwestern University, 53, 57, 62, 73, 96,
  138, 145
Northwestern University Settlement,
  109, 124
Norton, Alice P., 113
Nowicki, Stella, 124

Occupational Health and Safety Act, 174
O'Day, Hannah, 79
Ogilvie, Richard, 182
Old St. Mary's Church, 57
Olney, Nathan, 27
O'Neill, Lottie Holman, 119, 120
Order of the Eastern Star, 64
Organization for a Better Austin, 139
O'Sullivan, Mary Kenney, 78, 83-84
Otho S. A. Sprague Memorial Institute, 99
Ouilmette, Archange, 20
Ousley, Annie Fitzhugh, 53-54
Outreach Center, 138-139

Packinghouse Labor and Community
  Center, 176

Packinghouse Workers Union, 124
Paine, Eliza, 35
Palette Club, 102
Palmer, Bertha, 56-57, 66
Palmer, Potter, 56-57
Papieralski, Bernice, 109
Parents' Committe, 121
Parker, Francis, 90, 92
Park Ridge School for Dependent Girls, 83, 113-115
Parsons, Albert, 80
Parsons, Lucy, 80
Partee, Cecil A., 186-187
Peoria *Evening Star*, 122
Perkins, Lucy Fitch, 104
PEO, 60-61
Peoria petition, 54-55
Peosta, 17
Phyllis Wheatley Club, 68
Physician's Fellowship Club, 97
Pilsen Neighbors, 163
Piotrowski, Lillian, 130
Planned Parenthood, 122, 164, 166-168
Poetry: A Magazine of Verse, 103
Porter, Eliza Chappell, 41, 44
Porter, Julia, 96
Political Equality League, 87
Powers, Johnny, 74
Presbyterian Hospital, 97
prison reform, 34; legal serv., 155-158
Professional Organization for Women's Rights, 138
Professional Womtn's Club of Decatur, 121
Progott, Ira, 156
Progressive Era, 104, 112, 116, 118
Progressive Labor Party, 164
Progressive Miners of America, Ladies Auxiliary, 124
Progress reform movement, 65-66
Prohibition Party, 63
prostitution, 36, 75-76
protective legislation, 127
Provident Hospital Training School for Nurses, 97
public housing, 125
Public School Art Society, 60, 102
Pullman strike, 80-81
Putnam, Alice Whiting, 92

Rand, Sally, 125
rape, 16, 136, 150
Rape Action Committee, 150
Rape Crisis, Inc., 136
Rape Treatment Center Act, 137
Red Cross, 110, 127
red-lining, 139
Reid, Charlotte, 131
Relief and Aid Society, 56
religion, Baptist, 100; Catholic church, 21, 101; Catholic parish house, 71; Episcopal, 100; evangelists, 100; Free Methodist Church, 100, frontier, 28; Mormons, 100; orders, 45; societies, church, 59; Universalist Church 100; World Columbian Exposition, 67
Retail Lady Clerks Union, 77-78
Reynolds, Belle, 49
Richards, Ellen, 94
Richardson, Sukey, 25
right to life moevment, 141, 169
Rink, Susan, 143
Rittenhouse, Maud, 104
Robb, Isabel, 97
Robbins, Margaret Dreier, 83
Robertson, Mrs. 31
Rockford College, 70, 94, 143
Rockwood, Kaye, 155
Rodgers, Elizabeth Flynn, 77
Roosevelt, Franklin Delano, 124
Roosevelt, Theodore, 107
Rooseevlt University, 164
Rosary College, 143
Ross, Nellie Taylor, 115
Rothenberg, Sheribel, 154
Rouensa, Marie, 19
Rowe, Louise Osborn, 118
Rush Medical College, 95

Ryder, William H., 95

Safford, Anna, 60
Safford, Mary, 43
Saint Elizabeth's Day Nursery, 71
Saint Xavier College, 143
Saint Xavier Academy, 101
Salvation Army, 127
Sanger, Margaret, 121
Sanitary Commission, 41, 43, 44, 52, 95
Sanitary Fair (1863), 41
Saperstein, Esther, 119, 130, 181, 183, 185-187
Savickas, Frank D., 185
Schlafly, Phyllis, 132, 184, 188
Schloegel, Judith, 156
Schofield, Anna ,77-78
Schroeder, Josie, 77-78
Schubert, Helen and Leland, 157-158
Schultz, Kittie, 77-78
Scoville Institute, 93
Scrubwomen's Union and Janitors' Protective Association, 77-78
Seals, Connie, 160
Seippel, Clara, 108
servants, 34, 35, 69, 75
settlements, 69-74, 124, 143-144
Shapiro, Hannah, 81
Sharp, Katherine Lucinda, 93
Shaw, Annie C., 102
Sheppard-Towner Act, 119
Sherman, William T., 42, 43
Signal, The, 65
Sill, Anna Peck, 94
Simons, Mrs., 18
Sisters of Mercy, 45, 101
Sisters of the Holy Cross, 45
slavery, 21, 24, 34, 50
Smith, Amanda, 68, 69
Smith, Emma, 100
Smith, Joseph, 100
Smith, Julia Holmes, 99
social hygiene movement, 98
Social Service Bureau, 108
social work, 113
Socialist Party, 109
Socialist Workers' Party, 164
Society for Decorative Arts, 60
Soldiers' Aid Society, 91-92
Solomon, Hannah, 67, 108
Sorosis (New York), 61
Southern Illinois University, 146, 150, 151
Southwest College, 143
Southwest Rape Crisis Line, 136-137
Spock, Benjamin, 128-129, 144
Spokeswoman, 142, 160
Springfield Maternal Health Center, 122
Stanton, Elizabeth, 136
Starr, Ellen Gates, 70, 82
States Trades Assembly of Chicago, 77
Steinbacher, Roberta, 154
Stevens, Alzina, 78
Stevens, Helena, 115
Stevenson, Adlai III, 182
Stevenson, Sarah, 96, 97
Stiehl, Celeste, 188
Stone, Lucy, 36
"Stop ERA", 132, 184
Stringer, Charlotte, 95
Sturgis, Mother, 44
suffrage, 36, 51, 54-55, 61, 67, 83, 86, 105-108, 109, 110
Summers, Pauline D., 94
Summers College of Commerce, 94
support system, 29, 34 ,37, 124, 144, 145
Szold, Henrietta, 67

Taft, Lorado, 93
Taft, William H., 72
Talbot, Marion, 61, 94, 113
Task Force on Women's Rights and Responsibilities, 131
tax crusade, 106
Taylor, Lea, 124
Tecumseh, 19-20
temperance, 34, 36, 60-65, 106, 109
tea hour law (1909), 86
Terrell, Mary Church, 69

Textile Workers Union, 177
Thompson, William H., 117-118
Thompson, Mary Harris, 95, 97
Tillson, Christiana, 24, 33
Toynbee Hall, 70
Traveller's Aid, 76
Treaty of Prairie du Chien (1829), 20
Treaty of Tippecanoe (1832), 20
Trout, Grace Wilbur, 107
Tucker, Beatrice, 141
Tunnicliff, Sarah Bacon, 123
Turchin, Nadine, 49
Twist, Mrs. John, 32
Typographical Union, 78

Union College of Law, 53
Union of Bohemian Women, 63
unions, 57, 76-90, 115, 123-124, 137, 172-179
United Automobile Workers, 127
United Charities, 125
United Fund, 150
United Nations' Decade of Women, 153
United Nations' Year of Women, 153
United States Fuel Administration, 123
University and College Labor Education Association, 174
University and College Women of Illinois 138
University of Chicago School of Social Adminstration, 72-73; 73, 91, 94, 95, 99, 113, 122, 134, 135
University of Illinois, 83, 93, 99
University of Illinois Circle Campus, 138, 145
University of Illinois Medical School, 98

Van Cott, Maggie Newton, 100
van der Vaart, Harriet, 108
Van Hoosen, Bertha, 96
Vice Commission, 76
Vittenson, Lillian, 154
Vittum, Harriet, 109, 124
Voice of the Women's Liberation Movement, The, 135
volunteer, 112-113, 139, 168

Wait, Olive Stair, 36
Waite, Catherine V., 52, 55
Waite, Charles, 52
Walker, Dr. Mary, 48, 49
Walker, Sarah, 32
Wallace, Zerelda, 106
Walters, Annette, 156
war effort, Indians 20; frontier 33-34; Civil War 37, 38-40; World War II 127-128
Weinstein, Naomi, 134
welfare, 143
Wells, Ida B., 68, 69, 71
West, Mary Ellen, 53, 91
Western Association of University Women, 61
Westside Group, 135
Wheaton Planned Parenthood, 167-171
Whitmore, Mary Long, 125
Wieck, Agnes Burns, 124
Wilkerson, Mrs. John, 67
Willard, Frances, 33, 57, 61-63, 104, 106
Williams, Fannie Barrier, 67, 69, 97
Wilmarth, Mary, 84, 108
Wilson, Woodrow, 107
Winsor, Justin, 92
Wittenmeyer, Annie, 62
Wolf, Anna, 153

World Columbian Exposition, 66-76, 71; Board of Lady Managers, 66, Women's Building 66; Congress Auxiliary 66,83; World's Parliament of Religions 67; Jewish Women's Congress 67; Comparative Library Exhibit 93; "Columbian Ode" 103 women in occupations: work house, 1920's, 111; house Indians, 13-14, 17; house frontier, 22, 29; medicine, 31, 94-97, 98-99; nursing, 42-48, 97-98; law, 52-53; labor force, 75-77, 143; business, 101-102, 122; Art, 102-103, 125, 142; journalism, 104, 142; education, 115-116, 142-143; architecture, 125
Woman's Bureau (U.S. Department of Labor), 81
Woman's City Club, 73, 108
Woman's Club and Library Association (Cairo), 60
Woman's Party, 121
Women and Children's Protective Agency, 64
Women Employed, 137
Women for Peace, 141
Women Patriots, 119
Women's Action Alliance, 161
Women's Advisory Council, 127
Women's Bar Association, 162
women's centers, 137, 146-152
Women's Christian Temperance Union 57, 61-63, 65, 91-92, 99, 106
Women's Crusade Against Alcoholism, 61
Women's Equity Action League (WEAL) 131, 133, 139
Women's Hospital Medical College, 96
Women's International League for Peace and Freedom, 141
Women's Joint Congressional Committee, 121
women's liberation, 130, 134-136
Women's Medical Association, 99
Women's Medical College, 96
Women's Political Caucus (Carbondale), 146
Women's Radical Action Projects, 135
Women's Roosevelt Republican Club, 115
Women's Share in Public Service, 162
women's studies, 154
Women's Trade Union League (Chicago) 78, 81-85, 88-89, 113, 115, 141, 144
Women's World Fairs, 115
Wood, Elizabeth, 125
Wooden, Iva G., 107
Woods, Sylvia, 124, 127
Woolley, Celia, 70
Workers Alliance, 124
Wortheimer, Barbara 174
Wright, Sarah Peck, 97
Wyatt, Addie, 137
Wyatt, Edith, 104
Wylie, Philip, 128
Wythe, Mary K., 102

Yarros, Rachelle, 73, 98, 108, 121-122
Yarros, Victor, 98
Yates, Richard, 49
Young, Ella Flagg, 90-91, 108, 118
Young Women's Christian Association (YWCA), 65, 68-69, 70-71, 76, 110, 138, 141, 171, 181
Youth Against War and Fascism, 164

Zeisler, Fannie Bloomfield, 102-103
Zero Population Growth (ZPG), 166